D1715160

ALLEGORIES
OF
KINGSHIP

PENN STATE STUDIES
in ROMANCE LITERATURES

Editors
Frederick A. de Armas
Alan E. Knight

Refiguring the Hero:
From Peasant to Noble in Lope de Vega and Calderón
by Dian Fox

Don Juan and the Point of Honor:
Seduction, Patriarchal Society, and Literary Tradition
by James Mandrell

Narratives of Desire:
Nineteenth-Century Spanish Fiction by Women
by Lou Charnon-Deutsch

Garcilaso de la Vega and the Italian Renaissance
by Daniel L. Heiple

Allegories of Kingship:
Calderón and the Anti-Machiavellian Tradition
by Stephen Rupp

Acts of Fiction:
Resistance and Resolution from Sade to Baudelaire
by Scott Carpenter

Stephen Rupp

ALLEGORIES
OF
KINGSHIP

✛　✛　✛　✛　✛　✛

Calderón and the Anti-Machiavellian Tradition

The Pennsylvania State University Press
University Park, Pennsylvania

Publication of this book has been aided by a grant from The Program for Cultural
Cooperation Between Spain's Ministry of Culture and United States' Universities.

Library of Congress Cataloging-in-Publication Data

Rupp, Stephen James.
    Allegories of kingship : Calderón and the anti-Machiavellian
tradition / Stephen Rupp.
        p.   cm. — (Penn State studies in Romance literatures)
    Includes bibliographical references (p.   ) and index.
    ISBN 0-271-01456-3 (cloth : alk. paper)
    1. Calderón de la Barca, Pedro, 1600–1681—Political and social
views.   2. Monarchy in literature.   3. State, The, in literature.
I. Title.   II. Series.
PQ6317.H5R8   1996
862′ .3—dc20   94-41635
                                                                    CIP

To R. A. Nordman

Contents

✛   ✛   ✛   ✛   ✛   ✛

Acknowledgments

✢ ✢ ✢ ✢ ✢ ✢

This book marks the end of a project that began with my doctoral dissertation in Comparative Literature at Princeton University. Completing the dissertation left me with a number of questions concerning the conceptual background and internal development of Calderón's political theater. I have attempted here to answer these questions, a task that has involved further research in Spanish Golden Age drama and political thought and a thorough reformulation of my interpretation of Calderón. I am grateful to the members of my committee at Princeton—Alban K. Forcione, Alvin B. Kernan, and Robert Hollander—for counsel and support in all aspects of the dissertation, including my decision to leave it behind in order to examine Calderón's theater more intensively. From Alban Forcione, my director, I have learned a great deal about the forms of compassion and generosity that can inform scholarly inquiry. He has read through the project at each stage of its development, and the care that he has shown for my evidence and arguments has sustained my own attention over a long period.

Collegial support and guidance have assisted me in completing this work. Among the members of my department at the University of Toronto, James Burke, Mario Valdés, Keith Ellis, and Jesús Ara have offered encouragement and practical advice, and Gethin Hughes has helped me with the difficulties of translating Calderón's complex and inventive verse into English. For passages from *La cisma de Inglaterra*, I have also consulted the recent translation by Kenneth Muir and Ann L. Mackenzie (Warminster: Aris and Phillips, 1990). I am particularly grateful to those who read the manuscript and suggested changes and improvements: W. J. Callahan, J. H. Elliott, and the two readers who assessed the work for Penn State Press. In the long process of preparing and revising the manuscript on a word processor, I have received invaluable assistance from Rea Wilmshurst, who has worked through each chapter with care and encouraged me to clarify and reword my argument on various points.

Sections of Chapters 1 and 2 have been published in *Comparative Literature*, and part of Chapter 4 in the *Bulletin of the Comediantes*: "Reason of State and Repetition in *The Tempest* and *La vida es sueño*," *Comparative Literature* 42 (1990): 289–318; "Allegory and Diplomacy in Calderón's *El lirio y la azucena*," *Bulletin of the Comediantes* 41 (1989): 107–25. I thank the editors of these journals for the comments and suggestions that they supplied concerning this material and for permission to reprint it in its present form.

My approach to the literature of early modern Europe continues to rest on the basis established by the teachers who introduced me to the field: Lee Johnson at the University of British Columbia and Peter Marinelli at the University of Toronto. I warmly acknowledge the contribution that they have made to my intellectual life over many years. I also lament the sudden death of Peter Marinelli in the summer of 1993, an unexpected event that has deprived the scholarly community in Toronto of a generous and respected colleague.

I have dedicated this book to the teacher who, many years ago and in a field very different from the one that I now study, first introduced me to the pleasures of sustained attention to intellectual matters. In all my work I have tried to exercise the habits of respect and discipline that he taught me, although many faults of my own have persisted. The example of his teaching has guided and sustained me in this endeavor and in many others.

✝ ✝ ✝ ✝ ✝ ✝

INTRODUCTION

In the autumn of 1648 Philip IV of Spain undertook to marry for the second time. His chosen bride was his young niece Mariana of Austria, and the official betrothal was conducted by diplomatic proxy in Vienna in late November. On December 17 enthusiastic celebrations in honor of the royal engagement began in Madrid. The festivities involved the court and the city on various levels. The king appeared robed in an Italian cloth embroidered in gold and silver, displaying a splendor unseen in the capital since the death of his first wife Isabel of Bourbon in 1644; ambassadors, grandees, and councillors of state presented their formal congratulations; public pleasure was on offer in music, fireworks, two fountains that ran with wine, and windows that spilled forth gold coins.[1] The prominence of these events in Madrid's festive calendar is confirmed by Pedro Calderón de la Barca's decision to commemorate the betrothal in one of the *autos sacramentales* that he composed for the Corpus observances of 1649.[2] Presented under a title that clearly points to its immediate circumstances—*La segunda esposa y triunfar muriendo*—this *auto* dramatizes the details of the king's engagement and celebrates the approaching marriage for its prospect of spiritual and institutional renewal in Hapsburg Spain. Here, as in other *autos* that refer to affairs of statecraft and diplomacy, Calderón's complex allegory establishes correspondences between spiritual and political matters and urges an uncompromising ideal of Christian kingship on the Spanish Crown.

A brief account of the *auto sacramental* as a genre, and of the conditions in which such works were generally staged, will indicate why the *auto* could serve at times as a medium for offering counsel to the king. The origins of Spanish religious drama are notoriously difficult to trace.[3] It is clear, however, that the *auto* has antecedents in medieval tropes and pageants associated with key events in the religious calendar, and that the increasing prominence of the Feast of Corpus Christi as the day of performance was a crucial development in its history. By the late sixteenth century the genre had assumed recognizable conventions of

1. A contemporary document—Juan Francisco Davila's *Relación de los festivos aplausos con que celebró esta Corte Catolica las alegres nueuas del feliz Desposorio del Rey nuestro Señor Don Felipe Quarto* (Simón Díaz 499–506) —recounts in detail the festivities held in Madrid to celebrate the king's betrothal to Mariana. The arrangements for Philip IV's second marriage, and the response at court to the engagement, are also discussed by Stradling (338–39).

2. Although the political events this *auto* addresses are easily identified, the exact year of its performance is uncertain. In his edition of the *autos* Valbuena Prat suggests 1648 or 1649. Parker assigns *La segunda esposa* to the latter year, since it is likely to have been staged between the official betrothal in November 1648 and the royal wedding in October 1649 ("Chronology" 177). The importance of the betrothal celebrations in the public life of Madrid lends support to the argument for the later date.

3. The study of religious drama in medieval Spain suffers from a paucity of texts and documents. The earliest tropes of the Latin liturgy, and the forms of dramatic performance in the vernacular associated with prominent religious festivals (Christmas, Easter, Corpus Christi), are discussed by Shergold (1–84). Donovan surveys the extant liturgical drama in Latin, and suggests three possible explanations for the scarcity of such material in regions beyond Catalonia: the association in Castile between liturgical reform and the introduction of the French-Roman rite, the absence of dramatic tropes from the breviaries of the Cluniac monks who came to Spain, and the possibility that vernacular drama and religious theater developed simultaneously in Castile (see 67–73).

composition and presentation. As an integral part of the Corpus festivities in Spain's major cities, the *autos* consistently celebrated the Eucharist, both by dramatizing points of doctrine through the techniques of personification allegory and by closing the dramatic action with an elaborately staged discovery of the Host. These features impart a notable stability to the form. In its annual occasion and central purpose the *auto* is invariable. It turns a wide range of materials—topical images of human existence, events from sacred and secular history, biblical parables, diplomatic proceedings, and affairs at court—to a single celebratory end, in a civic contribution to the Corpus feast.[4]

The most striking aspect of the *auto* in performance is its relationship to the larger framework of the religious festival. Critical analysis should be attentive to this conjunction of theater and liturgy (Díez Borque 34), and to the implications that it holds with respect to the *auto* and its audience. Through its well-defined place in the Corpus ritual, the *auto* assumes a "quasi-liturgical role" that "gives the play something of the ceremonial and cultic function of Communion itself" and "confers upon the audience a participatory role analogous to that of the congregant or communicant" (Kurtz 21). Various features of staging reinforce the sense of public contribution and participation. The standard practice was to mount the sets and stage machinery for the *autos* on movable carts, so that the plays could be presented to different audiences in a series of venues. In Madrid temporary variations occurred on a standard order of performances. In the first half of the seventeenth century the city requested four *autos* each year; they were presented first to the king at one of the royal palaces, then to the principal governing bodies of the nation and the city—the Council of Castile, the various councils of state, and the municipality—and finally to the public at large. After 1648 the basic pattern displayed minor changes. The annual commission was reduced to two plays, and a more elaborate style of staging placed an increasing emphasis on the performances directed to the court, the councils, and the civic authorities.[5] These arrangements under-

---

4. The standard work on the origins and development of the *auto sacramental* is Wardropper's *Introducción al teatro religioso del Siglo de Oro*, and Shergold supplies an additional treatment of these subjects (85–112). Kurtz's excellent study of allegory in Calderón's *autos* offers an informative overview of scholarly opinion concerning the history of the genre (8–13).

5. This account of the evolution of the *auto*'s staging during the seventeenth century follows Shergold (esp. 424–29, 452–54). Valuable commentary on the transition in 1648 in

line the *auto*'s function as a civic tribute to church and state, offered in a spirit of instruction and celebration. In its ceremonial aura, and its appeal to a hierarchy of audiences, the *auto* aims to impart a sense of spiritual and ethical unity to its immediate community.

Calderón's success in meeting the demands of the Corpus festival in Madrid is beyond question. His *autos* became prominent in the city during the 1630s, and he later enjoyed a longstanding monopoly over the annual commission for new plays (1648–81). In *La segunda esposa y triunfar muriendo* he displays his talent for the genre by constructing a religious allegory from conventional and occasional material and by integrating elements of spoken drama, Christian liturgy, and stage spectacle.[6] This work is also typical of the *autos* that commemorate affairs of politics and the state in that much of its formative intent centers on the conduct of the king. Its allegory of the Eucharist is also an allegory of kingship, and the parallel development of its religious and political dimensions deserves close scrutiny.

In its central scenes *La segunda esposa* presents a conventional spiritual narrative. It depicts the birth of Man as a "pilgrim" on the earth (435b), and dramatizes his initial encounters with the demonic characters of Sin and Death, who attempt to seize him as their slave, and with Baptism, who promises to release him from their claim (435b–37b). The *auto* then traces Man's journey as he moves through the world, subject to the temptations of Sin and Death and aided by the comfort and instruction of the Sacraments. At the climactic point in his progress Man surrenders his life to the King (441a), who assumes and then sacrifices that life so that he may triumph for Man's benefit over the demonic opposition (442a–43b). The moral outline of this narrative is straightforward. The King represents Christ; his acceptance of Man's life, the Incarnation; his sacrifice and triumph, the Crucifixion. And Man's actions demonstrate the human capacity to seek salvation through the exercise of natural reason and free will, in accordance with the scriptural promise of eternal life for all who heed the Gospel (John 3:36, 11.25–26).

The image of human life as a pilgrimage, however, does not exhaust

---

conditions of performance is also available in Varey's "Calderón's *Auto Sacramental*," on the production of *La vida es sueño*.

6. In the course of his introduction to *La segunda esposa* Díez Borque draws attention to the technical diversity and artistic integration of the *auto* as a genre; he also stresses the central function of spectacle in creating a "symbiosis" among the theatrical, doctrinal, and liturgical components of the form (71).

the allegory of this *auto*. Man's progress toward redemption appears within a larger dramatic frame, in which the King plays a complex and crucial role. The frame relates the King's intervention on Man's behalf to two other acts: the promulgation of a new law and the founding of institutions to enshrine that law. These complementary acts are central to the text's formative aspect. In establishing new laws and institutions the King creates an order that will secure Man's salvation; he also offers a model for the structure of a Christian monarchy. The allegory as a whole traces correspondences between religious and political entities that have clear implications for the conduct of kings and their ministers.

The *auto*'s initial chorus summons all "mortals" to the prospect of eternal life (428a). The new law the King intends to put in force clearly underwrites this evangelical message, and the struggle over human redemption presents itself in the last analysis as a conflict of laws. The demonic characters insist that they hold Man enslaved by law and written authority (434b, 437b), and Death lays claim to a universal "empire" on the basis of her rights over humanity and the world (431b–32a). In contrasting the new law of the King to the old law of Sin and Death, Calderón alludes to the Christian doctrine that divides human history into three distinct eras according to the succession of three kinds of law. Before the declaration of the Decalogue natural law afforded humanity its sole ethical and spiritual guidance; during the Judaic era the Mosaic or written law supplied positive commandments for human conduct; since the coming of Christ the laws of the two previous epochs have been subsumed and sublimated into a new law of Grace.[7] In the *auto* Sin and Death ground their claims in the written law; they are bound to fail in their imperial ambitions because they deny the existence and efficacy of the new law promulgated for humanity's benefit. The evangelical promise of deliverance from mortality, issued to all in the King's name, rests on a renewal of the law.

The *auto*'s opening scene also makes explicit the institutional consequences of this legal renewal. The King enters here accompanied by the personified sacraments, to whom he turns for advice concerning his proceedings:

---

7. Kurtz outlines the historical scheme of the three eras, noting its Pauline sources in Romans 2 and 3, and discussing its presence in the allegory of the first of Calderón's two *autos* on the fable of Psyche and Cupid (*Psiquis y Cupido*, 1640?) (86–96).

saber espero
(pues Obras de Gracia quiero
medir, para más fineza,
con las de Naturaleza)
de qué una gran monarquía
consta desde el primer día
que se funda, porque en todo
nos ajustemos al modo
de una nueva Alegoría.

(428b)

(I hope to discover [since I wish, for greater excellence, to
measure Works of Grace with those of Nature] what a great
monarchy consists of, since the first day of its founding, so that in
all things we may conform to the mode of a New Allegory.)

The King's words indicate the interdependence of the law and the
institutions created to introduce and sustain it. To establish a "great
monarchy" is to translate the new law into practice through "works of
Grace." And since the law of grace sublimates the prior order of natural
law, the King must "measure" his works against those of nature. The
allegory here presents the founding of a kingdom as the institutional
enactment of principles embodied in a comprehensive system of laws.
The King's works, as he announces them in this scene, offer a model of
governance based on the rule of law.

In their response the sacraments assign to themselves the tasks of
establishing and ruling an ordered society. Baptism will oversee the birth
of the citizens destined for the kingdom; Confirmation will provide for
their education; Penitence (including Extreme Unction) will safeguard
their health; Communion will nourish the commonwealth; Priesthood
will furnish its justices; and Matrimony will ensure the due succession
of its governors (428b–29b). Through their dialogue the sacraments
emerge as the social institutions of an ideal monarchy, each with a crucial
role to fulfill for the benefit of the whole. And Matrimony speaks for the
interest of the community when he advocates a royal marriage. In its
appeal to etymology and analogy, his argument illustrates Calderón's
techniques for transforming current affairs into allegory. Through etymological play Matrimony relates Philip IV's first wife and his new bride
to the two covenants that God has extended to humanity. Isabel, or "Oath

of God," is the Synagogue; Mariana, or "Faith" and "Grace," represents the Church (429b–30a). Following a pattern established in earlier *autos*, this logic traces a correspondence between the royal betrothal and Christ's spiritual marriage to the Church.[8] The potential for spiritual and political renewal is implicit in the logic of the King's exchange with his advisers. By equating the sacraments with the institutions of monarchy, and by associating Mariana of Austria with the Church and its new covenant of grace, Calderón insists on the promise of a politics shaped by Christian principles and locates that promise in the rule of the Hapsburgs.

The political implications of the allegory become more pointed when the King endorses the advice that he has received from the sacraments:

> De vuestra razón de Estado
> ninguna cuerda consulta
> mi voluntad dificulta.
>
> (430a)

(No prudent counsel in your reason of state impedes my will.)

In the context of the political thought of early modern Europe, the King's praise for the "reason of state" proposed by his advisers takes on a definite resonance. Although Machiavelli makes no reference to *ragione di stato* in his writings, this term and its cognates in the languages of the major European monarchies (*razón de estado, raison d'état,* reason of state) appear repeatedly in the long debate concerning Machiavelli's conception of politics and princely power. Discussion of the term is constant, both in polemics designed to condemn and banish Machiavelli's ideas and in treatises intended to counter his example by defining a legitimate and Christian form of statecraft. The anti-Machiavellian debate consistently informs Calderón's political drama, and the ideas of Machiavelli and his critics will be explored in Chapter 1. At this point it is sufficient to note that in *La segunda esposa* the King's proceedings illustrate the Christian foundations of true reason of state, and that in

---

8. Neumeister has found antecedents for the treatment of a royal betrothal or wedding as an allegory of Christ's bond with the Church in two anonymous *autos* of the late sixteenth century (*Farsa sacramental de las bodas de España,* 1570; and *Los desposorios de la Infanta, moralizado a lo divino,* 1585) and in Lope de Vega's *Las bodas entre el alma y el amor divino* (1599) (35–36).

contrast Death is presented as a Machiavellian tyrant, whose imperial ambitions rest on her desire to claim legitimacy for power that she has gained through an act of usurpation (432b). The battle for Man's redemption develops as a conflict of laws, and as a struggle between Christian statecraft and its demonic or Machiavellian counterpart.

In the course of the *auto* Sin and Death pursue two related goals: to retain and strengthen their powers over Man and to impede the union of the King and his Bride. The King's victory over their designs secures the spiritual end of human liberty and the diplomatic conclusion of the royal marriage. The *auto*'s closing discoveries—staged on two carts which represent a castle and a pinnacle of rock—reinforce this conjunction of the spiritual and the political. In the final scene the first of the carts opens to disclose a lion, which opens to show a lamb, which in turn reveals a child bearing a cross; the second, in a similar sequence, displays an eagle followed by a dove. The characters on stage offer two complementary glosses on these images. The King and his Bride refer them to the sphere of politics and diplomacy: the heraldic lion of Spain and the imperial eagle of Austria have been joined, and possess in their union the mercy of the lamb and the sincerity of the dove (446a). Penitence and Communion appeal to religious symbolism: the lion enclosing a lamb is a "divine hieroglyph" of Christ's "power and kindness," the lamb itself represents the Eucharist, and the eagle and the dove together signify temporal death, whose harshness conceals for the faithful the "sweetness" of eternal life (446b–47a). The final emphasis on the Eucharist is conventional in the *auto*, but here it bears significantly on the political aspect of the allegory. Even as Calderón celebrates the emblems of Hapsburg imperial rule, he places those emblems within a larger sacramental order. In anticipation of the second royal marriage, he projects a renewal of the Spanish monarchy through a politics informed by Christian laws and institutions.

Written during the middle years of Calderón's long career as a dramatist, *La segunda esposa* addresses issues and ideas that appear consistently throughout his political theater. In *autos* that construct their Corpus allegories from affairs of state, and in secular *comedias* that dramatize political themes for audiences at court and in Madrid's public playhouses, Calderón examines questions of the law, of institutions of government, and of the larger significance of particular state occasions. Each of these concerns is central to his understanding of kingship, and each reflects the anti-Machiavellian principles that shape his thought.

To propose a political order founded on Christian ethics, and to center such an order on the conduct of the king, are common gestures in the political thought of Hapsburg Spain.[9] As Dian Fox has shown in her study of kingship and character in Calderón's works, the figure of the virtuous monarch enjoys a general currency:

> all Spanish political commentators, from Mariana to Quevedo, essentially agreed with Saavedra's rendition of the characteristics of the ideal ruler. The *príncipe político-cristiano* possesses the cardinal virtues, temperance, fortitude, justice, and the foremost, prudence. Able to rule over his own passions, he is an example for his subjects to emulate. He loves his people, favors the poor, exalts the Christian faith, and strives for spiritual glory. The worthy ruler delegates his authority to honorable men, opts for mercy over harshness in judicial matters, and eschews deception. (*Kings* 14).

This figure asserts itself in many of Calderón's political dramas. The allegorical program of *La segunda esposa* posits such an ideal ruler, capable of subordinating his desires to the demands of office and of establishing a Christian order in his kingdom; various secular plays set similar exemplars of royal constancy on the stage. When Prince Fernando refuses to allow that the Christian city of Ceuta be exchanged for his own freedom in *El príncipe constante* (1629), or when Ulysses abandons Circe's sensual delights at the command of Achilles' spirit in *El mayor encanto, amor* (1635), we are clearly in the presence of heroic princes whose conduct is bound by the cardinal virtues and the ethical obligations of sovereignty.[10] And Calderón is quick to exploit the double

9. The perfect prince, who renounces private concerns and emotions for the benefit of the realm, is a prominent figure in Western political thought. In *On Clemency* Seneca tells Nero that the just ruler declares through his deeds "that he belongs to the state" (159), and proves himself worthy of "high fortune" by displaying the "high spirit" of one who remains serene and self-possessed, even in the face of injuries for which lesser men would be free to seek redress (143–45). Aquinas's *On Kingship* expands on the dangers that unbridled passions hold for the ruler and for those over whom he rules. The true prince will seek the common good; the tyrant "will oppress his subjects in different ways according as he is dominated by different passions" (15–16) and so will render himself hateful and inhuman: "a man governing without reason, according to the lust of his soul, in no way differs from the beast" (18).

10. Recent studies have emphasized the ways in which these two plays develop the theme of kingship in relation to Spanish political theory and to the contemporary situation of the Hapsburg monarchy. Fox discusses Fernando's spiritual transformation into a

burden of this ideal type. The portrait of Philip IV in *La segunda esposa* is conventional and stylized, but the *auto*'s political logic suggests that the King will lose the right of dominion if he fails to answer the need for renewal in his kingdom. To paint the virtuous prince is to point to the dangers of decline into his tyrannical opposite.

The positive figure of the constant ruler, however, does not offer the sole pattern of princely conduct in Calderón's theater. Across the spectrum of his political plays, Calderón explores different forms of kingship and governance. The distinction between Christian statecraft and its Machiavellian or demonic counterpart is present throughout the corpus; the method of articulating and emphasizing this distinction varies as the author moves from secular to sacred forms of drama. In the *comedias* Calderón often dramatizes the failures of kings and princes who promote immediate political interests in defiance of legal and spiritual constraints; in the *autos* he defends true statecraft in theoretical terms and demonstrates its operation in the institutions and affairs of government. These two perspectives are complementary. Taken together, they present a comprehensive program for Christian monarchy, illustrated through the methods of example and counterexample.

Politics and drama are closely allied in the culture of early modern Europe. The theater's resources of rhetoric and spectacle lend themselves to the education and praise of kings, as well as to the broader scrutiny of princely conduct and political thought. In this context playwrights consistently address the ideas developed by Machiavelli or attributed to his influence, and they tend to draw on a common stock of materials and images: incidents from European history and contemporary diplomacy, chivalric ideals and legends, patterns derived from the long tradition of literary romances, Pythagorean and Neoplatonic images of universal order.[11] The various genres of Spanish drama allow Calderón

---

Christian prince and martyr in *El príncipe constante* (*Kings* 51–58); De Armas (*Return* 139–49) and Blue (151–69) interpret *El mayor encanto, amor* as a mirror of princes designed to warn Philip IV that the sensual pleasures of the Retiro may divert him from his royal duties and to urge that he attend more assiduously to the progress of the war against France. In her recent monograph on Calderón's mythological court plays, Greer offers a careful discussion of the latter work, describing the historical circumstances of its first performance and analyzing the strain of political criticism that lies beneath its spectacular surface (*Play* 77–95).

11. Calderón's political theater is part of the Spanish contribution to a large body of official drama and spectacle produced for the monarchies of early modern Europe. Works in this tradition share an interest in the different strains of contemporary political thought,

to offer a sustained and complex contribution to the political theater of the seventeenth century. The purpose of this study is to define the assumptions and principles that shape Calderón's understanding of kingship, and to examine the application of his political thought to specific conditions and institutions in Hapsburg Spain. Given Calderón's interest in the intellectual climate of his age, Chapter 1 discusses three issues of central importance in his political plays: the role of history in the education of princes, the reactions among Catholic thinkers to Machiavelli's reading of history's lessons, and the uses of allegory in the interpretation and composition of texts. Subsequent chapters analyze representative *comedias* and *autos*, with reference to three sets of questions that are prominent in *La segunda esposa*. The law, conceived as an ordered hierarchy and as an index to the progress of human history, is a central subject in the *comedia* and *auto* that share the title *La vida es sueño* (1635, 1674) and in *A Dios por razón de Estado* (1649); the principal institutions of the late Hapsburg monarchy—particularly the conciliar system of government and the rule of the royal favorite—are scrutinized in *La cisma de Inglaterra* (1627) and *El maestrazgo del Toisón* (1659); important occasions in Hapsburg ceremonial and diplomatic life form the basis of complex allegories in *El nuevo palacio del Retiro* (1635) and *El lirio y la azucena* (1660). Discussion of these plays will elucidate the terms of Calderón's engagement with the political thought of his age and illustrate his awareness of the particular institutions and proceedings of the Hapsburg state in the seventeenth century. Such commentary will also demonstrate the consistency of Calderón's theoretical position. Although his political theater evolves as the conditions of government change and as his own technical skill increases, it remains strikingly faithful to the anti-Machiavellian view of kingship and statecraft.

---

a stock of material appropriate for the counsel and praise of princes, and a concern with balancing the demands of text and spectacle. There are also points of contact between specific dramatic genres. Northrop Frye has classified the Spanish *auto* and the English court masque as analogous examples of the "myth-play," which "emphasizes dramatically the symbol of spiritual and corporeal communion" (282, 288), and the two genres parallel each other in their reliance on song and spectacle, their commitment to ideology, and their consistent recourse to idealization and abstraction. For commentary on the aesthetics and politics of the Stuart court masque, see Orgel's *The Illusion of Power*.

+ + + 1 + + +

HISTORY AND THE
ALLEGORIES OF KINGSHIP

Calderón shares the assumptions of contemporary thinkers concerning the primary audience and the basic methods of theoretical reflection on politics. In *La segunda esposa y triunfar muriendo* he directs his argument for renewal to the king, in accordance with the common view that the primary task of political theory is to secure the condition of the state by educating and improving the prince.[1] The tactics of analysis and persuasion in this *auto* are also conventional. Calderón relates a specific occasion in Hapsburg diplomacy—the betrothal of Philip IV and Mariana of Austria—to a larger christological pattern that can be traced through a long series of

---

1. Maravall has stressed the general didactic intentions of Spanish political thought, and the specific focus on cultivating self-knowledge and ethical conduct in the prince (*Teoría* 33, 250).

prior events and entities. The correspondences that link the king and his bride to Christ and the Church, and the institutions of government to the sacraments, confer meaning on present affairs by placing them in a comprehensive historical order. The tendency to find a "general significance" in specific events, to deduce a serviceable meaning from particular historical facts, is frequent among the humanists, and this intent reflects the continuing influence of medieval allegorical interpretation on Renaissance historical thought (Gilbert 167–68). The allegories that Calderón draws in his *autos* are directly indebted to medieval practices of scriptural interpretation, but political theory in this period is allegorical in a less specific sense, since readings in history consistently supply the basis for its lessons in the conduct of power. Political thinkers construct allegories of kingship from the historical record, and Calderón's political theater can be studied in relation to the competing readings of history that others offer to the princes of early modern Europe.

Three interrelated sets of intellectual and critical concerns inform Calderón's understanding of history and politics. The arguments that Spanish thinkers advance for the centrality of historical study in the education of princes clearly influence the political vision of his theater. The radical allegory of power and its maintenance that Machiavelli proposes in *The Prince*, and the counterposition that Catholic writers assume in response to Machiavellian ideas, shape Calderón's views concerning the theory and practice of true statecraft. Finally, a long tradition of allegorical reading and writing stands behind his theatrical practice in the *autos* and his general conception of history. The aim of this chapter is to outline some central issues and arguments in each of these areas.

The apprenticeship of Philip IV attests to the prestige of historical study in Hapsburg Spain. It is striking that the king saw fit to translate two books of Guicciardini's *Storia d'Italia* into Spanish, and that his own epilogue to the translation offers a careful account of his reasons for undertaking this task. Philip's stance here is initially defensive; in anticipation of those who might criticize him for having stolen time from the business of governing, he argues that his work on the translation has been "necessary and essential" for the affairs of the monarchy (printed as appendix to *Cartas* 231b). And he proceeds to comment in detail on the importance of history, stressing its place in his own education:

El leer historias también me pareció punto muy esencial para conseguir el fin a que encaminaba mis deseos de alcanzar noticias, pues ellas son la verdadera escuela en que el Príncipe y Rey hallarán ejemplares que seguir, casos que notar, y medios por donde encaminar a buenos fines los negocios de su Monarquía. (232b)

(Reading histories also seemed to me a very essential point for securing the end to which I directed my desires to obtain information, since they are the true school in which the prince and king will find exemplars to follow, cases to observe, and means through which to direct the affairs of their monarchy to good ends.)

A number of common assumptions concerning the centrality of history are present in Philip's justification. The statement that the "true school" of history offers "exemplars" of kingship implies that the outstanding virtues of past rulers can inspire the proceedings of their descendants in the present; the appeal to particular "cases" suggests that the specificity of historical knowledge can guide the prince in acquiring skills of administration and command that cannot be learned solely from general principles. The role of history in instructing by example, and in balancing abstract precepts against personal experience, is also a dominant theme. Philip himself insists that the prince must gradually acquire a direct knowledge of the demands of governing, but he regards historical study as an essential adjunct to such personal apprenticeship. The long tradition that informs this view of the education of princes invites further examination. The constitution of kingship as an art, and the bearing of history on that art, are central topics for the major writers on the theory of monarchy and empire in Hapsburg Spain. In *El concejo y consejeros del príncipe* (1559) Furió Ceriol anticipates the terms in which Philip IV defends the reading of history, arguing that this study is no mere "pastime" of princes, but rather a means of "saving time" that will impart to them in the compass of hours a body of knowledge accumulated over centuries (326a). The interrelations of history and royal education are delineated in the work's dedication, addressed by Furió Ceril to Philip II:

La institucion del príncipe no es otra, sino una arte de buenos, ciertos y aprobados avisos, sacados de la experiencia luenga de grandes tiempos, forjados en el entendimiento de los mas ilustres

hombres de esta vida, confirmados por la boca y obras de aquellos
que por su real gobierno y hazañas memorables merescieron el
título y renombre de buen príncipe. Los tales avisos, al príncipe
que los leyere y los pusiere por obra, son guia y camino trillado
para venir cierta y descansadamenta á la mas alta cumbre de
poder y gloria. (319)

(The education of the prince is nothing less than an art of good,
certain, and accepted directions, drawn from the long experience
of many ages, forged in the understanding of the most distinguished men of this life, and confirmed by the voice and deeds
of those who came to merit the title and fame of a good prince
through their excellent government and memorable exploits. For
the prince who will read them and put them into effect, such
directions are a guide and a well-trodden path for a sure and
unhurried ascent to the highest summit of power and glory.)

This argument proposes that the formation of princes is an art because it
can be studied from well-defined sources and because it supplies reliable
guidance for those who govern. The three areas in which true counsel
can be found—the experience of other eras, the wisdom of excellent
men, and the example of those who have won fame by ruling well—are
accessible in the records of the past, and the prince who consults these
sources will proceed securely to the height of honor. Although Furió
Ceriol makes no direct reference here to history, he is clearly stressing
the practical application of historical learning, and this passage parallels
his other assertions concerning the place of such study in the curricula of
the king and his councillors.[2]

2. Furió Ceriol devotes the greater part of his treatise to describing the perfect
councillor in terms of desirable talents and qualities, among which he includes an aptitude
for historical study and the capacity to apply the lessons of history to current affairs: "Es la
historia retrato de la vida humana, dechado de las costumbres y humores de los hombres,
memorial de todos los negocios, experiencia cierta y infalible de las humanas acciones,
consejero prudente y fiel en cualquier duda, maestra en la paz, general en la guerra, norte
en la mar, puerto y descanso para toda suerte de hombres" (History is a portrait of human
life, a pattern of the customs and humors of men, a memorial of all affairs, a sure and
infallible synopsis of human actions, a faithful and prudent counsellor in any instance of
doubt, a teacher in peace, a general in war, a lodestar at sea, a harbor and resting-place for
men of all kinds) (326a). Further discussion of Furió Ceriol's treatment of history and
politics is available in Fernández-Santamaría 157–58.

Later theorists develop two topics that remain implicit in Furió Ceriol's treatise: the relationship of historical learning to the knowledge that the prince acquires through personal experience and the unique value of history in the scrutiny and conduct of political affairs. In his *Tratado de la religión y virtudes que debe tener el príncipe cristiano* (1595) Pedro de Rivadeneira presents personal experience and reading in history as the two essential antecedents of the princely virtue of prudence: "no hay cosa que más nos enseñe que la experiencia de lo que nosotros mismos probamos y tocamos con las manos, y en leer los libros de los que fueron prudentes" (there is nothing that teaches us more than the experience of what we try for ourselves and touch with our own hands, as well as reading the books of those who were prudent) (566b). The nature of the lessons that the prince can draw from history is apparent in Rivadeneira's discussion of statecraft and religion. This issue is central to the intellectual program of his treatise, and he argues with force and insistence that civil concord depends on the authority of inviolable religious belief. To persuade princes of this political truth, Rivadeneira urges them to scrutinize the contrasting histories of kingdoms destroyed by religious confusion and preserved through fidelity to Christian doctrine (501a). The classification of history according to the categories of example and counterexample is typical of Rivadeneira, and the gesture of turning to the past for exemplary patterns and figures is repeated in a long series of treatises on kingship. Saavedra Fajardo's *Idea de un príncipe político cristiano* (1640) — a representative work in this tradition — reaffirms the importance of historical study in the formation of the perfect prince. The argument that history complements the prince's personal acquaintance with the practices of power by encapsulating the experiences of past rulers finds its most direct expression here, in the defense of history as the best school in the arts of government:

> La historia es maestra de la verdadera política, y quien mejor enseñará a reinar al príncipe, porque en ella está presente la experiencia de todos los gobiernos pasados y la prudencia y juicio de los que fueron. Consejero es que a todas horas está con él. (1:114)

> (History is the schoolmistress of true politics, and the one who will best teach the prince to rule, because within her the experience of all past governments, and the prudence and judgment of

those who once lived, are all present. She is a counsellor who is
with him at all times.)

Saavedra Fajardo favors the image of history as an ever-present "counsellor." Throughout his treatment of prudence he describes works of
history as "faithful and true friends" of the prince, who will not hesitate to
furnish him with honest advice concerning the perils of his office and the
ills of the kingdom. According to this argument, history affords both an
"anatomy" of politics and a naval cartography for the ship of state:

> Gran maestro de príncipes es el tiempo. Hospitales son los siglos
> pasados, donde la política hace anotomía de los cadáveres de las
> repúblicas y monarquías que florecieron, para curar mejor las
> presentes. Cartas son de marear, en que con ajenas borrascas o
> prósperas navegaciones están reconocidas las riberas, fondeados
> los golfos, descubiertas las secas, advertidos los escollos, y señala-
> dos los rumbos de reinar. (2:33–34)

> (Time is a great schoolmaster of princes. The past centuries are
> hospitals, where politics anatomizes the cadavers of the republics
> and monarchies that once flourished, in order to better treat the
> states of the present. They are charts to navigate by, on which,
> through the squalls and prosperous voyages of others, the shore-
> lines have been identified, the gulfs sounded, the sandbanks
> discovered, the reefs marked, and the courses of governing laid
> out.)

Yet for all the force of his technical metaphors, Saavedra Fajardo places
qualifications on the exemplary value of history and on the concept of the
book as counsellor.[3] He is particularly eager to dissuade princes from

---

3. Saavedra Fajardo argues that the prince must be cautious in proceeding on the basis
of historical examples because the circumstances of the present, in their human complexity,
will rarely correspond in every detail to those of the past. Only in the exercise of immutable
virtues, endorsed by natural and human law, is it safe to trust in the exemplary value of
history: "Solamente aquellos ejemplos se pueden imitar con seguridad que resultaron de
causas y razones intrínsecamente buenas y comunes al derecho natural y de las gentes,
porque éstas en todos tiempos son las mismas; como el seguir los ejemplos de príncipes que
con la religión, o con la justicia o clemencia, o con otras virtudes y acciones morales se
conservaron" (The only examples that can be imitated safely are those that followed from
causes and motives which were intrinsically good, and common to natural law and the law

consulting works that advocate dubious political expedients, and for this reason he would center their historical reading on the historical books of the Bible:

> Pero no todos los libros son buenos consejeros, porque algunos aconsejan la malicia y el engaño; y, como éste se practica más que la verdad, hay muchos que los consultan. Aquéllos solamente son seguros que dictó la divina Sabiduría. En ellos hallará el príncipe para todos los casos una perfecta política, y documentos ciertos con que gobernarse y gobernar a otros. (2:34)

> (But not all books are good counsellors, because some counsel malice and deceit; and, since the latter is practiced more often than the truth, there are many who consult them. The only trustworthy books are the ones dictated by divine wisdom. In them the prince will find a complete politics for all occasions, and reliable documents for governing himself and governing others.)

Through their readings of history the political theorists of this period accommodate old standards and values to a changing order of institutions and ideas. In deducing general rules from the experiences that historians have condensed and codified, they attempt to understand politics in modern terms as a "rational method" rather than as "an arcane and mysterious art" (Pocock 28), yet in the moral perspective that they bring to the scrutiny of history, and in the injunctions that they draw from this exercise, they display a marked traditional cast. When Saavedra Fajardo asserts that the prince will learn from scriptural history "to govern himself and to govern others," he is invoking the exemplary figure of the constant monarch. Like the majority of Spanish theorists, he draws on the past to reinforce the ethical and customary limits of the king's authority.

Despite their consensus on the character of the true prince, Saavedra Fajardo and his contemporaries were aware that historical studies did not afford unqualified support for their position. The broad range of humanist discourses concerning both history itself and the application of its

---

of nations, because these causes are the same in all periods; as in following the examples set by princes who prevailed through religion, or through justice and clemency, or through other virtues and moral actions) (2:41). For further commentary on the problems of history and exemplarity in Saavedra Fajardo, see Fernández-Santamaría 249–55.

lessons to political affairs opens the way for competing views of princely conduct, some of them decidedly at odds with the traditional ideals of Christian monarchy. Saavedra Fajardo's reference to books that "counsel malice and deceit" points to the most challenging of the alternative views of kingship. In the political lexicon of the period these terms apply to the techniques of governance associated with Machiavelli and reason of state, particularly as they are described by hostile critics. Machiavelli alarmed the counsellors of princes by pursuing allegorical interpretation "in a purely secular way" and by applying the method to dubious and unstable instances of political authority (Gilbert 168, 163). Because of its prominence in the debate on the nature and limits of statecraft, his allegory of kingship must be examined in detail.

Machiavelli's attempt to comprehend the order of secular history presumes a cyclical pattern of political change. His synopsis of political history in *The Discourses* (1:2) proposes that six forms of government follow one another in succession as each regime that promises to establish or renew civil order declines into a corrupt variant of itself: monarchy into tyranny, aristocratic rule into oligarchy, democracy into anarchy (Mesnard 54–55). From this cycle Machiavelli does not infer that repetition is inevitable; he argues instead that the cycle will end only when republican government establishes a stable constitutional balance among the powers of the prince, the nobility, and the people. The transition from existing forms of government to a republican regime is a crucial issue in his political thought. Under the conditions of public life as Machiavelli knows them, only a strong ruler will have the power to overturn custom and to create the conditions of political and constitutional renewal. Without such a prince there can be no republic; Machiavelli's thought rests on the principle of autocracy preparing the way for republicanism (Mesnard 84–85), and his counsel for princes stresses the qualities of command that will enable them to break the patterns of custom and tradition.

To convince us that successful dominion depends on the exercise of these qualities, Machiavelli makes extensive reference to historical events. A specific example from the third chapter of *The Prince* will illustrate his approach to history and the lessons that he draws from its record. This chapter concerns the difficulties that a ruler will confront in attempting to govern a new territory annexed to his realm. Although he concedes that such possessions are hard to control, Machiavelli asserts that success will fall to those who can anticipate political dangers and act decisively to eliminate them. His argument proceeds from historical example to technical analogy. He cites the Romans for their foresight in balancing the powers and interests of their colonies in Greece, and compares the ruler's task to that of a physician who must prescribe the correct "medicine" before a disease becomes so manifest as to be "incurable." In developing this analogy he insists on the parallel between the "remedies" of the physical body and the body politic:

> Così interviene nelle cose dello Stato, perchè conoscendo discosto (il che non è dato se non ad un prudente) i mali che nascono in quello si guariscono presto: ma quando, per non gli aver conosciuti, si lasciano crescere in modo che ognuno li conosce, non vi è più rimedio. (192)

> (Thus it occurs in affairs of state, because when the state's ills are recognized with much anticipation [as only a prudent person is able to do] they are soon cured: but when, because they have not been recognized, they are allowed to increase to the point that everyone may see them, there is no longer any remedy.)

The dilemma addressed in this passage—that of the political innovator who must displace the established customs of a society with a new order which will legitimate his regime—is central to the secular allegory of Machiavelli's treatise. The ruler who attempts to extend his realm puts himself in the position of the "new prince" to whom Machiavelli devotes so much of his attention. *The Prince* may be described as "an analytic study of innovation and its consequences" (Pocock 156); for this reason it turns to history for case studies of princes who are aware of the precariousness of their power and determined to secure that power by any means at hand (Sasso 328). Machiavelli regards these new princes as locked in opposition to old ways of government; he applies the term *stato* to the "limited" and "partly legitimized" political order that they are able to maintain (Pocock 175). By its unstable and provisional nature, *stato* exposes the prince to the dangers commonly attributed to *fortuna*, and the successful innovator must counter these dangers by exercising *virtù*. Instead of supplying a single definition of *virtù*, *The Prince* indicates the abilities that the innovator must demonstrate in a broad range of political circumstances. Foremost among these is a capacity for foresight, which Machiavelli identifies with the phrase *veder discosto* (Sasso 357) or, as here, with the equivalent expression *conoscere discosto*. Such anticipation will be of little avail, however, unless the prince is prepared to take whatever action may be required to conserve his regime, even if that action violates accepted precepts of morality and religion. In the execution of *virtù*, a willingness to enter into evil conduct is the necessary complement of the princely foresight associated with the phrase *veder discosto* (Sasso 402–3). This acceptance of evil implies a new understanding of politics. The "prudent one" to whom Machiavelli confides the task of successful innovation recognizes that the political world is one of images and appearances, in which he must safeguard the *stato* not by preserving a timeless essence mistakenly ascribed to it, but by adjusting his policies to the shifting forces of time and necessity (Lefort 429). The art of ruse—crucial to the prince's political labor and dangerous in that it places his honor and reputation at risk—is the soul of *virtù* (Lefort 412–13).

Machiavelli's analysis of political history in terms of the axis of *virtù* and *fortuna* exemplifies the radical character of his thought. *The Prince* resembles earlier treatises on princely conduct in its attention to the past, but its distinctive view of history urges rulers to adopt new standards of judgment and action in affairs of state. Whereas the constant prince of traditional political thought possesses immutable virtues that enable him to stand firm in the face of time and change, Machiavelli's prince derives his strength from rejecting the idea of constancy, from opening himself and his conduct to the unending flux of Fortune and Nature (Manent 18–19). Machiavelli proposes an ambitious revision of the modes and assumptions of discourse on politics; he sets out to rob the reader of any support in the "established truths" of humanist and Christian thought, and proceeds to "a slow and methodical destruction of traditional political teaching" (Lefort 365, 399). His interpretation of the forces that have shaped the trajectory of temporal power attempts to displace all other historical allegories of kingship.

An attack on this scale was bound to draw defenders to the side of tradition, and theorists of the period are eager to condemn Machiavelli for promoting a politics of deception and calculation. His accusers quickly isolate the most daring and original aspect of his thought—the attempt to separate the practical claims of politics from the moral and spiritual demands of religion—and they place this point at the center of their critique. A counterargument that insists on the priority of religion is repeated in one treatise after another, in various rephrasings of a single key proposition: that a purely secular politics is doomed to failure because God controls the unfolding of human history through providence. Spanish theorists participate fully in this polemic. In his treatise on the Christian prince Rivadeneira asserts that providence will sustain the faithful prince who trusts in God and bring ruin to those who invest their confidence in the designs and stratagems of human invention:

> la providencia que Dios tiene de todas las criaturas, y especial-
> mente de los hombres buenos y reyes fieles, . . . es el funda-
> mento en que debe estribar el gobierno y confianza del príncipe
> piadoso, que está colgado de Dios y echado en sus brazos, y
> reposa en su divina providencia, y para deshacer las marañas de
> los políticos, que de tal suerte enseñan á gobernar los estados,
> como si el Señor no tuviese providencia dellos, y el mundo se
> gobernase acaso ó con sola la malicia y astucia humana. (470b)

> (the providence that God has for all His creatures, and especially
> for good men and faithful kings, . . . is the foundation which
> should support the government and trust of the pious prince, who
> depends on God and lies in His arms, and relies on His divine
> providence, and the basis for undoing the stratagems of so-called
> men of state, who so maintain that states should be governed, as
> to imply that God had no care of them, or that the world were
> governed by chance or solely through malice and human cun-
> ning.)

For all the force of this anti-Machiavellian discourse, conservative thinkers do not limit themselves to railing against the errors of secular politics. A substantial and diverse body of theory attempts to define principles of statecraft that can be reconciled with religious teaching, in order to furnish Christian rulers with appropriate guidance for the tasks of governing a temporal kingdom. In the influential treatise *Della ragion di stato* (1589) Giovanni Botero rehearses the standard argument for the priority of religion in secular matters, and argues from this position that true reason of state—defined as "knowledge of the means suitable for founding, maintaining and enlarging a State"—must take account of the force that providence exercises in human affairs (Meinecke 67, 69). Botero was read in Spain (Elliott, "Self-Perception" 54–55), and many Spanish theorists apply themselves to the task that he sets out: to distinguish between bad reason of state, detrimental to both religion and politics, and good reason of state, consonant with religious doctrine and beneficial to the realm (Meinecke 120). His influence is evident in Rivadeneira's work. In his preface Rivadeneira announces his intention to offer the prince "rules of prudence" for political conduct, and dwells on the dual nature of reason of state:

> porque ninguno piense que yo desecho toda la razon de estado (como si no hubiese ninguna), y las reglas de prudencia con que, despues de Dios, se fundan, acrecientan, gobiernan y conservan los estados, antes todas cosas digo que hay razon de estado y que todos los príncipes la deben tener siempre delante los ojos, si quieren acertar á gobernar y conservar sus estados. Pero que esta razon de estado no es una sola, sino dos: una falsa y aparente, otra sólida y verdadera; una engañosa y diabólica, otra cierta y divina; una que del estado hace religion, otra que de la religion hace estado; una enseñada de los políticos y fundada en vana prudencia y en humanos y ruines medios, otra enseñada de Dios, que estriba en el mismo Dios y en los medios que Él, con su paternal providencia, descubre á los príncipes y les da fuerza para usar bien dellos, como Señor de todos los estados. (456)

> (so that no one may think that I reject all reason of state [as if there were none at all], and the rules of prudence with which, after God, states are founded, augmented, governed, and conserved, I say before all else that there is reason of state and that all princes should keep it always before their eyes, if they wish to succeed in governing and conserving their states. But that this reason of state is not one, but two: one false and apparent, another sound and true; one deceitful and diabolical, another sure and divine; one that makes a religion of the state, another that governs the state through religion; one taught by men of state and based on vain prudence and contemptible human measures, another taught by God, which rests on God Himself and on the measures that He, with his paternal providence, reveals to princes, giving them strength to use them well, as Lord of all states.)

In stressing the grounds of distinction between the two kinds of statecraft, and associating true reason of state with divine providence,

Rivadeneira is typical of a particular strain in the development of Spanish political thought. J. A. Fernández-Santamaría has argued that the theory of statecraft in Hapsburg Spain began as an "ethicist" reaction to Machiavelli and modulated into a "realist" inquiry into politics as a field of knowledge and practice. Both schools accept the primacy of religion and religious ethics, but they adopt different approaches to defining true reason of state: "the ethicists . . . thought that they could arrive at this *verdadera razón de Estado* by stressing the time-honored figure of the Christian prince and exposing the teachings of the *políticos* as false *razón de Estado*, whereas the realists endeavored to build their own reason of state on a pragmatic, if Christian, approach to political problems" (Fernández-Santamaría xvi). The two approaches are not mutually exclusive, and in the seventeenth century they exist side by side, but the realists follow a distinct line of inquiry into the status and the applications of statecraft.

Historical study is central to the origins of realist theory. The conception of history as a repository of past experience from which principles of judgment and action could be deduced encouraged the development of politics as an independent discipline. Free to speculate within a well-defined field of historical investigation, the realists could set the claims of religion and ethics to one side and pursue questions of primary political interest. The shift in emphasis is marked. Such issues as the intellectual status of statecraft as an art or a science, and the necessity of cultivating a balance between theoretical analysis and practical competence, become prominent in the realist school. And the pragmatic inclination of the realists leads them to redefine the qualities and virtues of the true prince in terms that contrast with the ethicists' insistence on conformity with the order of providence. Saavedra Fajardo proposes that the prince must possess the prudence to anticipate shifts in time and circumstance, and the capacity to accommodate his character to such changes (2:105). Baltasar Gracián, in his encomium of Ferdinand of Aragon, associates princely excellence with the intellectual virtues that will secure quick and prudent responses to the multiple occasions of governing (58). The priority in these arguments of practical considerations attests to the difficulties of reconciling religious values with adequate counsel for political action. The effort in early modern Europe to isolate a Christian reason of state has been described as "an attempt . . . to fit Machiavelli's world into Augustine's universe" (Raab 101), and the discomforts of this task make themselves felt among Spanish thinkers of the realist school.[4]

Through his theater Calderón presents an articulate and detailed defense of the ethicist position. In placing the figure of the virtuous prince on stage, and in contrasting true and false versions of reason of state, he aligns himself with the conservative theorists of Christian statecraft. And in the line of such thinkers as Rivadeneira, he centers his response to Machiavelli on the force of providence in the affairs of kings and princes. The counterexample of rulers who subject their kingdoms to the priority of temporal ends, and the positive model of diplomatic proceedings and political institutions that conform to Christian patterns, illustrate the necessity of recognizing the divine presence in history and of governing in accordance with its demands. Calderón's reading of history stresses that a divine context surrounds and limits royal conduct, and the two dominant genres of his political theater present this lesson by different means. In *comedias* and *autos* alike, however, emphasis falls on the unfolding of God's intentions in human history and on the consequences of the prince's disposition in relation to the providential order.

Many of the *comedias* consider the results of resorting to manipulative statecraft, whether for personal motives or for reasons of public interest. The terms in which Calderón articulates his critique of secular politics correspond to a crux in the cyclical framework of Machiavelli's thought. The transition from the autocracy of the decisive prince to republican government is an essential step in the political cycle, yet Machiavelli himself recognizes, at least implicitly, that this transition cannot be guaranteed. The new prince, in exercising his *virtù*, may simply reproduce the conditions that he has attempted to overcome and so reduce the realm once again to tyranny (Sasso 430). For all his insistence on astuteness and resolution, Machiavelli regards the politics of unbridled power as a politics of mere repetition (Lefort 428). Following the assumptions of Spanish political theory Calderón excludes the republican option, but he gives full weight to the threat of repetition inherent in Machiavellian procedures. In their treatment of statecraft his political *comedias* emphasize two fundamental principles: that recourse to secular reason of state will reduce public life to a repetitive cycle of intrigues and usurpa-

---

4. This account of realist political theory in Spain follows the outline of Fernández-Santamaría's discussion in the second part of his monograph (esp. 166–71, 246–65, 293–96).

tions, and that the only remedy for this cycle is a return to the virtues and limits of traditional kingship. And Calderón's commitment to this view inspires in his work a pronounced skepticism concerning the realist attempt to separate technical issues in statecraft from ethical questions and to reconcile political flexibility with Christian principles. Calderón is clearly aware of the discomforts of this enterprise, and one of the somber lessons of his *comedias* is that any form of political manipulation will induce a cycle of Machiavellian expedience.

Calderón locates the antidote to secular politics in the traditional princely virtues because he maintains that the Christian king can amend the state by aligning its actions and institutions with the due order that providence has established for human affairs. The genre in which he develops this argument is the *auto sacramental*, and a complete discussion of his allegory of kingship should include commentary on the explicitly allegorical techniques of the *autos*. Drawn from diverse sources in traditional religious theater and in Christian exegesis, these techniques illustrate the complexity of Calderón's allegorical practice and the central place of allegory in his conception of history.

In the literary culture of the seventeenth century, the *auto* as a genre is notable for its adherence to the conventions of extended allegory. The dominant literary theory of the period is generally hostile to allegory, and offers no account of fictions organized as continuous allegorical wholes (D. Wilson 53). In neo-Aristotelian treatises allegorical procedures are subsumed under the category of rhetoric, or adduced to legitimate the representation of characters and actions that defy the standard canons of verisimilitude (D. Wilson 54–56). In this limited view allegory is an ornamental trope or, in the defensive phrasing of Jacopo Mazzoni, the "medicine of the impossible" (quoted in Montgomery 48b). And a mounting mistrust of the intellectual capacity of the audience for literature prompts many theorists to prefer clear exposition over any form that attempts to convey a hidden meaning beneath an intricate surface (D. Wilson 59). In their annual contributions to the Corpus festival, however, Spain's major dramatists show little regard for the theoretical resistance to allegory. *Auto* after *auto* celebrates the significance of the Eucharist through complex and recondite allegorical means.

Calderón's own fidelity to allegory can be traced to various motives. The importance of allegory in the generic development of the *auto* is one significant factor. Calderón respects the conditions of Madrid's annual commission for *autos*, and prides himself on his ability to compose new

works within the accepted conventions of the genre. In the prologue to
the collection of his *autos* published in 1677, he defends his repeated
recourse to a limited set of personified characters, arguing that he has
directed these allegorical "means" to different theological "ends" and that
the creation of many works centered on the same characters is in itself a
sign of exceptional artistry.[5] The didactic potential of allegory also
contributes to Calderón's interest in the mode. Northrop Frye has
observed that an allegorical text invites a particular kind of interpretation,
so that "actual allegory" appears "when a poet explicitly indicates the
relationship of his images to examples and precepts, and so tries to
indicate how a commentary on him should proceed" (90). In keeping with
the intent to supply instruction on the Eucharist and its feast, Calderón's
autos offer extensive interpretive direction to the audience: characters
introduce themselves and explain their identities, aspects of costume and
stage spectacle appeal to traditional icons and emblems, entrances and
discoveries are glossed for their symbolic significance. Direction of this
kind appears frequently in such genres of Renaissance spectacle as the
court masque. Calderón nonetheless departs from a stance common
among the authors of these genres in his refusal to privilege the discur-
sive meaning of his allegories by separating the intellectual "soul" of the
work from its tangible and spectacular "body."[6] The prologue to the 1677
collection apologizes for the tepid quality of the printed page and invites
readers to imagine the effects of sound and staging that the medium
cannot convey. In Calderón's view text and spectacle contribute by
distinct means to the *auto*'s allegory of the Eucharist.

The genre's sacramental occasion is another factor that accounts for
Calderón's commitment to allegory. His *autos* are openly allegorical in
their recourse to personification, a technique that can be described as "a
staple of allegory and the most trustworthy evidence of its presence" (D.

5. Valbuena Part reprints the text of the 1677 prologue in his edition of Calderón's *autos*
(41a–42b).

6. Conflicting claims for priority in determining the "fable" or "invention" of a court
entertainment—that is, the enduring poetic "soul" that animates its ephemeral "body" of
spectacle—form the ground of conflict between the writers and designers who contributed
jointly to such forms of court drama as the English masque. D. J. Gordon has examined this
issue in relation to the English masque, with detailed reference to the polemic between Ben
Jonson and Inigo Jones. In her analysis of *Las fortunas de Andrómeda y Perseo* (1653), Greer
contrasts the standard argument concerning the poet's position with Calderón's "poly-
phonic" conception of court theater, and discusses the "synthesis" of diverse elements
(music, dance, scenery, stage machines) in his dramatic practice (*Play*, 54–76).

Wilson 66). Yet the kind of allegory associated with personification—variously known as moral allegory, reification, or *allegoria in verbis*—rarely appears in isolation in Calderón's works. A second variant of allegory—figural allegory, typology, or *allegoria in factis*—is also central to his sacred dramaturgy.[7] Stephen Barney has observed that these two kinds "have divided the world of allegory between them" (60), and the task of combining the two in a genre dedicated to the Corpus feast undoubtedly draws Calderón to the allegorical mode.

Moral and figural allegory are distinct in their origins and procedures. The first, derived ultimately from late Hellenic interpretations of Homer, treats the text as a fiction or fable that conveys a moral truth through techniques of metaphor and analogy; the second, expounded by the church fathers and traditionally applied to Scripture alone, presents the text as the record of providential history, in which crucial agents and actions are anticipated or prefigured by others that have occurred earlier.[8] The fundamental distinction between the two procedures lies in the relationship between the text and its significance. Whereas moral allegory locates a timeless, internal truth beneath an external fiction, figural allegory establishes a correspondence of "figure" and "fulfillment" between a series of personages (for example, Moses and Christ) or events (Exodus and the Redemption) that are both regarded as true and historical. This insistence on "the historicity both of the sign and what it signifies" is a unique and characteristic feature of figural allegory (Auerbach 54).

Each variant of allegory also pursues specific issues and interests. Stephen Barney has noted that moral allegory tends to "personal reflection on one's self, one's relation to nature, and one's connection with others" and figural allegory to "social reflection on history" (38). Calderón's practice corresponds in large measure to this distinction. In the *autos* that address providence and its laws in abstract terms, he resorts primarily to moral allegory, in order to examine the individual's accommodation to the divine order; in those that commemorate actions and

7. Various contrastive terms have been employed to distinguish one kind of allegory from the other. In recent scholarship the contrast is often drawn between moral and figural (or theological) allegory; Barney (30–38) and Neumeister (40–41) supply definitions of the other terms cited here.

8. Seznec discussed the classical and medieval origins of moral allegory (84–121); D. C. Allen surveys its history during the Renaissance. The classic study of Christian or figural allegory, as applied to Scripture, is Lubac's *Exégèse médiévale*.

personages in the public life of Hapsburg Spain, he uses figural allegory to trace correspondences between sacred history and contemporary events. Although personification and metaphor appear throughout the corpus of his *autos*, the prominence of typology in works dedicated to occasions and affairs of state is striking.[9]

Figural allegory is appropriate to the political *auto* because it functions as a method of historical interpretation. Barbara Kurtz has observed that in his mythological *autos* Calderón assumes the stance of an "editor or transmitter" who presents his own "inventions or interpolations" as an "explicative or illustrative gloss" on the meaning of his subject (101). The same principle applies to the *autos* inspired by political affairs, in that these works identify and explicate figural patterns assumed to be present in current events. Typology proposes that all of history is centered on two definitive moments of revelation: the Incarnation, through which the figures or types of the Old Testament find fulfillment in Christ; and the Last Judgment, which represents the "ultimate fulfillment" of history itself (Auerbach 58). Kurtz has supplied an informative and detailed account of typology's application to the present, conceived as the historical period that lies between these two events. During this interregnum history can be viewed as "postfigurative," that is, as generative of patterns that recall the life of Christ and the apostles and anticipate the Apocalypse (155). Through this "secularization of typology" significant current events— including the proceedings of kings and their ministers—are granted a place in the sacramental order of Christian history. The assumption of continuity between the figures of the present and their fulfillment in sacred history "informs Calderón's circumstantial *autos* and gives them their theological and allegorical power" (141). *La segunda esposa y triunfar muriendo* is representative of these *autos* in its figural treatment of the persons and instruments of the Hapsburg state. To present the King and his Bride as types of Christ and the Church, and the institutions of government in figural relation to the sacraments, is to extend scriptural typology to contemporary political affairs. Through such figural tech-

---

9. Analysis of typology in Calderón's *autos* has tended to center on the dramatization and exegesis of figural patterns in individual works, particularly those based on material from the Old Testament (Glaser, Foster, Cilveti). In contrast to the limited focus of such studies, Kurtz's recent treatment of the subject is both comprehensive and detailed. Her monograph traces the origins and development of Calderón's complex allegorical technique, and examines his sophisticated use of typology not only in *autos* on scriptural themes, but also in works devoted to classical mythology, national history, and contemporary affairs.

niques the political *autos* trace a sacramental pattern in the unfolding of Spain's imperial history.

The exact typology of the *autos* is the keystone of the larger allegory of kingship that Calderón constructs in his political theater. Providence asserts itself in human history through the repetitive patterns of figure and fulfillment, and the presence of these patterns in Spanish statecraft and diplomacy shows us that the state's proceedings can confirm and promote the providential design. In contrast to the Machiavellian stratagems of the *comedias*, the *autos* exemplify true or Christian reason of state, and the two kinds of statecraft lead to two distinct modes of historical repetition. The pursuit of a politics designed for secular ends induces a destructive cycle of deception and violence; the alignment of the state and its instruments with providence sets the realm in the positive sequence of repetition delineated by Christian typology. As in the allegory of power and its maintenance that he attempts to counter, Calderón applies a particular reading of history to the conduct of kings and princes. His theater follows the anti-Machiavellian tradition in stressing that true reason of state commands those who govern to respect the order of providence and the limits of temporal authority.

2

KINGSHIP AND THE LAW
La vida es sueño (*comedia* and *auto*) and *A Dios por razón de Estado*

In the secular theater of early modern Spain the king often assumes responsibility for rendering justice in matters related to honor, feudal obligations, and political rights. In such cases the king's decision bears directly on the resolution of the dramatic conflict, and his ability to reconcile competing demands and interests varies from one play to another. At times royal authority is able to satisfy the aggrieved parties and to respect the principles of justice; on other occasions the best it can offer is a provisional remedy that maintains only the appearance of a just order. In each instance the king's capacity for equitable judgment reveals his personal character and exposes the conditions under which power is exchanged in his realm. A true monarch can secure a just outcome and inspire fairness in others, while a partial or misguided king condones unjust or dishonorable conduct and sets the pattern for a general tyranny.

Fidelity to the law, and to procedures consistent with legal principles, is the most secure guarantee of just conduct on the king's part. A number of well-known *comedias* attest to the centrality of the law, although the king's willingness to secure its influence over himself and others is subject to marked variations. In Lope de Vega a just monarch often stands in opposition to an abusive and self-indulgent member of the landed aristocracy. As Dian Fox has shown, Lope's kings are notable for their accessibility to commoners and their willing involvement in matters of justice and equity (*Refiguring* 136, 91). These royal prerogatives are particularly evident in *El mejor alcalde, el rey* (1620–23), in which the modest hidalgo Sancho turns to Alfonso VII for aid in recovering his captured bride from his feudal lord Don Tello and in redressing the patent offense to the couple's honor. Contempt for the law marks Don Tello as a local tyrant. Sancho asserts that his lord has arrogated to himself the authority to declare and revoke laws within his lands (1437–40); the servant Nuño remarks that he recognizes no law beyond his own pleasure (1895–96); and Don Tello limits his legal consideration of Sancho's case to quibbling over the exact status of his marriage (1540–49). The king, in contrast, attempts to curb the despotic lord to the law's demands and proceeds through legal means. He gives Sancho a letter ordering that his bride be returned, and, when Don Tello refuses to comply with this written order, Alfonso comes to the village to act as his own investigating officer and to dispense justice in person. Fox has observed that Sancho is cast "as a sort of David whose weapon against the giant is the law" (*Refiguring* 83), and the king himself ensures the law's efficacy. When Alfonso first agrees to hear Sancho's complaint, the courtier Don Pedro praises his "piety" and "clemency," and offers him as an "example" to other monarchs in his respect for "holy laws" (1321–24). Through the conflict of Alfonso and Don Tello, Lope clearly marks the division between a king who grounds his authority in the law and an oppressive aristocracy.

La Estrella de Sevilla—a *comedia* once attributed to Lope but now generally considered to be of uncertain authorship—reverses Lope's typical view of the relations between the monarchy and the nobility.[1] In

---

1. In the preface to his edition Foulché-Delbosc rejects the traditional attribution of *La Estrella de Sevilla* to Lope de Vega and argues, on the basis of parallels with other plays of

this work Sancho IV pursues the noble Estrella Tavera and so threatens the honor of her brother Busto. The stratagems of erotic desire repeatedly compromise the royal commitment to justice and the law. The king shows undue preference for Busto, extending the offer of a military command when more qualified petitioners have presented their cases; he orders Estrella's suitor Don Sancho Ortiz to kill the unyielding Busto; and he attempts to secure a pardon for Don Sancho without revealing his own part in Busto's death. The counsellor Don Arias abets the king, contriving procedures to serve his desires and assuring him that within the realm the sovereign's pleasure is the only law (1188–89). At each stage, however, the local aristocracy resists or protests the king's injustices in the name of the law and due process. Busto consciously limits his ambitions to what the law allows (298–307) and asks that the command be given to the more worthy of the two petitioners; Don Sancho questions the harsh sentence pronounced on Busto (1487–96) and acts against him only because he believes that the king's laws must be obeyed (1752–54); the justices of the city refuse to pardon Don Sancho without proper cause (2915–21). The play stresses the importance of local authority and presents the law as the instrument that allows the Sevillian nobility to induce shame and repentance in the errant king of Castile.

Calderón's treatment of the law is comprehensive and sophisticated. His secular theater insists in the first instance on the law's force in royal justice. *El médico de su honra* (1635?) is typical of the honor plays in its portrayal of a flawed monarch who proves unable to provide justice because he fails to rely on the law. Pedro I must remedy a set of interrelated grievances of honor. Don Gutierre is the object of a complaint from Doña Leonor, who maintains that he has abandoned her after giving her a promise of marriage; he also believes that he has suffered a personal affront because the king's half-brother Enrique has approached his wife Mencía. On principle the king believes that he is bound to observe and sustain the law. When he responds to Leonor's petition he describes himself as "un Atlante en quien descansa / todo el peso de la ley" (an Atlas on whom all the weight of the law rests) (675–76), and Gutierre echoes this phrase when he addresses his sovereign as "español Apolo" and "castellano Atlante" (Spanish Apollo, Castilian Atlas) (2053–

the period, that its composition must antedate April 1617 (*La Estrella* 529–30). Ruth Lee Kennedy offers more recent commentary on these questions, and assigns composition to 1623, the year of the diplomatic visit to Madrid by Prince Charles of Wales.

54). In practice, however, Pedro is not faithful to these high standards. He is given to patrolling Seville by night in search of "novelties" and vain "offices" and to drawing his sword on those involved in these affairs (1405–40); he intervenes directly in the intrigues of honor, and in investigating the claims and counterclaims he resorts to the "ill-conceived device of hiding the plaintiff behind the tapestries as he confronts the accused" (Fox, *Kings* 72). The king's personal involvement in matters of justice renders him incapable of applying the law on an impartial basis, and in the end he finds himself obliged to condone the secret death that Gutierre has "prudently" arranged for his wife (2792–93). The king's proceedings are inconsistent with his stated respect for the law and cannot secure justice for his subjects.[2]

Calderón offers Pedro I as a counterexample of a monarch's infidelity to law and legal procedures. In other works he presents a positive view of the application of law to human affairs. This view appeals to a systematic hierarchy that extends from human positive law to the eternal law of providence; it also stresses the conversionary process through which human beings accommodate their conduct to the law's demands. Calderón places this process at the center of political, moral, and spiritual life, and he proposes that human attempts to comprehend and act upon the law at any level in the hierarchy can lead to conversion. In *La vida es sueño* Segismundo becomes a Christian prince who understands the hierarchy of laws and promises just rule for his kingdom; in the *auto* of the same title Man enters a world governed by divine law and learns that God will enable him to abide by its precepts; in *A Dios por razón de Estado* the figure of Ingenio apprehends God's existence and providence by scrutinizing the laws of distinct human religions. In each case the law in its various forms offers humanity a guide to just conduct.

The force of law in questions of justice, and in the broader sphere of politics, is a central theme in Spanish political thought. Prominent thinkers consistently argue that the king can best preserve the legitimacy of his powers and the security of the state by observing the law. Rivadeneira asserts that "el verdadero rey está sujeto á las leyes de Dios y de la naturaleza; el tirano no tiene otra ley sino su voluntad" (the true

---

2. Fox presents a detailed analysis of political issues in this play and draws parallel conclusions concerning the theme of justice and the law: "Although the King prides himself on his equity, the execution of the law in his reign is consummately inconsistent. There is no such thing as equal justice in Pedro's domain, hard as he tries to be impartial" (*Kings* 71–72).

king is subject to the laws of God and of nature; the tyrant has no law other than his will) (532b), and Saavedra Fajardo defines tyranny in similar terms, as the king's usurpation of the superior authority that resides in the law: "no es otra cosa la tiranía, sino un desconocimiento de la ley, atribuyéndose a sí los príncipes su autoridad" (tyranny is nothing other than a disregard for the law, in which princes attribute the law's authority to themselves) (1:261–62). Saavedra Fajardo also maintains that Christian rulers must respond to the demands of the law, rather than to the immediate exigencies of desire or necessity, when they set the political course of their kingdoms. His answer to Machiavelli rests on the concept of a higher law that guarantees the king's authority, and his treatise is emphatic on this point: "Sobre las piedras de las leyes, no de la voluntad, se funda la verdadera política. Líneas son del gobierno, y caminos reales de la razón de estado" (True politics is founded on the stones of the law, and not on the will. The laws are guidelines of government, and highroads of reason of state) (1:260).

Calderón's view of the law's application across the entire spectrum of human conduct appeals to the system of laws elaborated by Neoscholastic theorists of natural law in the sixteenth century. Discussion of legal questions in his theater should begin with an outline of this system. As the terminology of *La segunda esposa* has shown, the concept of law has a temporal dimension that defines the successive convenants between God and humanity. In Neoscholastic thought, however, its definitive feature is the vertical axis that sets the distinct kinds of law in an ordered hierarchy. At the highest position stands the eternal law through which God disposes the order and destiny of all things in the universe. Beneath this supreme law are ranged, in descending order, the three kinds of law that apply to religious and political life: divine law, which God has revealed to humanity in the two testaments of Judeo-Christian Scripture; the law of nature, which God has implanted in the mind so that human beings may discern through reason the fundamental principles of ethics and the design of Creation; and human law, which men themselves have enacted for the ordering and government of their societies.[3] The hierar-

3. This outline of the Thomist hierarchy of laws follows the accounts in Hamilton (5) and Skinner (2:148). Hamilton stresses the centrality of this hierarchy in the major political thinkers of sixteenth-century Spain (11) and surveys their application of natural-law theory to such issues as the laws of the community, the rights and duties of the sovereign, and international law. Her discussion deals in detail with the limits of royal authority; she remarks of the authors whom she reviews (Vitoria, Soto, Molina, and Suárez) that "in their

chy is harmonious and internally consistent, since the supreme law ultimately secures the integrity of each level within the system. All lesser laws, insofar as they accord with reason and fundamental justice, proceed from the eternal law.

This conception of the law has significant implications for human knowledge and human society. It proposes "a universe ruled by a hierarchy of laws" (Skinner 2:148), and it assigns humanity a privileged position in that hierarchy. For Aquinas the eternal law is coequal with divine providence; it is "the plan of divine wisdom directing all things to the attainment of their ends" (Copleston 220). In the fulfillment of God's plan, free will and reason distinguish humanity from the rest of Creation. Where other objects and creatures are directed by nature or by instinct to act in accordance with the eternal law, human beings can choose to obey or to refuse its commands. The three subordinate kinds of law thus exist solely for the instruction and guidance of mankind. And human possession of these laws, particularly of the law of nature, determines the character of ethical and social existence. Because the mind bears the imprint of natural law, human beings can govern themselves according to the principles of morality and justice without direct knowledge of divine law. Natural-law theory holds as a fundamental assumption "that man has the capacity to use his reason in order to supply the moral foundations of political life" (Skinner 2:148). And the temporal character of human society follows as a corollary of this assumption. Through the exercise of reason men have made laws and institutions for their own governance, but no form of political society has been directly ordained by God. In the words of the Catholic theologian Robert Bellarmine, "the foundation of dominion is not in grace but in nature" (quoted in Skinner 2:167).

Although political institutions are human inventions, the superior kinds of law determine the validity of the laws of society and the status of its rulers. Human laws are necessary because natural law is not sufficient in itself for the governance of human communities. Its precepts cannot address all that society requires for "preservation and good government" (Hamilton 43), nor does the fallen condition of humanity allow all to sustain a peaceful and just existence without the ordinances and sanctions of human positive law (Skinner 2:159–60). All the laws that men ordain for their societies must nonetheless have a valid basis in natural

---

theories all these four men are constitutional thinkers in the sense of advocating monarchy under various restraints" (38).

law, and human law must respect in all cases the precepts of the laws that stand above it in the hierarchy. In Catholic political theory "the laws of the community are constantly referred to and judged by the laws of nature and of God" (Hamilton 30). Because of its harmony with the other laws in the hierarchy, human law has the capacity to bind all the members of a community. Despite the logical difficulties of making the sovereign subordinate to the laws of his own state, Neoscholastic thinkers maintain that the king must obey the laws of the society that he governs. To argue this point they generally resort to the distinction that Aquinas draws between the "coercive power" and the "directive force" of the law (*Basic Writings* 2:797). Although there is no superior authority in society that can command the king's obedience by imposing legal sanctions, the king is bound in conscience to respect the moral force of the laws that he has enacted for others. According to Domingo de Soto, "by the very fact that a prince makes a law, he becomes subject to it himself by the law of nature."[4]

Calderón's understanding of the law reflects a profound engagement with the political thought of his contemporaries. His conception of society and its governance follows the principles of natural-law theory, while his larger view of the law's functions in human existence embraces the Neoscholastic hierarchy as a whole. And his comprehensive treatment of conversion and the law has clear political implications. As a turning point in the life of the spirit, conversion frees the individual from the state of sinfulness; as part of the education of the prince, it releases the political state from the repetitive and destructive cycles of political expedience. It is Calderón's view that the state can flourish only by fulfilling the designs of providence, and that true reason of state obliges the prince to proceed in accordance with the eternal law.

The nexus of repetition, statecraft, and the law is a central subject in *La vida es sueño*. This work attests to Calderón's conviction that those who fail to respect the law, or who live in a society where it is not adequately

4. Hamilton notes that the theorists examined in her study "are in no doubt about the king's being in some way bound by the laws" (64), and surveys the arguments that Vitoria and Soto offer on this point (64–67). The absence of specific coercive powers to be exercised against the king, in conjunction with the insistence on his subordination to the laws, leads to conceptual difficulties that neither Vitoria nor Soto can fully resolve. Of particular interest is Hamilton's observation that "the complexity of these problems also serves to explain the spate of books which appeared in the sixteenth century dealing with the character and education of Christian princes" (67).

observed, will be trapped in a cycle of repetitive violence. The experience of major and minor characters in the play confirms this principle. The deceived Rosaura paints herself as a "portrait" and "copy" of her ill-fated mother (2770–73), and Clarín, in accepting his allotted role as one more of Poland's "counterfeit princes," becomes an ironic double of Segismundo (2264–65).[5] The issue of the royal succession, however, offers the most significant framework for examining the politics of repetition. The casting of Segismundo's horoscope has placed Basilio in the paradigmatic position of the Machiavellian ruler. Basilio has found in his son's character an innate disposition to cruelty and impiety that will expose the kingdom to the dangers of treason and division, and he has attempted to apply this prior knowledge to the task of conserving the political order. Astrology has served here as an instrument of Machiavellian foresight, and to prevent the afflictions that he anticipates Basilio has acted as a political innovator who is prepared to suspend the traditional rights of the populace and the hereditary prince. The harsh irony of this situation is that Basilio's measures have the potential to induce the political conditions that he hopes to avert. If Segismundo proves to be a tyrant, his regime will simply reiterate the failings inherent in his father's rule. In attempting to alter the course of the succession, Basilio discovers the dangers of political calculation. To the degree that his statecraft departs from the law, it threatens to reduce the politics of the kingdom to a cycle of tyranny. The ethical and legal implications of Basilio's conduct in relation to his son, and of Segismundo's response to that conduct, are central to the play's scrutiny of the uses and limits of royal authority.

The principles of seventeenth-century political theory indicate that Basilio's proceedings are neither prudent nor just. Hailed at his first entrance as a learned king, Basilio misapplies his learning to the tasks of government and places unwarranted confidence in a science generally regarded as too inexact to provide an appropriate guide to political action. He is not alone in his commitment to learning—Fernández-Santamaría notes that realist political thought is marked by "an almost obsessive faith

---

5. The text of the *comedia* carefully elaborates the parallel between prince and servant. If Segismundo endures a troubling "dream" that ultimately instructs him in the order of providence, Clarín is plagued by a nightmare in which flagellants rise and fall in a parody of Fortune's wheel (Paterson 159); if the rebel soldiers acclaim Clarín their natural prince, he concludes that the practice of selecting a prisoner for a day's rule is a local custom (2243–46); if the rebels greet him as Segismundo, he accepts that all "counterfeit princes" are given the name (2264–65).

in the power of knowledge as a means of understanding and controlling"
(xx)—but he pursues knowledge through suspect means and applies
what he has learned to dubious ends. Paterson remarks that Basilio "is
forever driven by the need to know" (168); Cascardi asserts that, in his
attempt "to submit an entire society to science," the king "confuses the
natural and social orders" (14). Contemporary thinkers would have been
quick to find fault in such impulses and actions. In his fourth *empresa*
Saavedra Fajardo concedes that princes cannot rule without learning
(1:106), but argues that the demands of government require only a
general knowledge of the arts and sciences and of their practical effects
(1:112). He cautions against extremes in learning, since excessive study
will impede the execution of other duties (1:110), and he classifies judicial
astrology, with its false claims to knowledge of the future and its presumption upon divine providence, among the disciplines in which princes
lose themselves and earn the distrust of their subjects (1:114–15). In
comparing different forms of learning, Saavedra Fajardo consistently
praises historical study as the key to the princely virtues. The twenty-
eighth *empresa* of his treatise presents history as a school of true
prudence. And to contrast the benefits of history with the dangers of other
disciplines, Saavedra Fajardo returns to his argument against astrology:

> Por estos aspectos de los tiempos ha de hacer juicio y pronosticar
> la prudencia de vuestra alteza, no por aquellos de los planetas,
> que, siendo pocos y de movimiento regulado, no pueden (cuando
> tuvieran virtud) señalar la inmensa variedad de accidentes que
> producen los casos y dispone el libre albedrío; ni la especulación y
> experiencia son bastantes a constituir una ciencia segura y cierta
> de causas tan remotas. (2:35)

> (Your Highness should judge and prognosticate on the basis of
> these aspects of past times, and not on those of the planets which,
> being few in number and regular in movement, cannot [even if
> they had such power] indicate the immense variety of contingen-
> cies that circumstances produce and free will disposes; nor are
> speculation and experience sufficient to constitute a sure and
> exact science from such remote causes.)

Saavedra Fajardo's views are typical. That prudence is the key to
successful and just rule, and that it can best be acquired through

historical study, are common propositions among the thinkers whom Fernández-Santamaría classifies as realists (87,160). This background of accepted political opinion casts Basilio's failings into sharp relief. As presiding monarch he expresses a genuine and positive concern for the future of his nation, but, since he believes that astrology is an "exact science," he acts imprudently to protect the realm. Faced with the prospect of tyranny, he seeks a solution not in history, but in speculative science; as R. D. F. Pring-Mill has noted, his treatment of Segismundo is an "experiment" designed to determine if a wise king—in this case Basilio himself—can turn aside what is decreed in the stars (54–55). This procedure exceeds the legitimate dissimulation that political theorists were willing to allow because it violates the principles of charity and justice enjoined upon the ruler by natural law. To turn aside the threat of Segismundo's horoscope, Basilio has acted with Machiavellian decisiveness, but he has ignored the principles of true political prudence.

The conditions that Basilio imposes on his sole heir will perpetuate the errors of his own regime. In his conviction that Segismundo must be removed from society, Basilio fails to recognize that isolation and imprisonment can do nothing to correct his son's violent inclinations. Pring-Mill observes that the king has no grasp of the principle that education should foster the positive capacities of the individual and restrain the negative ones (58–59); Frederick de Armas notes that his actions intensify the saturnine melancholy that Segismundo has inherited from the stars ("Planeta" 908). Although Basilio has taken pains to supply formal instruction for his captive son, by the standards of natural law his curriculum is questionable both in its general intentions and in its specific details. Segismundo tells Rosaura that he has studied the "politics" of beasts and birds (214–16); Basilio informs the court that Clotaldo has instructed him in "sciences" and in "Catholic law" (756–58); Clotaldo himself enumerates the topics that he has discussed with his difficult pupil:

> con él
> hablé un rato de las letras
> humanas que le ha enseñado
> la muda naturaleza
> de los montes y los cielos,
> en cuya divina escuela

> la retórica aprendió
> de las aves y las fieras.
>   (1026–33)

(I spoke with him for a time of the humane letters that the mute nature of the hills and heavens has taught him, in whose divine school he learned the rhetoric of the birds and beasts.)

Basilio and Clotaldo assume that nature's example will instruct Segismundo in the principles of order and justice. Their logic is hopelessly flawed, in that it takes no account of the ways in which humanity differs from nature in its participation in the eternal law. As the devotional literature of this period tirelessly demonstrates, all natural creatures tend to their rightful ends in the order of providence, but they do so with neither understanding nor volition. Human beings, in contrast, must cooperate actively with providence, under the direction of the subordinate laws that God has ordained for their guidance. This distinction between the orders of nature and of humanity underlines the central failing in Segismundo's curriculum. His tutor has set him to learn "politics" and "humane letters," but these subjects cannot be mastered solely on the basis of the natural world that has been the object of his study. Although nature may stand before him as a "divine school," it can offer no instruction in the laws that God has created for humanity alone, nor can the prince easily learn "rhetoric" from something "mute" and without reason. And even if his lesson were better presented, Segismundo's circumstances would impede any true understanding of the human community. Set apart in his tower, he enjoys none of the exchange of needs that makes society and its laws both necessary and desirable for human beings. In his skins and chains, the imprisoned Segismundo confirms Domingo de Soto's axiom that "a solitary individual, unless he leads an angelic life, must be a beast" (*De Justitia et Jure*; quoted in Hamilton 32). Finally, as Pring-Mill has argued, Segismundo's solitude also denies him the personal experience essential to the virtue of prudence (62). His education has dealt exclusively in abstract principles; he has neither experience nor historical knowledge to aid him in applying and evaluating what he has learned. For all that he desires to avert the threat of tyranny, Basilio unwittingly ensures that his failings will be duplicated in his son. Lacking in prudence himself, the king can offer Segismundo no opportunity to become a prudent ruler.

The imprisonment of the prince scandalizes the law on two accounts. In addition to stultifying Segismundo's capacity to understand law and society, it violates the positive laws that should guide all human conduct. Basilio acknowledges the legal implications of his position when he addresses the court in act 1. In his desire to ensure a proper succession he has realized that, although Segismundo may be a potential tyrant, he is also a legitimate prince to whom "human and divine law" have granted an inalienable right to govern (771). Basilio has thus decided that he must test his son to discover whether his free will has made him capable of acting as a just ruler. This procedure again illustrates Basilio's determination to plot and control the course of political events. Pring-Mill remarks that when the king ceases to hold his son prisoner, and decides instead to test his will, he abandons his first experiment and begins a second (55). Basilio is heedless of the obvious contradictions in this project. He does not admit that the first experiment may determine the outcome of the second (Pring-Mill 54–55), nor does he see any difficulty in making his test dependent on the very quality—human free will—that most theorists regarded as undermining the scientific approach to politics.[6] Whatever its limitations, the test appeals to Basilio because it offers an apparent solution to the legal dilemma that has suspended him between the potential tyranny of Segismundo's rule and the effective tyranny of denying his right to the crown.

De Armas states that, in view of the conditions and the curriculum that Basilio has prescribed, "the test he gives his son is an impossible one" ("Planeta" 910). Segismundo's own conduct reveals his incapacity to shoulder the princely burdens imposed upon him. Far from governing with prudence and mercy, he acts as a despot who will only intensify his father's misrule. His failure, however, attests equally to his violent character and to the inadequacies of his education. And nowhere does his education fail him more thoroughly than in his understanding of the law and legal rights, particularly the rights that he enjoys as the prince. One of the principles that Segismundo has inferred from his study of the

6. According to Fernández-Santamaría "the question of whether political knowledge is a science . . . is of exceptional interest to the study of Spanish views on the nature of statecraft" (xxi). Opinion on this question is not univocal (140), but the majority position, as expressed by the Tacitist Alamos de Barrientos, is that politics cannot be rigorously scientific. Even though political thinkers may deduce rules on the basis of human nature, the rules will not apply in every specific case since free will allows human beings to act contrary to their natural inclinations (205).

natural order is the priority of liberty, and he has asked himself what form of law or justice could have denied him a "privilege" that all of nature seems to enjoy (167–72). When he awakens in the palace, to find himself at liberty and installed in his rightful position as hereditary prince of the realm, he quickly turns upon those who have held him captive. Accusing his tutor Clotaldo of threefold wrongs—against law, king, and prince—he threatens to kill him for his treachery (1305–11); confronted by his father, he reproaches him for the years of unjust captivity:

> Tirano de mi albedrío,
> si viejo y caduco estás,
> muriéndote, ¿qué me das?
> ¿Dasme más de lo que es mío?
>   Mi padre eres y mi rey;
> luego toda esta grandeza
> me da la naturaleza
> por derechos de su ley.
>   Luego, aunque esté en este estado,
> obligado no te quedo,
> y pedirte cuentas puedo
> del tiempo que me has quitado
>   libertad, vida y honor;
> y así, agradéceme a mí
> que yo no cobre de ti,
> pues eres tú mi deudor.
>
> (1504–19)

(Tyrant of my free will, if you are old and senile, what are you giving me as you die? Are you giving me more than what is mine? You are my father and my king; thus nature grants me all this grandeur by my rights under its law. Thus, although I may find myself in this state I am not obliged to you, and I can call you to account for the time during which you deprived me of liberty, life, and honor; and so, be grateful to me that I make no claim on you, since you are my debtor.)

Segismundo's exchanges with Clotaldo and Basilio reveal what he has made of the law. Educated in the principles of sovereignty, he is well aware of the "rights" that he enjoys through natural law. He possesses the "grandeur" of power by right; Basilio, in assuming the authority to grant or deny this right, has acted as a "tyrant." Segismundo's knowledge of the law allows him to understand that he has been injured. He realizes that he could call his father to account for denying him not only his patrimony, but also the most fundamental of human liberties. His understanding is, however, dangerously one-sided, in that he fails to recognize that natural law also limits his own conduct. In threatening to kill Clotaldo with his own hands he forsakes justice for personal revenge; in suggesting that Basilio has released him only because old age and senility forbid the old king from continuing to govern, he assumes that others act, as he does, to serve their own desires and interests. The contradiction here is self-evident. Even as Segismundo reproaches his father for violating natural law, the only standard that he applies to himself is his own satisfaction. When a court servant attempts to defend Clotaldo, Segismundo insists that the king has no right to impose unjust laws: "en lo que no es justa ley / no ha de obedecer al Rey" (in what is not just law the king should not be obeyed) (1321–22); yet when the same servant warns him of his own excesses, he replies that justice depends solely on his will: "Nada me parece justo / en siendo contra mi gusto" (Nothing seems just to me if it runs counter to my pleasure) (1417–18). His knowledge of law and legal rights, instilled in him as part of Basilio's educational program, leads him to disastrous conclusions. Although he is keenly aware of the legal injuries that he has suffered, he feels no obligation not to malign or injure others. The test of his capacity to govern ends in a second legal impasse. As true heir to the throne Segismundo possesses an inalienable right to rule, and he has now asserted that right; as a prince who cannot grasp that legal constraints apply to himself as they do to others, he is a tyrant who threatens to destroy the positive laws of the kingdom. The king's immediate solution to this problem is of course to return Segismundo to the tower; however, Basilio himself has been exposed as a tyrant who has failed to prepare his son to rule. Through his Machiavellian scheme against tyranny, Basilio has brought events to a troubling moment of stasis.

This moment ends when the popular rebellion acclaims Segismundo the true prince and demands that he seize the crown from his father. As Dian Fox has noted, the rebellion embodies a force that Basilio has omitted from his political calculations (*Kings* 110), and when it arises he perceives the vanity of his attempts to control the kingdom. Initially, however, the rebels offer no release from the cycle of repetition; by deposing Basilio in favor of Segismundo, they will simply exchange the lesser tyranny of the father for the greater tyranny of the son. This outcome is averted only because events encourage Segismundo to overcome the threat of repetition through a correct and full apprehension of the law. His trial at the court, designed by Basilio as a speculative experiment, becomes in Segismundo's mind a true experience that, when fully incorporated, enables him to observe the limits of temporal power and to apprehend the eternal law that guarantees all legitimate authority. This process of conversion is central to Segismundo's development. When he is first brought to the court, the prince understands the law solely as it applies to his immediate interests; when he returns to power in triumph, he has learned that its constraints are divinely sanctioned and bear upon his own conduct.

Embracing the law is Segismundo's final and most effective defense against the pattern of repetition that threatens prince and kingdom alike, but he arrives at this gesture only after he has tried other, provisional solutions. During the final act he encounters this threat on several occasions, in a sequence that forces him to respond to it with increasing insight and sophistication. When the rebels first arrive to release him from the tower, he dismisses them because what they have to offer so closely resembles his previous experience of an apparently false liberation:

> ¿Otra vez (¿qué es esto, cielos?)
> queréis que sueñe grandezas
> que ha de deshacer el tiempo?
> ¿Otra vez queréis que vea
> entre sombras y bosquejos
> la majestad y la pompa
> desvanecida del viento?
> ¿Otra vez queréis que toque
> el desengaño, o el riesgo
> a que el humano poder
> nace humilde y vive atento?
>   (2307–17)

(Once again [whatever is this, oh heavens!] do you want me to dream of grandeurs which time must destroy? Once again do you want me to see, amidst shadows and shapes, majesty and pomp

dispelled by the wind? Once again do you want me to touch the
disillusion, or the risk, under which human power is humbly born
and mindfully lives?)

Piling question upon question, Segismundo pieces together his response
to the rebels. It is clear that he regards their action as a recapitulation of
what Basilio has already done. The reiterated phrase "otra vez" reveals
that he draws no significant distinction between his previous "dream" of
power and the rebellion that promises to return him to the throne. He
resembles Clarín in assuming that the "grandeurs" and "majesty" that the
rebels offer are essentially counterfeit, but differs from him in refusing
to trade in such worthless currency. Experience has taught Segismundo
that human authority is so profoundly at risk as to expose those who
wield it to deposition and disillusion. Having once experienced this
pattern of liberation and imprisonment, he is unwilling to leave the tower,
and he expresses his refusal in the classical language of *desengaño*
(2326–27). To the extent that he sees his own experience as repetitive, he
acts to remove himself from a self-defeating cycle.

This withdrawal from his princely role is Segismundo's first attempt to
break the pattern of repetition. It is a negative gesture, in that it rests on
his assumption that he cannot stop events from repeating their former
course. He realizes the importance of his own conduct only when one of
the rebels suggests that he may interpret his "dream" as an "omen" of
his due ascent to power. The possibility of distinguishing between the
images of his former "dream" and the reality of the present rebellion
allows Segismundo to reconstruct his experience in another light. The
dream has taught him that all earthly authority is limited and transient;
he may now take this lesson into account as he attempts once again to
assume control of the kingdom. Armed with two fundamental principles
of kingship—that prudence is the best safeguard against disillusion, and
that all power is "lent" to those who exercise it (2366–67, 2370–71)—
he is prepared to seize his fortune at its height. His gesture here is
Machiavellian, but, because he is determined not to repeat his former
errors, he performs it with a non-Machiavellian respect for Christian
ethics: "Mas, sea verdad o sueño, / obrar bien es lo que importa" (But
whether this is truth or a dream, to live well is what matters) (2423–24).

Criticism of *La vida es sueño* has emphasized the role of reason in
Segismundo's conversion. Everett Hesse tells us that in the last act
"Segismundo uses his reason to help him deliberate the issues carefully

before arriving at a decision" (126), and Pring-Mill has argued that he acts as a "rational man," using his memory and understanding to apply past experience to present conditions and his will to hold his passions in check (68). Reason functions here within the field of natural law; it has allowed Segismundo to act in accordance with the fundamental moral principles that all human beings possess. His recognition that these principles must govern his own conduct marks an advance in his understanding of the law, and from this new perspective he is capable of apprehending the eternal order that sustains the law in all its forms. A movement from natural law to the eternal law will complete the process of his conversion.

The encounter with Rosaura on the battlefield forces Segismundo to take this final step. Like the second liberation from the tower, this episode is disturbing in its initial effects. When Rosaura reveals that she has seen Segismundo in the palace, and describes her own efforts there to recover her lost honor, she challenges the proposition that his experiences at court were simply a private and prophetic "dream" of the power that he should now accept as real. And this challenge threatens to collapse the distinctions that have shaped the prince's conduct in the final act; confronted with Rosaura's testimony, he questions the very possibility of distinguishing between living and dreaming, between true and false glories, between an original and its copy (2934–49). The last set of terms here reopens the difficult issue of repetition. The copy that perfectly reproduces the original is for Segismundo an image of the exact repetition of things that has already threatened him with absolute disillusion. The return of this threat initially leads him to despair of ethical conduct. If events repeat themselves in a sequence beyond our comprehension or control, we are best advised to grasp immediate pleasures, without considering what may follow: "soñemos dichas agora, / que después serán pesares" (let us dream of pleasant things now, which later will be sorrows) (2965–66). By undermining Segismundo's moral logic, Rosaura's narrative has undone his resolve to abide by natural law.

Segismundo regains his ethical bearings when Rosaura's challenge forces him to alter the terms of his reasoning. Under the pressure of the knowledge that he has acquired from her, Segismundo comes to a crucial realization about human achievement: that from the perspective of providence all earthly glories, whether real or imagined, are equally illusory. This sudden apprehension of a reality beyond human experience transforms his understanding of his actions and their consequences. Having learned to distinguish between the "vainglory" of this world and the true "glory," which is divine (2969–71), he perceives earthly pleasure itself as transitory and resolves to embrace "the eternal" with its promise of "lasting fame" for the worthy (2982–85).[7] The immediate situation demands that he translate this principle into practice. His new awareness of the eternal determines his final response to Rosaura. Although he desires her for himself, and has been prepared to violate the law in the name of his love (2960–63), he now realizes that as the legitimate prince he is obliged in conscience and law to supply her with a marriage that will restore her honor:

> Rosaura está sin honor;
> más a un príncipe le toca
> el dar honor que quitarle.
> (2986–88)

(Rosaura is without honor; it is more a prince's part to confer honor than to withdraw it.)

Dian Fox has observed that in Calderón's *comedias* "the capacity to recognize and value the eternal over the temporal is fundamental to the proper enactment of social roles" (*Kings* 112). Segismundo's renunciation of Rosaura illustrates this proposition. The eternal, as the principle that secures the universal hierarchy of laws and rewards those who live by the law, confirms Segismundo's decision to act virtuously in his role as prince of the realm. His reeducation in the law, and in his political duties, is now complete.

At the end of *La vida es sueño* Segismundo undertakes to restore due order to the realm that Basilio has divided. This resolution can occur because father and son have come to accept the limits of royal authority. The failure of Basilio's program, and the unforeseen conversion of Segismundo, have demonstrated that the welfare of the nation is better entrusted to God's design than to the plotting of kings. Political calculation can only decline into a cycle of oppression; providence holds the promise of just governance under the aegis of the law. This movement from tyranny to justice may invite us to interpret the play as a defense of

---

7. For a complementary reading of this speech, emphasizing the "logical and semantic" difficulties that Segismundo encounters in deciphering the metaphorical equivalence of the terms "life" and "dream," see Lipmann 380–84.

a dominant aristocratic ideology. In his recent study of public theater in England and Spain, Walter Cohen classifies *La vida es sueño* as an example of "tragicomic romance," in which "long periods of suffering ultimately issue in the triumphant reconciliation of family and of nation" (384). Through its "transcendence of tragedy" this variant of romance recognizes the contemporary failure or crisis of the aristocracy, and yet takes that failure as a "point of departure" for "asserting the triumphant adaptation of that class in the future" (389–90). According to Cohen, Calderón finds the sole alternative to "the persistent conflict of the present" in "a utopian view of the future" that celebrates the final restoration of social harmony (391). In a parallel reading of the play's dimensions of myth and romance, De Armas has argued that "the figure Rosaura-Astraea" can be interpreted "as the embodiment of returning justice and truth" and that her presence in the final scene signals the restoration of these virtues in "a new golden age" (*Return* 98, 89). Calderón's concept of the law appears to confirm this view of the play. To the extent that Segismundo applies the principles of his conversion to the tasks of governing, the hierarchy of laws will secure the promised social order. Yet the final moments of *La vida es sueño* emphasize the difficulties of pursuing justice in secular society, rather than the concord of the new regime. Despite Segismundo's conversion through the law, his first actions in government offer an uncertain prospect of Utopia.

After his victory over the old king Segismundo must address the law as it applies to human conduct in society, in order to render justice to those who have been drawn to the opposing sides of the civil war. In discharging this task he demonstrates an acute and unexpected understanding of the insecure relationship between legal principles and the conditions of social existence. He recognizes that the basic precepts of natural law are not sufficient in themselves to weigh human conduct in all circumstances, and that he cannot invoke the law to justify the pursuit of personal vengeance. Despite the injuries that he has suffered because Basilio and Clotaldo have violated natural law, Segismundo pardons their errors and offers them his generosity and respect. Yet the spirit of his judgment suddenly changes when the rebel soldier steps forward to ask what portion he will receive for his part in the popular rebellion. The prince's response—to condemn the soldier to life imprisonment in the tower—displays an unyielding rigor in enforcing the law against tyranny. The severity of this sentence, and the contrast between Segismundo's merciful reception of his father and tutor and his summary treatment of

the soldier, have led critics to question the quality of judgment that the new prince has brought to his government. In his seminal article on this question, H. B. Hall asserts that the soldier's fate shows us that Segismundo has become a "calculating, cruel Machiavellian" who is prepared to inaugurate his reign with "an act of gratuitous repression" (197, 200).

Segismundo's conduct may be surprising, but it is not indefensible, particularly in the light of contemporary political thought. Alexander Parker's answer to Hall—that the soldier, in seeking personal profit from his contribution to the rebellion, makes himself subject to just censure and punishment ("Calderón's Rebel Soldier" 124)—has found general support among critics who have scrutinized the soldier's motives or related the scene to the traditional belief in the king's obligation to punish traitors even if he has benefited from their actions.[8] Through this strict enforcement of a legal sanction against treason, Segismundo also confirms his intention to submit all the estates of his kingdom to the rule of law. Dian Fox has argued that Basilio's tyranny lies in part in his refusal to grant the common people a voice or presence in the affairs of state, and that Segismundo recognizes this alienated constituency when he imposes the sanction for treason on the rebel soldier (*Refiguring* 50–52). In Fox's view the sentencing of the soldier is an act of enfranchisement that assigns the commoners a legitimate place within "a nation of laws" (51). At the beginning of his regime Segismundo revives the tower that Basilio has had constructed, but the change in the tower's function emphasizes the "passage from injustice to justice" in the course of the play (Connolly 13).

Segismundo has learned that the law offers the best defense against the threat of repetition, and he attempts to govern according to the most exacting standards of law and justice. He has good reason for each of the judgments that he delivers during the final scene. As men who have

8. Critics who see the imprisonment as just are in general agreement that the rebel soldier acts on the basis of personal interest and shows no concern for the body politic. He has been described as self-serving (Halkhoree 10), and as a violent character who threatens the social order (Connolly 13; J. B. Hall 346). C. Christopher Soufas supplies a concise statement of this position: "by demanding an immediate reward for his participation, the Rebel Soldier suggests that his reason for joining forces was personal and not civic, that he has come to think of the rebellion as an end in itself and not simply as a disagreeable yet necessary means of restoring the rightful rulership and succession to the Polish throne" (205). For the tradition of castigating the traitor, see Heiple. Scholarly opinion concerning the rebel soldier is surveyed by Lipmann (388–89n) and C. Soufas (296n).

shared in the prince's experience of *desengaño*, Basilio and Clotaldo have a strong claim on his prerogative of mercy, and the imprisonment of the rebel soldier inaugurates a rule of law for all the citizens of the kingdom. Yet the concord that Segismundo is able to strike does not possess the stability and harmony that political thinkers would attribute to such a legal order. The challenge of applying the law to life in society exacts a human cost from both the governor and the governed. In sentencing the rebel soldier Segismundo must turn upon one of the first subjects to have supported his legitimate right to rule, and the soldier himself is made to sacrifice his liberty for the enfranchisement of his estate. Through his treatment of the hard choices that confront the victorious Segismundo, Calderón reads us one of his most telling lessons concerning the nature of kingship. The true king finds the pattern of just government in the hierarchy of laws, but he also faces the task of adjusting that pattern to the particular debts and desires of men in society. Segismundo's rule is fragile because its justice depends on his ability to reckon the fair cost of ruling by the law and on his willingness to pay that cost. Should he fail in the economy of justice, the tyranny of his father's regime will repeat itself.[9]

Segismundo leaves us to question the permanence of his conversion. It is clear that the task of balancing the law against the claims of the parties in the rebellion is simply the first in a series of similar challenges that he will encounter during his reign, and that the costs of rendering justice will always impinge upon his resolution to act by legal principles. His apprehension of the eternal law is genuine, but it does not make him certain or secure in his judgment of particular moral or political circumstances. The central motif of this *comedia*—the process of human accommodation to the eternal law through conversion—is reconsidered in the late *auto* that shares its title.[10] Although Alexander Parker is correct in asserting that

9. H. B. Hall describes the order that Segismundo establishes in the final scene as "extremely fragile" (200), and other critics have entertained the possibility that his government will decline into tyranny. May argues that the young king's judgment of the rebel soldier is the first error of his reign (74) and that history will repeat itself as the son's rule becomes as unjust as the father's; C. Soufas maintains that Segismundo's decision is just, but concedes that his regime will become unstable in the "unlikely but possible event" of his abandoning what he has learned in the course of the play (296).

10. In my discussion I refer to the version of *La vida es sueño* performed in 1673 and published in Calderón's *Autos Sacramentales alegóricos e historiales* (Madrid, 1677). Valbuena Prat uses this edition as his copy text; he also prints in an appendix (1859–75) the manuscript version of the same *auto*, which he attributes to Calderón and describes as an

the *auto* is not simply "the *comedia* interpreted *a lo divino*" (*Allegorical Drama* 203), the *auto* presents Man as a counterpart of Segismundo, in that both characters learn through reason that eternal law governs Creation and that human beings must live in accordance with providence. The depiction of humanity as a single personified character indicates that moral allegory is the dominant mode of this *auto*, and Calderón resorts to this abstract mode in order to scrutinize the human capacity to find and retain a place in the providential order that governs the affairs of individuals and of nations.

Parker has grouped *La vida es sueño* with a number of other late *autos* that dramatize the dogma of the Redemption. The focus on this dogma, however, does not limit the scope of Calderón's dramatic argument. *La vida es sueño* exploits the timeless aspect of moral allegory in order to set the Redemption within its universal context: the conflict between the forces of the demonic and the divine. The significant events that mark the course of this struggle—the war in heaven against the rebel angels, the creation of the world and of humanity, the Fall of Man, the Incarnation, the death and the Resurrection of Christ—appear in the *auto* through retrospective narrative or allegorical representation. This inclusive argument allows Calderón to dramatize the action of the eternal law in its various domains, particularly in the creation of the world and in the ethical life of humanity. The role of redemption in relation to the law, however, leads to a crucial distinction between *comedia* and *auto*. In the *auto* divine wisdom intervenes to redeem Man when he violates the precepts that have governed his life in Eden and to establish the sacraments that will enable him to live in harmony with the eternal law. Because the sacraments promise to secure his capacity to abide by the law, they spare Man the dilemma that confronts Segismundo at the end of the *comedia*. Reason allows Segismundo to break the cycle of Machiavellian politics; divine grace, through the agency of the sacraments, aligns Man's spirit with the pattern of salvation. *Comedia* and *auto* both empha-

---

intermediate step between the *comedia* and the mature *auto* (1860a). This version of the *auto* closely follows the outline of the *comedia*, and it anticipates several features of the late *auto*, particularly in the ordering of the elements (1826b), the creation of Man and his reception in the garden (1865b, 1868a), and the use of the *glosa* (1869b–70a). Its argument, however, does not consistently address man's accommodation to the law, nor does it conclude with the securing of that accommodation through the institution of the sacraments. The late *auto* is less faithful to the details of the *comedia*, but more cogent and sophisticated in the treatment of its themes.

size that human beings must accommodate themselves to the eternal law; the *auto* stresses that divine aid will assist in initiating and securing the process of conversion.

Discussion of the eternal law in this *auto* should begin with the first of the domains in which it functions: the creation of the physical world. Parker has shown that Calderón follows Augustine in distinguishing two distinct phases in the act of creation, "first, the creation of 'materia informis' and second, the raising of this into actuality by endowing it with 'forms'" (*Allegorical Drama* 205). The *auto* opens on the spectacle of the four personified elements battling among themselves, each one claiming precedence over the others. They suspend their conflict only when the persons of the Trinity—Power, Wisdom, and Love—enter to divide the elements and impart forms to them.

Each of the three persons makes a specific contribution to this task, and each of their labors advances our understanding of the operation of the eternal law in the process of creation. Power undertakes to reconcile the elements by bringing their contending qualities into equilibrium; Wisdom, to define their "positions" and "offices" in the order of the world; Love, to enrich them with divine gifts, so that the world will be filled with plants and animals. In the course of the *auto* the eternal law continues to act through the assignment of offices and the bestowing of gifts. The most significant contribution of the Trinity, however, is the initial disposition of the elements, since by this action Power establishes the general principles of order among all created things.

Power proceeds from the recognition that the elements can act upon each other through "sympathy" and "antipathy" (1388b), and that variety and harmony depend on the presence of both these phenomena. Sympathy alone will reduce all the elements to a single unity; antipathy alone will induce absolute division between one element and another. Due order rests on maintaining a balance between the unifying and opposing "qualities" inherent in matter, and Power summons the elements into such an arrangement:

> pues en una parte opuestos
> y en otra parte benignos,
> es fuerza que eslabonados,
> cuando vaya a dividiros
> el odio, os tenga el Amor;
> y que amigos y enemigos

duréis conformes y opuestos,
lo que duraren los siglos.
(1388b–89a)

(so opposed on the one hand and on the other in accord, it is
necessary that, in your linkage, whenever hatred divides you Love
will hold you together, and that, as companions and contraries,
you endure in agreement and in opposition as long as time may
endure.)

E. M. Wilson has described the conception of a stable equilibrium among
the elements as a classical "doctrine" that has been "incorporated into the
scholastic system" (34). In dramatizing the origin of this equilibrium
Calderón alludes to a complex of ideas first elaborated by Empedocles
but generally associated in Renaissance thought with Neopythagorean
cosmology. This complex posits four fundamental qualities of matter, and
assigns these qualities to the elements in pairs. The presence or absence
of shared qualities among the pairs allows the elements to be arranged in
a balanced tetrad that may be represented as a circle. Those elements
that have no quality in common and so exert a force of mutual repulsion—earth (cold and dry) and air (hot and moist), water (cold and
moist) and fire (hot and dry)—are placed directly opposite one another.
In the resulting arrangement of elements around the circle's circum-
ference—earth, fire, air, and water—each set of adjacent elements
shares one quality and so exerts a mutual attraction that counteracts the
repulsion of the other elements. As Calderón puts it, the elements are
forever linked together through the balanced forces of primordial "love"
and "hatred."[11] This equilibrium distinguishes the order of the tetrad
from the indiscriminate conflict of the opening scene. The disposition of
the elements represents the operation of the eternal law in giving form to
the physical world.

11. I follow Heninger in this account of the structure and dynamics of the tetrad
(158–64). Heninger discusses the origins of the tetrad in Empedocles (170–74); he also
comments more generally on the syncretic character of Neopythagorean thought in the
Renaissance (xv). In the manuscript version of Calderón's *auto*, the command of the divine
Word to the elements is less precise in its engagement of the Neopythagorean model:
"porque assí / unidos y desunidos, / por una parte contrarios / y por otra parte amigos, /
durará la oposizión / por los siglos de los siglos" (because in this way, united and disunited,
opposed on the one hand and on the other in accord, their opposition will endure forever
and ever) (1862b).

The *auto*'s account of creation initially draws our attention to the parallels between the elements and Man. In the human domain, as in the physical world, the eternal law operates through the institution of offices, of gifts, and of order. Man is created to preside over the world as its "viceroy" and "prince" (1390a, 1391b); he receives abundant gifts from the Trinity and the elements; he must balance the conflicting impulses of his own nature if he is to make appropriate use of the gifts and privileges that he has been granted. Within this parallelism Calderón reproduces the Neoscholastic distinction between natural and human participation in the law. While Power summons the elements into equilibrium, he leaves Man free to find his own balance. As Parker has noted, Man's freedom places him in an intermediate position with respect to the elements and the Trinity: "the order and harmony of the world, expressed in the obedience of the Elements to the higher authority of Man, is dependent upon the obedience of Man to the higher authority of God" (*Allegorical Drama* 211).

Human obedience cannot be taken for granted, since the freedom of Man's will implies the possibility of his fall. Power introduces the dilemma of human freedom before the "court" of the elements when he reviews his decision to proceed in the creation of Man (1390a–91b). Lucifer's rebellion has prompted Power to fear that if Man is created he may also defy providence, and Wisdom has foreseen the Fall of the first man and the somber fate of his descendants. In the face of this testimony concerning Man's future, Love has spoken in favor of proceeding with his creation, arguing that Power must endow Man with freedom and with adequate faculties of perception and judgment:

> si los cinco
> Talentos que le has de dar
> han de ser cinco Sentidos,
> si tres Potencias los tres;
> y si uno Razón y Juicio,
> deja que el Entendimiento,
> con el racional instinto
> le advierta del bien y el mal,
> dándole un libre Albedrío
> con que use del mal o el bien.
> (1391b)

(if the five Talents that you will give him are to be five Senses, and
if the three are to be three Powers, and if I treat Reason and
Judgment as one, let Understanding advise him of good and evil
by means of rational instinct, giving him a Free Will with which he
may make use of evil and of good.)

Love's argument outlines the Scholastic view of the constitution of the
human soul. The act of creation will endow Man with five exterior senses
and three superior powers. He will also possess a "rational instinct" that
will inform these powers, allowing his Understanding to advise and his
Free Will to act in matters of good and evil. This instinct corresponds to
the natural law.[12] It will be imprinted in Man's soul, and it will grant him
innate knowledge of the fundamental principles of ethics. The primary
counsel that Man will receive through his Understanding—that good
is to be sought and evil avoided—stands among the precepts that
Spanish thinkers attributed to the natural law.[13] To the extent that he
abides by the principles that he can discern through reason, Man will
respect God's laws. In this *auto*, as in the *comedia* of the same title, human
participation in the eternal law begins in the apprehension of natural law.

Man's progress during the *auto* follows the scheme that the Trinity
sets out in this exposition. To prepare and receive Man as the world's
governor, the elements extend their gifts on several occasions. They
supply the physical material that Power requires for Man's creation
(1392a); they summon nature's abundance to Man's service when he
enters the garden (1395b); they enrich Man with objects that will enhance
the honor and dignity of his office (1397a–98b). Man himself enters
accompanied by Understanding and Free Will, who will assist him in
knowing and executing his position. As Parker has demonstrated, these
two powers have distinct functions in relation to Man: "Understanding
explains his *nature*, Free-will informs him of his *purpose*, and Understand-

12. The parallel passage in the manuscript version refers specifically to the concept of
law: "después / que vida y alma le dés / ley aluedrio y auiso, / le traslada al parayso /
adonde sepa quien es" (after you give him life and a soul, law, free will, and counsel, place
him in paradise, where he may discover who he is) (1866a).

13. Hamilton emphasizes the generality of these precepts: "Natural law was thought to
be very general, and there seems to have been no attempt to make its fundamental
principles any less so: perhaps it was felt to be unwise. *Do good and avoid evil*—a
question-begging precept to a modern mind—and, more reasonably, *Do unto others as you
would they should do unto you* were the two self-evident principles, and from these followed,
both logically and reasonably, prohibitions of murder, theft, and adultery" (13–14).

ing reconciles the disparity between the two by emphasizing the necessity of *obedience to law*, whereby the dualism of his being may be converted into the harmonious unity of love" (*Allegorical Drama* 216). Understanding delivers his counsel in terms that introduce the concept of human accommodation to an eternal law. When Man asks why he was born of the "sepulcher" of the earth, Understanding replies by defining the conditions upon which Man's "high fortune" depends: "si a la Ley no te ajustas, / quedó en la cuna labrada / la materia de la tumba" (if you do not abide by the law, the material of your tomb lay fashioned in the cradle) (1397a). Yet this admonition does not guarantee that Man will execute his office in accordance with God's laws. Since Man inclines to the "assurance" of Free Will rather than to Understanding's "severity" (1396a), he indulges himself in the vainglory of temporal authority and yields to the temptation of Sombra and the Prince of Darkness, the two demonic characters who intervene in the *auto* to disrupt the ways of providence.

In the temptation scene Sombra exploits Man's weakness for authority and distorts his comprehension of power and the law. The demonic characters plan to concoct a potion that will prompt Man to violate the conditions of his reign, and to use this potion to infect one of the gifts that the elements have supplied to ennoble his office. When this strategy is on the point of failing, Sombra interposes herself between Man and Earth and offers him a "golden apple" as proof of her power over the elements. Man's exchange here with Sombra reveals the motifs of his temptation and the reasons for his fall.

When Man first greets Sombra he expresses wonder at her beauty and daring:

> ¿Quién eres, bella zagala,
> que sobre la Tierra triunfas,
> tan dueña de sus caudales,
> que para ti los usurpas,
> sin que ella te los defienda;
> y nueva Aurora segunda,
> das a entender que amaneces
> en bella oposición suya,
> compitiendo con las selvas,
> donde las flores madrugan?
>   (1398b)

(Who are you, beautiful shepherdess, who triumphs over the Earth, so possessed of her riches that you usurp them for yourself, without her protecting them from you; and, a new second Dawn, you appear to rise in rivalry with her loveliness, competing with the woods where the flowers open at first light?)

That Man chooses to address Sombra as a "beautiful shepherdess" is significant, since his greeting draws on the forms and topics of pastoral literature. It is structured as a *glosa* on a pastoral lyric in a traditional style, and it juxtaposes two of the major themes of Renaissance pastoral verse: the capacity of art to perfect nature and the rivalry of human and natural beauty.[14] Sombra takes possession of Earth's untamed riches by cultivating them through the arts of agriculture; she rises before Man as a "second Dawn" who presumes to set her beauty against nature's own light and variety. In their application to Sombra these pastoral topics take on a demonic cast. Through her ability to usurp Earth's abundance and to oppose Dawn's splendor, Sombra challenges the order of providence in the natural world. And by voicing wonder at her powers Man shows himself subject to temptation. He admires Sombra not because she conforms to the order of Creation, but because she seems to set herself above that order, and Man himself may succumb to the desire for such powers.

In her response Sombra sustains the pastoral tone of Man's greeting and plays on his interest in her dominion over nature. As she continues the *glosa* that Man has begun, she reveals to him the putative source of her powers, claiming that scrutiny of the elements' "hidden qualities" has granted her a privileged knowledge of nature and its phenomena. Like Circe in *El mayor encanto, amor*, she portrays herself as a sorceress who finds mysterious "characters" in the products of the earth, "oracles of fire" in the stars, secret "books" in the surface of waters, and "flights" of prophecy in the movement of birds (1398b). And as in Circe's reception of Ulysses, the object of Sombra's discourse is enchantment. By attributing an occult system to nature and associating her powers with that

14. The *glosa* is based on the initial lines of a *romance* by Antonio de Mendoza, which appear in several of Calderón's dramatic works, including *Los encantos de la culpa* and *El maestrazgo del Toisón* (Wilson and Sage 24). Rivers's study of the "pastoral paradox" in Garcilaso's Third Eclogue discusses the concordance and rivalry of art and nature in the Renaissance; see in particular his commentary on the concept of artifice (140–42).

system, Sombra hopes to blind Man to the authentic order the eternal law has established in the physical world and to tempt him to defy that law.

Sombra conjoins the arguments of her enchantment when she presents the golden apple:

> Si una vez su sabor gustas,
> verás que no solamente
> en ti mis ciencias infunda;
> pero que inmortal te haga,
> para que no puedas nunca,
> igualándote al poder
> del rey, perder de esta augusta
> majestad la acción, que hoy
> no puedes decir que es tuya.
> Del tiempo que allá en la Tierra
> te ocultó, venga la injuria;
> come, y como el rey serás
> eterno, edades futuras.
>
> (1399a)

(If once you taste its savor, you will realize that not only will I instill my learning in you, but that I will render you immortal, so that, by attaining kingly power, you can never lose the force of this august majesty, which today you cannot call your own. Avenge the injury for the time he concealed you below in the Earth; eat, and like the king you will be eternal through future ages.)

As she tempts Man to taste her gift, Sombra draws an explicit connection between knowledge and power. The apple will "instill" her occult learning into Man's mind, and it will preserve his "majesty" for all time by making him immortal. Through this promise of eternal dominion Sombra invites Man to join in her defiance of providence. According to her counsel Man can best secure his position in Eden not by accepting what the eternal law has decreed, but by pursuing a sovereignty that recognizes no limit. Whereas Understanding has warned Man that his power is lent and rests on a higher law, Sombra offers to make him equal to the author of that law. And to persuade Man that he has due cause for challenging divine authority, Sombra reduces the law itself to an economy of injury and retribution. Under Sombra's tutelage Man learns that he has been injured, and that the secret powers of the apple will enable him to secure satisfaction for his injury. This prospect of power and vengeance induces Man's first transgression of the law.

Nowhere does Man more closely resemble Segismundo than in his temptation and fall. Both characters are tested to determine if they are fit for their allotted offices, and both fail because they accept an incomplete and one-sided conception of the law. Sombra exploits for demonic purposes the innate legal sense that Man possesses through the imprint of natural law, and the position that she urges upon him parallels Segismundo's reproach of Basilio in its emphasis on personal injury. Like Segismundo, Man falls because he pursues unlimited power and private retribution. Yet Man also reminds us of Segismundo in his capacity to apprehend the eternal law by applying reason to his experience. The role of reason is not at odds with the *auto*'s central theme of redemption, since Man's salvation here is a dual process. Wisdom intervenes to release the demonic bonds of the Fall, but Man himself meditates on his condition and so discerns the immanence of the eternal and the force of its laws. In his fallen state Man at last grasps the importance of his own accommodation to providence.

The Fall initially subjects Man to a condition of extreme isolation. In his desire for power Man has cast aside Understanding, and after he has tasted the apple Free Will and the four elements withdraw from him. In this abandonment Man falls into a deathlike sleep, and he begins to contemplate his experience when he awakens and finds himself again reduced to the somber and limited circumstances of his birth. The sudden loss of Eden forces Man to consider his nature and his true place in the order of Creation.

Man voices his reflections in a soliloquy that recalls Segismundo's awakening at the end of the second act of the *comedia*. Like Segismundo, Man proceeds from the false prospects of vainglory to an awareness of the uncertain and fragile character of human existence, and his discourse unfolds according to the pattern of his alternating desires and fears. He begins to speak while he is still submerged in sleep, insisting in his dreams on the patrimony that Sombra has persuaded him to claim for his own. Although he recognizes the earth as his mother, Man is convinced that his occult "learning" will allow him to challenge the authority of his divine father and to govern the world as its "immortal prince" (1401b). At the moment of his awakening, however, this assurance gives way to a profound sense of doubt and dislocation:

¿Adónde estoy?
¿Esta no es de mi fortuna
la primera prisión fiera?
¿No es ésta aquella primera
bóveda, que fué mi cuna?
¿No es ésta la desnudez
en que primero me vi?
(1401b)

(Where am I? Is not this the first harsh prison of my fate? Is not this that first cavern which was my cradle? Is not this the nakedness in which I first saw myself?)

Through these successive questions, urgent in their threefold repetition of "primero," Man confronts the cyclical pattern of his experience and attempts to discern its significance. On facing the reversion of his confinement to the earth and the sudden loss of his majesty, he draws the most direct inference: that he has known his dominion only in a dream. As his reasoning proceeds Man finds value in what he has dreamed by assuming that it has shown him his true identity, and resolves to reclaim the "high estate" that is his due. To the extent that it confirms Man's conviction of his physical immortality this assumption is misguided, and his attempt to act on these heroic ambitions serves only to disclose the full consequences of the Fall. When Man tries to leave his birthplace, he discovers that a chain holds him captive and that the elements have turned the physical world against him. Where Eden once promised Man all of nature's gifts, the world now offers him the diet of Adam: "que Pan de dolores coma / y Agua de lágrimas beba" (that I shall eat the Bread of sorrows and drink the Water of tears) (1402a). Man's realization of the sudden and radical change in his estate leads him to question his capacity to distinguish waking from dreaming:

¿Quién me dirá cuál ha sido
en mis mundanzas más cierto,
lo que allá soñé despierto
o que aquí veo dormido?
(1402a)

(Who will tell me which has been more certain amid my changing fortunes: what there I dreamed awake or what here I see asleep?)

Like Segismundo, Man reaches a point of crisis when he despairs of the distinctions that have given meaning to his experience. As in Segismundo's case, further reflection allows Man to overcome this crisis by refining his understanding of the relationship between the states of dreaming and of temporal existence. This process begins in Man's dialogue with Sombra, who emerges now as his constant and reproachful companion. Sombra's assertion that any past "happiness" can be known only as a dream prompts Man to recognize that there is a habitual distinction between true and feigned phenomena and that his dominion, if viewed in this light, is not illusory. Although the fall has undone his claim to immortality, Man is nonetheless "hereditary prince" of the world, and he intends to pursue the "majesty" appropriate to his office (1402b). When Sombra insists on the futility of his project, Man presses her reasoning to its logical conclusion:

> SOMBRA. Sueño fué para este empeño,
>   que toda la *Vida es sueño.*
> HOMBRE. Luego ésta lo es: con que se halla
>   tu réplica convencida,
>   porque ¿si la *Vida es*
>   *sueño,* no es fuerza después
>   que duerma esta triste Vida,
>   que a mejor Vida despierte?
>
>   (1402b)

SOMBRA. For all that it was a dream, since all of *Life is a dream.*
MAN. Then this life is one: with which your argument turns on itself, because, if *Life is a dream,* does it not follow that after I have dreamed this sad Life I will awaken to a better Life?)

In this exchange Man uses his innate reason to overcome the limitations of Sombra's demonic thinking. He admits the equivalence of living and dreaming, but he scrutinizes and refines the terms in which Sombra has stated her argument. The proposition that life can be nothing more than a dream is consistent insofar as we limit our thinking to life in this world; if we consider the question from a larger perspective, we must concede that we may "awaken" from the dream of temporal existence into the "better life" of eternity. In Man's experience, as in Segismundo's, this apprehension of the eternal completes the process of conversion. After he has grasped the principle that informs and sanctions all laws, Man is prepared to accept the necessity of his own accommodation to the law. The prospect of eternity, as Man discovers it in his dialogue with Sombra, exhorts him to align his conduct with the design of providence.

As Man continues to exercise his innate moral judgment, he recovers the faculties that he has lost. Understanding returns to his side, and informs him that he can summon and direct Free Will through reason. In these actions Man gains control over his unstable nature and prepares himself to assume his allotted office in the world. Until this point the process of Man's conversion has run in parallel to that of Segismundo. Now, when Man instructs Free Will to petition the Creator for pardon of his sins, the *auto* diverges from the *comedia*. In response to this petition Wisdom intervenes to execute and secure Man's redemption, through a process that falls into two well-defined stages. In the Crucifixion, Wisdom offers satisfaction for Man's transgression and triumphs over the demonic characters; in the institution of the sacraments he grants Man the means to remain in the converted state. Through reason Man has overcome the cycle of sinfulness, and he is freed so that he may participate in the regular reenactment of Wisdom's sacrifice. The ritual repetition of the sacraments will ground his existence in the pattern of salvation.

The reluctance of the demonic characters to relinquish their hold on Man underlines the need for the sacraments. After Wisdom's victory the Prince of Darkness continues to pursue a twofold claim on humanity, arguing that the Fall has "corrupted" the matter of which Man's descendants will be formed and that Man's propensity to sin will always place his liberty at risk. To negate the first of these claims Wisdom promises that an "element" will remove the "stain" of Man's inheritance; to deny the second, Power pledges that he will assist Man in his spiritual life:

> Elemento habrá que tenga
> materia también en quien
> otro *Sacramento* sea
> preservación de ese daño,
> dando al Espíritu fuerzas;
> con que en aumentos de Gracia
> pueda durar en la enmienda.
>
> (1406a)

(There will be an element which also contains substance, in which
another Sacrament will be a safeguard against that injury, by
giving strength to the Spirit; with which, through increments of
Grace, Man will endure in his reform.)

Power stresses the centrality of the Eucharist in the life of the human
spirit. This second "sacrament" will protect Man against the potential
"injury" of turning once again to sin. Strengthened by its influence, his
soul will persist in its condition of spiritual renewal. The intervention of
grace fulfills the process of conversion and redemption. Meditation on his
experience has enabled Man to recognize his place in the order of
providence, but only the agency of grace can maintain his hold on that
place. Natural law has led man through reason to an apprehension of
eternity; the Eucharist will now sustain his final adjustment to the eternal
law.

The inauguration of the sacraments allows the eternal law to operate
fully in Creation through its principles of order, service, and the exchange of gifts. In its closing scenes the *auto* celebrates an order in which
Man and the elements exist in alliance and harmony. Man is prepared to
assume his position as God's viceroy in the world and to make appropriate use of the prerogatives of his office. And the elements participate
jointly in Man's service, as each one makes a particular contribution to
the creation of the sacraments. Water brings the waters of Jordan for
Man's baptism; Earth supplies in sheaves and vines the "primary material" of the Eucharist; Air pronounces "mysterious words" to transform
this material into flesh and blood; Fire reveals the "form" of the Host, in
which the spark of divine love is contained. This final exchange of gifts
secures the mutual participation of Man and the elements in providence.
Alexander Parker has described the significance that this *auto* assigns to
the conventional discovery of the Eucharist: "The bond of love between
the Elements and Man—the harmony of the world—is restored in the
Sacraments. Matter is made the visible medium through which Man's
spiritual life is renewed, each Element contributing to Man's regenera-
tion. The Eucharist, finally, is the supreme sign and symbol of the unity
and harmony of creation—the Elements, Man and God united in a
sacramental union of love that perpetuates the sacrificial union" (*Allegorical Drama* 224). This "sacramental union" fulfills a providential design.
Through the eternal law Power has disposed the elements to create a
world for humanity, and he now empowers Man to take full possession of

this patrimony. With the spiritual aid of the sacraments, Man will remain faithful to the principles of God's governance in Creation. Whereas the cycle of temptation and sin defies the order of providence, the repetition of the Mass will secure Man's accommodation to the eternal law.

That the sacraments possess a unique power to sustain the human spirit is a point of doctrine that ethicist political thinkers are quick to urge upon the king. In his treatise on the Christian prince Rivadeneira argues that the "evangelical law" of the Church commands obedience because of its superiority to other forms of religious law, and he enumerates the qualities in which its spiritual excellence resides:

> que es una ley celestial y divina, que enseña lo que debemos hacer, y nos da la voluntad y fuerzas para lo hacer. Y que los sacramentos que tenemos en nuestra religion, los cuales ninguna otra ha tenido en el mundo, son los instrumentos que Jesucristo, nuestro redentor, instituyó para darnos este espíritu y esta gracia. Porque los sacramentos de la nueva ley, no solamente sinifican la gracia, mas la obran y causan en el ánima del que dignamente los recibe. (463b)

> (that it is a celestial and divine law, which teaches us what we should do, and gives us the will and strength to do it. And that the sacraments that we have in our religion, which no other religion in the world has had, are the instruments that Jesus Christ, our Savior, instituted to give us this spirit and this grace. Because the sacraments of the new law not only signify grace, but also put it into effect and produce it in the soul of one who worthily receives them.)

Rivadeneira draws attention to the agency of the sacraments and to the historical succession in divine law from the old covenant of the Mosaic commandments to the new law of Christian evangelism. The progression from one law to another bears on the spiritual lives of individual believers and on the conduct of kings and governors. As the instruments of grace, the sacraments induce and secure the conversion of the individual; as the most effective revelation of God's plan for humanity, the new law indicates to the rulers of society the principles of true governance. Although *La vida es sueño* ends in the inauguration of the sacraments, it does not deal with the historical dimension of the law, nor does it directly address the political implications of the new law. The force of divine law in conversion, and in the progressive discovery of the providential design, is the central theme of *A Dios por razón de Estado*, an *auto* that scrutinizes the various kinds of laws in an attempt to define true reason of state.[15]

A Dios por razón de Estado sets the phenomenon of conversion within the context of early Church history. Its allegorical mode is appropriate to such a historical subject, since it combines moral and figural techniques. Its text is typical of Calderón's *autos* in its extensive use of personification and abstraction, but it presents conversion as a specific historical act through which the individual realizes the cyclical pattern of salvation in his own existence. Whereas *La vida es sueño* dramatizes the role of the eternal law in the universal processes of creation and redemption, *A Dios por razón de Estado* addresses the operation of providence in human history and in the lives of the first Christians.

For the argument of this *auto* Calderón turns to the account in the Acts of the Apostles of Paul's mission to Athens (Acts 17:16–34), in which the apostle preaches in the Areopagus on the theme of the unknown god to whom the Athenians have erected an altar and persuades several of their number to join the early Church. Dionysius the Areopagite is named among those who have heeded the Pauline lesson, and the *auto* dramatizes the process of his conversion. Critical opinion has stressed the importance of reason in this process. The text allegorizes Dionysius as Ingenio, and its main action can be interpreted as an exploration of the human capacity to discover God by the exercise of natural reason.[16] The rational path, however, is not the only way to God in this *auto*. Its text also incorporates Paul's own conversion through the direct agency of divine

15. There is no exact evidence for the date of *A Dios por razón de Estado*. Valbuena Prat assigns it to the decade 1650–60, but offers no rationale for his decision. Alexander Parker notes of this *auto* that "on stylistic and technical grounds alone it would have to be placed in the period 1647–1657" ("Chronology" 181), and proposes the following argument for 1649: a document from 1651 shows that the *loa* printed by Pando with *Los encantos de la culpa* was performed in 1649, and evidence within the text of the *loa* suggests that in fact it was written for *A Dios por razón de Estado*; therefore the *auto* should be assigned to the same year as its *loa* (178–81). The appearance of the phrase *razón de estado* (430a) in *La segunda esposa y triunfar muriendo* (also dated 1649 by Parker), and the representation of Christian statecraft in this *auto*, lend support to Parker's argument.

16. Fiore asserts that "in this *auto sacramental* Calderón dramatizes an ethical problem related to natural law—man's knowledge of God as the first cause by use of natural reason complemented by divine revelation obliges him to acknowledge and worship God" (79); Hillach remarks that "el problema expuesto aquí por Calderón en forma alegórica . . . es el del conocimiento de Dios con los recursos naturales de la razón" (the problem Calderón

grace, and it is particularly concerned with the relationship between the two modes of conversion that Calderón discerns in the history of the early Church. Through true reason of state man can apprehend the laws that manifest God's order in Creation, and so attain the religious conviction that is also granted by faith alone. In Calderón's view reasons of state and reasons of faith lead to the same spiritual end.

A desire to understand the order of things motivates Ingenio's actions in the course of the *auto*. When he introduces himself to Gentility in the opening scene, Ingenio calls attention to his intellectual curiosity and to his dual role in applying his intellect to the events on stage. Like many of Calderón's personified abstractions, Ingenio resorts to a series of etymologies to explain his own significance. He derives the term "ingenio" from the Latin *ingenitus*, and draws on the supplementary evidence of Greek and Hebrew to define his characteristic faculty as an "extension of the understanding" that arises from within the soul itself (852b). To complement this basic statement of his identity, Ingenio adds that in the "new allegory" of this *auto* he possesses a proper name that reinforces the idea of his sublime understanding and indicates his aptitude for such practical matters as the arts of warfare.[17] "Dionisio," he asserts, signifies "the pure and supreme part" of man's divine soul, while "Areopago" points to his expertise in the skills of Mars or Aries. Taken in conjunction his various names reveal the duality of his functions within the text:

> con que haciendo
> a Dionisio Aries y Pago

---

sets out here in allegorical form . . . is that of the knowledge of God through the natural means of reason) (90).

17. The activities that Calderón associates with *ingenio*—intellectual inquiry and mechanical invention—reflect the common semantic range of the term. According to Covarrubias "vulgarmente llamamos ingenio una fuerça natural de entendimiento, investigadora de lo que por razón y discurso se puede alcançar en todo género de ciencias, diciplinas, artes liberales y mecánicas, sutilezas, invenciones y engaños; y assí llamamos ingeniero al que fabrica máquinas para defenderse del enemigo y ofenderle" (commonly we define *ingenio* as a natural force of the understanding, which investigates what can be attained through reason and thought in all branches of learning, all disciplines, and the liberal and mechanical arts, as well as in deceits, fabrications, and tricks; and so we call someone who constructs engines for defense and assault against an enemy an *ingeniero*) (737b). The *Diccionario de Autoridades* supplies a similar definition: "facultad ò poténcia en el hombre, con que sutilmente discurre ò inventa trazas, modos, máchinas y artificios, ò razones y argumentos, ò percibe y aprehende facilmente las ciencias" (a faculty or power in man, through which with acuity he contrives or invents means, ways, engines, and devices, or reasons and arguments, or perceives and understands learning with ease) (4:270a).

> cabal mi nombre, a ser vengo
> a dos luces por los dos
> sentidos, en el primero
> el de Dionisio Areopago,
> en el segundo el Ingenio.
>   (853a)

(and so, making from Dionysius, Aries, and Pagus my complete name, I have come to be [from two perspectives because of the two senses] in the first sense Dionysius the Areopagite and in the second, Ingenio.)

Through this exposition Ingenio establishes his importance for the unity of the *auto*'s action. He has told Gentility that its allegory is twofold— "yendo de historial sentido / y alegórico compuesto" (being composed of a historical and an allegorical sense) (852b)—and now he explains that he encompasses this duality by possessing a particular name and identity for each of the two senses. In the abstract terms of moral allegory he is Ingenio; in relation to the history of the early Church he is Dionysius the Areopagite. The significance of the *auto* rests on the unfolding of its two senses through the development of the complementary identities of its central personified abstraction. As Ingenio this character applies his powers of understanding to the task of discerning God's law in Creation; as Dionysius he performs the specific historical act of converting to the Church that honors and propagates that law. The conversion of Dionysius is the logical endpoint of Ingenio's intellectual project.

Ansgar Hillach has noted that Ingenio's search for the true law follows from his capacity to question what others accept on the basis of sensory evidence or traditional belief (94). Ingenio himself emphasizes his propensity for doubt and inquiry. He refers to each contradiction that he encounters as a "mystery" or "enigma" that demands his attention, and he describes his own "excellence" as the ability to investigate and comprehend the unknown through questioning: "saber preguntar, / para saber responder" (knowing how to question, to know how to reply) (857b). The general structure of the *auto* corresponds to the order of Ingenio's inquiry. As the dramatic action unfolds, Ingenio examines three distinct sets of questions or "enigmas" in an ordered sequence. The rites of Gentility in Athens lead him to query the rationale for attributing existence to an unknown God (851b); the sudden appearance of distur-

bances in the created universe prompts him to wonder that a god who is
the first cause of Creation should be capable of suffering (855b); Synagogue's account of her prophecies moves him to raise a series of
theological issues concerning the nature of the Judeo-Christian deity
(864a). The progress from one set of questions to another gradually
refines Ingenio's understanding of the law and of reason of state, and so
prepares him for the final act of conversion.

The concepts of law and of reason of state appear in conjunction at the
end of the long opening encounter with Gentility, when Ingenio decides
that he can best explore the enigma of a suffering god by searching for
such a divinity among the various human religions. The possibility of this
search is implicit in the book of Acts. During his discourse in the
Areopagus, Paul tells the Athenians that God has created a variety of men
who share a common origin and a common inclination to religion: "And
he made from one every nation of men to live on all the face of the earth,
having determined allotted periods and the boundaries of their habita-
tion, that they should seek God, in the hope that they might feel after him
and find him" (Acts 17:26–27). This Pauline understanding of human
diversity suggests the mode of pursuing the divine that the *auto* explores.
Ingenio has decided to examine the different confessions through which
men in the world's diverse regions have elected to seek God. The terms
in which Ingenio defines his search, however, are more comprehensive
and more explicit than those of Paul's discourse:

> Discurriendo
> el mundo por cuantas leyes,
> cuantos ritos, cuantos fueros
> una y otra religión
> tienen, hasta que mi anhelo,
> haciendo razón de Estado
> la que ahora de dudar tengo,
> la causa halle de las causas
> que tenga (toda oídos siendo,
> toda ojos, toda manos)
> la conveniencia de serlo
> para padecer.
>
> (856a–b)

(Ranging the world, through all the laws, rites, and statutes that
each religion possesses, until my yearning, by turning the reason

I now have to doubt into reason of State, finds the cause of causes
which [being all ears, all eyes, all hands] has the ability to contain
all things including suffering.)

Ingenio openly announces his interest in religious rites and observances.
In contrast to the Pauline reference to "every nation" of humanity, he
speaks of the diverse "religions" he intends to examine. And in the "laws"
and "statutes" of these religions he hopes to find the "cause of causes"
whose enigmatic effects he has observed in the alterations of the physical
world. This procedure will resolve his doubts about divinity by locating a
rational order in which a god who suffers can exist. Ingenio's reason of
state functions within the field of divine positive law, and it will scrutinize
that field in order to determine the true rationale of an omnipotent and
suffering deity. Because it introduces the concept of reason of state and
associates that concept with religious law and the divine order, this
passage assumes a central place in Calderón's treatment of the law.

Ingenio's progress from one religion to another underlines the comprehensive character of his search. Since moral allegory transcends the
normal limits of space and time, Ingenio can survey a broad sector of
human religions, including those that lie beyond the ancient world known
to Saint Paul.[18] The text presents each religion as a personified abstraction, and associates each one with a particular region: Gentility and
Rome, Atheism and America, Africa (as the character is named) and
Islam, Synagogue and Jerusalem. Through his dialectic Ingenio sets out
the fundamental tenets of these religions. Gentility believes in a multi-
plicity of gods; Atheism in none; Africa in a single god who has yet to
enunciate his law through a prophet; Synagogue in one god who has
given his law to the chosen. Ingenio's search draws him at the last to
Synagogue, who stands alone in possessing a religion of laws that centers
on a single omnipotent deity.

The recent disturbances in the natural world color Synagogue's encounter with Ingenio. Synagogue has put Christ to death, and she
concedes that storms and earthquakes occurred at the moment of his
execution. She refuses, however, to accept Christ's divinity or to acknowledge any change in her privileged status before the godhead. Indeed, she

---

18. Ingenio himself acknowledges that his inquiry can be comprehensive because of its
allegorical cast: "que no se da / en lo alegórico tiempo / ni lugar" (since in the allegorical
neither time nor place exists) (857a).

mentions her laws as she enumerates the favors that God has conferred upon her:

> si entre tantos beneficios
> fue el mayor darme su ley
> en mármol escrita, siendo
> su mismo dedo el cincel,
> por quien la ley natural
> vino a elevar y crecer
> su primer candor, subiendo
> de dos preceptos a diez.
>
> (863b)

(if among so many benefits the greatest was to give me His law written in marble, with His own finger acting as the chisel, through which natural law came to refine and enhance its first splendor, increasing from two precepts to ten.)

Synagogue's discourse reviews Scholastic thought on providence and the succession of laws.[19] According to Aquinas natural law is the "participation of the eternal law in the rational creature" (*Basic Writings* 2:750). The fundamental precepts of natural law constitute a limited set of "self-evident principles" to which all men have access and from which all the specific injunctions of this law can be derived (2:774, 777). The Decalogue enunciates a divine positive law that supplements the principles of natural law by supplying a secure and uniform code that applies to all forms of human conduct, including hidden or interior acts. The divine law is particularly concerned with man's spiritual destiny. As Aquinas puts it, "since man is ordained to an end of eternal happiness which exceeds man's natural ability," he must be "directed to his end by a law given by God" (2:752–53). This understanding of the relationship between natural and divine law supports Synagogue's conviction that the written law is the most significant of the divine favors she has received. In granting Synagogue a law that subsumes the two precepts of natural law under the Ten Commandments, God has shown his particular care for the destiny of her people.

19. For a parallel commentary on the succession from natural law to divine positive law in this passage, see Fiore 93–94.

In Synagogue's religion Ingenio has found a single deity who is the first cause of all things (863a), but he finds her prophecies enigmatic. He cannot understand why Synagogue expects her god to double himself as both Father and Son, nor can he grasp how a human being could have claimed to be her Messiah (864a). During the closing scenes of the *auto* Saint Paul addresses this last set of mysteries in a long dialogue with Synagogue and Ingenio. As Hillach has shown, Paul explains the Trinity in terms drawn from Saint Augustine and Richard of Saint Victor (94). His logic demonstrates that Christ is a person of the godhead who has suffered as a man in order to redeem humanity, and so confirms Ingenio's supposition of an omnipotent and suffering god. In conjunction with this doctrine Paul announces the establishment of a "third law" entrusted to Gentility (867b). Ingenio's search for an adequate deity has led to a new law that shapes his understanding of reason of state.

A concluding series of *apariencias* sets out the sequence of laws that Ingenio has discovered in the course of his search. The three kinds of law present themselves as personified abstractions in the order of their historical succession. Natural Law announces the two fundamental principles that sufficed for the moral governance of humanity before the Fall; Written Law recites the commandments that have prevailed from the age of Moses to the Crucifixion; the Law of Grace introduces the seven sacraments that will now "fortify" the commandments by enhancing the human capacity to abide by them. The spectacle of the personified sacraments encircling the Host completes the *auto*'s exposition of the Scholastic system of laws. In accordance with Aquinas's synthetic bias, one kind of divine law does not supplant the other. Just as the Decalogue grants men superior guidance by elevating the basic precepts of natural law, so the new law is ordained for the perfection of those who have known the spiritual preparation of the old: "God . . . gave one law to men while they were yet imperfect, and another more perfect law when, by the preceding law, they had been led to a greater capacity for divine things" (2:755). The new law of Christian grace incorporates and sublimates the other kinds of law, and offers to perfect humanity through divine love.

In response to the spectacle of the law, Ingenio bows to the creator of such a complete and harmonious order:

> que debe el ingenio humano,
> restituido al papel

de Dionisio Areopagita,
llegándose a convencer
de la doctrina de Pablo,
con la experiencia de que
nada su ley nos propone,
que bien a todos no esté
el creerlo y el amarlo,
llegando a amar y creer
por razón de Estado cuando
faltara la de la fe.

(868b)

(that human Ingenio—restored to the role of Dionysius the
Areopagite, and having been convinced by Paul's teaching, together with the experience that His law proposes nothing to us
that is not beneficial to all—should believe in Him and love Him,
coming to love and to believe through reason of State, when
reason of faith is lacking.)

Ingenio returns here to his identity in history. As Dionysius the Areopagite he embraces the God of Pauline evangelism and explains the rationale
of his conversion. By "doctrine" and "experience" he accounts himself
obliged to love and believe in the deity whose "law" has established a
rational order beneficent to all humanity. And he now perceives the law in
its fundamental unity. The various kinds of law discovered in the final
apariencias are all specific manifestations of the eternal law through
which God has created and ordered the universe. The *auto*'s procedure of
applying reason of state to the diverse laws of human religion has ended
in an apprehension of the one supreme law. Because reason disposes
the human soul to put itself in harmony with the eternal law, this
procedure alone is sufficient to lead man to God. Dionysius has turned to
the Christian confession for reasons of state, in an act that parallels Paul's
conversion for reasons of faith.

Ingenio's return to his role as Dionysius the Areopagite confirms the
primacy of the historical sense in this *auto*. Calderón uses the abstractions of moral allegory to dramatize the rational process that has led to
Dionysius's conversion, but he presents the conversion itself as a specific
act that occurs within a well-defined historical context. This act marks a
dual fulfillment in history of the pattern of salvation. Dionysius has

enacted this pattern in his own life, and he has participated in the founding of the Church that will disseminate the sacraments in the world. The parallel between the lives of Dionysius and Saint Paul indicates that conversion by law coexists with conversion by faith. Since the religious laws that God has granted to humanity are consistent with the eternal law, if man applies his reason to these laws he can discern the providence that has been ordained for the profit of all and act to accommodate himself to its design. As divine governance unfolds in history, its beneficence urges men to convert for reasons of state.

A Dios por razón de Estado defends the medieval ideal of a universe ordered by eternal law (Hillach 95). Because the eternal law informs all that stands beneath it in the fourfold hierarchy, this defense bears on the laws and the reason of state through which kings govern their communities on earth. Calderón appeals here to the Neoscholastic concept of law in order to refute the postulates of Machiavellian statecraft and to question the assumption of realist political thinkers that the Christian prince may isolate a limited field in which he is free to proceed according to the demands of secular politics. Calderón's strategy of applying reason of state to divine positive law denies the autonomy that Machiavelli claims for the political sphere, but it is consistent with the Neoscholastic view that all laws are ranged in a single coherent hierarchy. And the proposition that reason of state enjoins obedience to the eternal law has clear implications for those who preside over human society. In this *auto*, as in many political *comedias* of the period, the law stands as the pattern of a beneficent order, and human actions are just to the extent of their conformity with the higher laws. Through this argument Calderón offers an astute and sophisticated defense of the central axiom of ethicist political thought: that true reason of state cannot be separated from the orders of law and of providence. He sustains this anti-Machiavellian position throughout his political theater, both by exploring the haste with which the procedures of realist politics descend into a self-replicating tyranny and by aligning the institutions and diplomacy of the Hapsburg monarchy with the cycles of providential history. In the affairs of a Christian state, as in the spiritual life of an individual believer, fidelity to the law secures human participation in the order of Creation.

✛ ✛ ✛ 3 ✛ ✛ ✛

KINGSHIP AND THE STATE
La cisma de Inglaterra and
El maestrazgo del Toisón

In his political theater Calderón
does not limit himself to considering the state as an abstract entity. His
engagement with theories of statecraft is complex and subtle, but it does
not represent the full extent of his political concerns. In addition to
addressing the prerogatives and duties of the monarch, his works examine the role of the officers who exercise authority in the king's name and
the order of the institutions in which those officers perform their tasks.
This attention to bureaucrats and bureaucracy reflects an acute interest
in the practice of monarchy in Hapsburg Spain. Federico Chabod has
observed that in early modern Europe the authority of the ruler and the
hierarchy of his officials came to constitute the two "poles" of the state
(604), and in turning his attention to the offices and institutions of
government Calderón takes account of the distribution of power and of

the shifting balance between the Crown and the state apparatus. This scrutiny of the Hapsburg monarchy and its bureaucracy offers a practical complement to his theoretical examination of the law and Christian reason of state.

Discussion of these matters should begin with some commentary on the place of bureaucracy in the centralized European monarchies. Recent historical studies have argued that in the currency of power the institutions of government proved to be a coin with two faces. In its early stages the bureaucratic hierarchy enhanced and extended the king's power over the realm, but as its officials came to perceive themselves as a distinct professional class they began to pursue their own concerns and interests at the expense of the central authority. Geoffrey Parker has remarked on the inherent conflict between the loyalty of officials to their own institutions and their duty as royal servants to king and nation (57), and Jaime Vicens Vives has proposed that the practice of administrative bureaucracies in "containing or distorting the ruler's wishes" contributed to the seventeenth-century crisis of sovereignty (69). A central factor in the evolution of the early modern state is this consolidation of bureaucratic interests, in at least potential opposition to the Crown.

The Spanish experience conforms to the general pattern. In the late fifteenth and early sixteenth centuries the monarchy attached to itself a large group of conciliar bodies, some concerned with specific problems of administration and some with particular regions, and charged them with reviewing affairs of state in their assigned areas and with preparing written reports or *consultas* from which the ruler could draw personal decisions. The councils were meant to preserve the principle that sovereignty should reside solely in the monarch—John Elliott remarks that they had the effect of "grafting a modern-style bureaucratic system on to a society that was still essentially medieval" (*Imperial Spain* 181)—but in time the tensions and contradictions inherent in the system emerged more and more insistently.[1] Although nominally free to exercise his own judgment, the king became increasingly dependent on his councillors and officers and on the written documents that they supplied to him. Elliott has noted that under Charles V and Philip II the Spanish monarchy

1. Elliott supplies a concise account of the structure and evolution of the conciliar system and its role in relation to the Crown, under the heading "The Organization of Empire" (*Imperial Spain* 170–81). For the complexities that arose within the system in the early seventeenth century, including the increasing pressures on the king and the proliferation of *juntas* or subcommittees struck to address urgent matters, see Lynch 2:19–23.

shifted from "government by the spoken word" to "government by paper" (*Imperial Spain* 170), and the point is apparent in contemporary writings about the court. In the autobiographical sketch appended to his partial translation of Guicciardini, Philip IV describes how he "learned the office of King" through observing and then gradually taking an active part in the sessions of his various councils and the drafting of official despatches (232a–b). And if the education of the prince had become in large measure a bureaucratic process, this change points to the increasing strength of the conciliar bodies, and to their corresponding tendency to act on their own concerns rather than those of the king. The professional mentality of the bureaucratic corps contributed to this development, as did their aspirations to aristocratic status and their willingness to defend the vested interests of that class.[2] And legal considerations influenced the relations of the Crown and its councils. Through their judicial functions the councils were empowered to enforce the laws that safeguarded traditional rights and placed effective limits on the king's powers. According to I. A. A. Thompson, the rule of law offered genuine protection from arbitrary measures on the part of the Crown: "The councils provided the only firm framework of legality and constituted an independent system of checks and balances and reciprocal controls within the apparatus of government itself. Conflicts of jurisdiction and competence were not just marginal issues . . . , but real limitations on the effectiveness of executive authority and the most accessible channel of legitimate resistance to the royal command" (231).

At its best the conciliar system and its bureaucratic apparatus set functional bounds on royal authority and so secured a significant degree of correlation between the practice of government and the theory of limited monarchy. The division of power nonetheless provoked uneasiness among the governed, particularly when it threatened to concentrate authority in hands other than those of the king. In plays concerned with the practice of statecraft Calderón often turns to an issue that attracted attention and anxiety in seventeenth-century Spain: the rise of the royal

2. Vicens Vives discusses the "process of refeudalization" in seventeenth-century Europe, through which the aristocracy made use of the administrative apparatus to reassert its authority within the state, and notes that this process required the "complicity" of the bureaucratic class (81). In relation to the aspirations of the latter class, Stradling remarks on "the constant gravitation of bureaucracy towards the condition of aristocracy, an unceasing process of mutation which transformed the surgical knife of revolution from above into the thick, leathery skin of resistance from below" (146).

favorite (*privado* or *valido*) as a prominent figure in the monarchy and of the favorite's office as an institution (*valimiento*). Geoffrey Parker has noted that at this time the rulers of the major European monarchies became increasingly dependent on this office, as they attempted to oversee the complex administrative structures of their centralized states (57–58). In Spain the favorite's role as the king's chief minister and his intermediary with the councils shifted during the century, from the autocratic regimes of Lerma and Olivares to the moderate administration of Luis de Haro and the later favorites. Calderón's theater reflects changes in the institution of *valimiento* and in attitudes toward the favorite's authority. First recorded in connection with production at court in 1627, *La cisma de Inglaterra* addresses the issues that concerned political thinkers and observers in the years of Olivares's ascendancy.[3] It centers on the relationship of monarch and favorite, presenting Henry VIII as a king misled by his own passions and by the self-serving stratagems of Cardinal Wolsey. Through Wolsey's practices it offers a negative example of false statecraft, and it resembles *La vida es sueño* in associating such proceedings with the violation of divine law and with a destructive cycle of tyranny. *El maestrazgo del Toisón*, written for the Corpus observances of 1659, extends a positive model of a state struc-tured on Christian principles. Its figural allegory, based on the founding of the Order of the Golden Fleece, traces a series of correspondences that relate the king of Spain and his officers to Christ and the apostles. By using the order of the apostles as a typology for the structure of the state, this allegory carefully redefines the favorite's role. As a postfiguration of John the Baptist, the favorite serves as first minister to the Crown and occupies a position of parity with the other councillors. The contrast between *La cisma de Inglaterra* and *El maestrazgo del Toisón* marks the institutional changes that distinguish the *valimiento* of Olivares from the administration of Luis de Haro.

Political thought and popular theater share the general preoccupation with the power of the favorite. Attention to this issue was particularly acute in the early decades of the seventeenth century, due in part to the marked contrast between the personal authority of earlier Spanish kings and Philip III's notorious reliance upon Lerma. Charles V and Philip II

---

3. As Shergold and Varey have noted, fiscal records kept by the Royal Chamber show that *La cisma de Inglaterra* was performed for Philip IV and the queen as a private entertainment on 31 March 1627 (274, 277). This is the earliest date recorded for the play.

had governed with the assistance of untitled royal secretaries who had little influence beyond administrative affairs; Philip III inaugurated a monarchy dependent upon highly placed favorites who enjoyed the king's friendship and intervened directly in his name in the instruments and policies of government (Lynch 2:26–27). This development seemed to announce a profound and disturbing historical change. In the reign of Philip III "the novelty of a weak king and a powerful favorite so impressed contemporary Spaniards that they regarded the year 1598 as the end of an age" (Lynch 2:18).

Political theorists reflect this attitude, although they respond to shifting conditions at court and their views are not univocal.[4] Early commentary tends to condemn the favorite, describing his rule as a kind of tyranny. Such writers as Juan de Santa María (publ. 1619), Jerónimo de Zeballos (publ. 1623), and the Quevedo of the first part of *Política de Dios* (1626) argue that the king who governs through a favorite surrenders part of his sovereignty to another, diminishes his personal majesty, and, in general, endangers his kingdom by placing personal friendship above the interests of the realm. With the accession of Philip IV and the rise to power of Olivares, however, the dominant trend of opinion begins to change. Responding perhaps to Olivares's stringent regime of reform, or perhaps to his personal influence at court, the theorists turn from dismissing the favorite to justifying his role and outlining the virtues that will ensure that he fulfills it to the benefit of the monarchy as a whole. A literature now arises devoted to educating the favorite. Defining the proper relationship of prince and favorite is a central concern in this material. Whether they limit the favorite to acting as a superior adviser to the monarch, or allow him to exercise certain powers independently, the later theorists accept the existence of *valimiento* and attempt to reconcile it with the concept of inalienable royal sovereignty. Many urge the favorite to cultivate a spirit of fortitude and self-control, in accordance with Olivares's own devotion to the Neostoic formula of "iron resolution, imperviousness to vicissitude, dedication to work and self-sacrifice" (Stradling 60);[5] others accom-

4. This summary of seventeenth-century political theory concerning the favorite is based on Maravall (*Teoría* 303–17). The standard study of *valimiento* as a political institution (although recently questioned by Stradling for its account of Philip IV's government after the fall of Olivares) is Tomás y Valiente's monograph.

5. Elliott (*Richelieu and Olivares* 25–27) and Stradling (60–61) both stress Olivares's intellectual debt to Lipsius. For a discussion of Lipsius's political thought, and of his general influence on the official ideologies of early modern Europe, see Oestreich (esp. 90–117).

modate his role to an explicitly Christian model of the state, claiming on occasion that monarchy and *valimiento* are both divinely inspired institutions.[6]

A parallel development appears in theatrical treatments of *valimiento*. In the 1620s the favorite emerges as an important character in Spanish drama, particularly in *comedias* concerned with royal justice. *La Estrella de Sevilla* follows this tendency. The play's action portrays Don Arias as a false servant who indulges his master's passions and practices a statecraft of preferment and secrecy. In inviting the king to desire and pursue the noble Estrella, and in concealing the consequences of his indiscretion, the favorite turns the powers of sovereignty to dubious ends. As he twice remarks to the king, the royal prerogatives of generosity and favor can conquer the will of others and overcome scruples of honor (198–204, 457–63). His position distorts the uses of magnanimity—one of the defining virtues of the true prince—and promotes unjust conduct. By finding measures to meet immediate needs, Don Arias abandons the servant's duty to offer true counsel. His dereliction demands that others undertake this task. Since the young king has suffered ill service from his favorite, the Sevillian nobility must educate him in the sanctity of justice.[7]

The fragility of justice in a court dominated by *valimiento* is also a major theme of *El burlador de Sevilla* (before 1625). This play centers on the difficulties of containing Don Juan, a character anarchic in his personal energies and treacherous in his dealings with others.[8] Although Don Juan shows no respect for rank or person, he believes that the

6. José Laynez argues that the authority of the true favorite enjoys divine sanction in *El privado christiano* (1641): "Dios elige Privado como Rey; da los Imperios y las bases en que se afirman" (God chooses both Favorite and King; He grants Empires and the foundations that secure them) (quoted in Maravall, *Teoría* 312).

7. Kennedy interprets *La Estrella de Sevilla* as a pointed commentary on kingship and *valimiento* during the inaugural period of Philip IV's reign. Her discussion traces several correspondences between the actions of Don Arias and the conduct of Olivares, particularly in the exchange of royal honors and in the favorite's willingness to satisfy the king's sensual desires (118–23).

8. Wardropper notes Don Juan's propensity for treachery and comments on Don Diego's role as a false favorite who uses his position to protect his son, even at the expense of the interests of Crown and kingdom ("Tema" 9–10, 14–15). In a complementary analysis of the play, Varey discusses Tirso's concern over the "moral degeneracy" of those who dispense power and justice in society: "the specific attacks are aimed at the dependence of the Crown on unworthy favourites, and suggest the need for the King to take a more direct role in the administration of justice" ("Social Criticism" 215).

privileged position of his family will always allow him to act with impunity. Many of the events in the play justify this conviction. Don Juan's successive acts of deceit and violence seem to occasion no consequences. In Naples he enjoys the protection of his uncle Don Pedro, Spanish ambassador and confidant of the local monarch; in Seville he is assured that his father, favorite of the king of Castile, will avert any challenge to the family honor. Under these conditions no lasting claim can be made against Don Juan. His victims converge on Seville in a movement that suggests a tragic narrowing of possibilities, but they can expect little satisfaction, since they must address their appeals to the Castilian king. In the moral world of the play, however, justice is not limited to human agency. An exchange between Don Juan and his servant Catalinón contrasts the proceedings that the favorite can control with the implacable judgment of God (1958–65), and this superior power finally exacts retribution. As Wardropper has argued, Don Juan's death is a miraculous event that God performs to secure the justice that kings and their ministers have denied ("Tema" 16).

In *El burlador* and *La Estrella de Sevilla* the favorite stands in the king's shadow, influencing events that directly touch the lives and honor of other characters. A significant subgenre of the *comedia* takes the favorite's career as its principal subject. The spectacular scandal that ended in 1621 in the beheading of Rodrigo Calderón—a prominent member of the administration of Philip III and a political dependent of Lerma—supplied a focus for the general debate concerning *valimiento*, and this subgenre dwells on the tragic figure of the fallen favorite and on the lessons in mutability and human weakness that can be drawn from his fate. Mira de Amescua's *Adversa fortuna de don Alvaro de Luna* (1621–24) is typical, both in portraying Luna as a historical exemplar of the overreaching favorite and in developing the conventional themes of fortune, envy, and inconstancy.[9] Yet despite its moralizing aspect the play does not offer a one-sided view of its central character. Don Alvaro dedicates himself to

---

9. Together with *La próspera fortuna de don Alvaro de Luna y adversa de Ruy López de Avalos*, this play forms a pair of interrelated works in which Mira de Amescua examines the favorite's fall by dramatizing events at the fifteenth-century court of Juan II. MacCurdy's monograph offers comment on both plays, emphasizing the primary role of Ruy López in the first and of Don Alvaro in the second (122–44). MacCurdy also discusses the contemporary impact of the case of Rodrigo Calderón (38–47) and the characteristic moral themes of the fallen-favorite plays (80–89).

exacting standards of duty and fortitude; his betrayal of those ideals, and the failings of the king whom he serves, lead to his fall from favor. The text does not scant his virtues. Don Alvaro possesses the traditional aristocratic attribute of excellence at arms; his servant Hernando de Robles announces that he intends to refuse all honors that he has not won through military action against the Moors (27–32), and he later leads a successful assault to recapture the city of Trujillo from the Aragonese. He also displays a Stoic detachment from the accusations of others, choosing to retire into voluntary exile when the nobles first complain to the king of his influence at court. From one perspective Don Alvaro merits the image that Robles evokes of him, as a man in whom nature's gifts have conquered the ways of fortune (19–22). The progress of his career, however, reveals a propensity for political calculation. Don Alvaro arranges for the king to marry Isabel of Portugal, acting neither on the royal will nor on diplomatic considerations, but rather on the conviction that he will be immune to envy if the queen stands in his debt (1575–82), and he bends his master to his will by threatening to retreat once again from the court. The shift from reliance on talents granted by nature to deliberate manipulation of fortune's power is a Machiavellian turn that puts Don Alvaro at risk. Calculation proves to be endemic in the courtly circle, and the weakness that the king shows in agreeing to marry Isabel leaves him equally susceptible to the tactics of the favorite's enemies. In the face of renewed opposition to Don Alvaro's rule, the king signs his death warrant and surrenders him to the "tragic theater" of the executioner (3021–23). The play's main interest lies not in rejecting *valimiento* as such, but in exploring the dangers of a regime formed of a weak king and an ambitious favorite. Its text incorporates an excursus that appeals to the historical ubiquity of the favorite and defends his role in sharing the burdens of rule (1367–88), and the king himself delivers a closing lesson on the Crown's obligation to protect those who serve:

> Reyes deste siglo, nunca
> deshagáis vuestras hechuras.
> ¡O, quien a mis descendientes
> auisara que no huyan
> de los que bien eligieron
> para la pribança suya!
>   (3055–60)

(Monarchs of this age, never undo those whom you have created. Oh, would that I might admonish my descendants not to shun those well chosen for their favor!)

This apostrophe to posterity suggests that the system of *valimiento* can function well if king and favorite are faithful to the virtues of true statecraft. Quevedo's *Cómo ha de ser el privado* (1626) —a *comedia* closely aligned with Olivares's plan for reforming the favorite's office—sets out this possibility in programmatic terms. The play is set in Italy, but the characters and actions clearly evoke Spanish models. In the opening scene the young Ferdinand, as he inaugurates his reign as king of Naples, surveys the princely virtues in order to determine the tenor of his rule and the courtier best suited to serve as his favorite. His preference for the marquis of Valisero—the name is an anagram of Olivares—invites us to view the Neapolitan court as a mirror of *valimiento* in the administration of Philip IV. Elliott has shown that the king's choice of virtues produces a "combination of a *rey justiciero* and a *ministro desinteresado*," and that the play's development alludes to such recent events as the suspension in 1623 of the diplomatic attempts to arrange a Spanish marriage for Prince Charles of Wales and the English assault on Cádiz ("Quevedo" 235–36). The dramatic action also illustrates the force of the political virtues in practical affairs. Although disinterest is not a quality that lends itself to the stage, Quevedo constructs his plot to emphasize its centrality in the favorite's conduct of internal audiences and external affairs. In receiving petitioners at court Valisero is patient and impartial; in negotiating the king's marriage he advises that religious law must not be compromised for considerations of state. The marquis also exemplifies a Stoic resolve that sustains the virtues of king and favorite alike. Fully aware that those who govern are exposed to fortune, he meets personal adversity with equanimity and urges the king to respond to challenges from abroad by ordering a general reform of morals and justice within his kingdom. Valisero is equally notable in his devotion to duty. One of his initial rivals for the favorite's position later remarks on his tireless application to the office:

> Y un esclavo, sin salir
> del espacio de su celda,
> de medio día a media noche
> nota, escribe, oye y espera,

o con ministros en juntas,
ocupado en mil materias:
secretarios cuyas plumas,
siguiendo su acento, vuelan.

(622a)

(And a slave, never leaving the space of his cell, from midday to midnight he records, writes, hears, and waits, or in meetings with ministers he is occupied in a thousand matters: secretaries whose pens fly to follow his voice.)

The emphasis here on the labors of government points again to Quevedo's concern with the conditions of *valimiento* in Hapsburg Spain. Possessed of fortitude and discretion, the marquis also commands the administrative expertise to secure effective action on the king's behalf. A constant servant and devoted bureaucrat, he is a model of the perfect favorite in the context of early modern statecraft.

Spanish opinion concerning the favorite's rule clearly shapes the interpretation of English history in *La cisma de Inglaterra*. In considering the interest that the events of Henry VIII's reign might have held for Calderón and his audience, modern critics have drawn attention to the Hapsburgs' commitment to confessional unity in Europe and to the state of diplomatic relations between Spain and England, both during the Reformation and in the period immediately preceding the play's first performance. To the various points of contact in Spanish and English affairs—the place of Catherine of Aragon in Henry's court, the abortive effort to negotiate a Spanish match for Prince Charles, the prospect of extending the war on heresy to British territory—it is appropriate to add the parallels between the royal favorites who had risen to prominence in the two monarchies.[10] Rivadeneira expresses an awareness of this his-

10. Two recent studies offer contrasting interpretations of the historical basis for Calderón's interest in the English Reformation. Mario Bacigalupo notes the prior significance for a Spanish audience of Henry's divorce from Catherine of Aragon, and suggests that Calderón found in Queen Mary's failure to return England to the Catholic community a "dilemma between religious belief and history" that he attempted to resolve by turning to contemporary thought concerning religion and reason of state (212–13). John Loftis argues that "a series of spectacular victories" in 1625 had reinforced Spain's commitment to religious war and raised the prospect of invading England to restore the kingdom to Catholicism (17–19).

torical correspondence in his treatise on the Christian prince, when he compares the case of Alvaro de Luna to the fate of Henry's favorites:

> El ejemplo de don Alvaro de Luna basta por todos, si no está ya olvidado, y si lo está, los del cardenal Volseo y Tomas Cronuelo nos pueden enseñar esta verdad; pues en nuestros días, en tiempo de Enrique VIII, fueron como reyes de Inglaterra y murieron condenados, como lo escribimos en nuestra *Historia eclesiástica* del scisma de aquel reino. (559a)

> (The example of Don Alvaro de Luna is sufficient for all, if it has not been forgotten already, and if it has, those of Cardinal Wolsey and Thomas Cromwell can show us this truth; since in our age, in the time of Henry VIII, they were like kings of England and they were condemned to death, as we have written in our *Ecclesiastical History* of the schism in that kingdom.)

In classifying these figures as negative exemplars, this passage urges the prince and his ministers to avoid the consolidation of authority in the hands of a powerful favorite. Rivadeneira's history of the English Reformation (1588) was in all probability the principal source for *La cisma de Inglaterra*, and the play also turns the past to formative purposes.[11] Calderón portrays Volseo as a false minister who plays on Enrique's weaknesses and practices a politics of deception, and he attributes the schism in large measure to this injurious association of king and favorite.[12]

11. Parker discusses the evidence in the text of *La cisma de Inglaterra* for Calderón's dependence on Rivadeneira's history, and the ways in which Calderón departs from his narrative source in presenting the central figures of Henry, Wolsey, and Anne Boleyn ("Henry VIII" 332–35).

12. Attention to the play's substantial political dimension calls into question Parker's widely circulated view that its ethos is one of irremediable confusion and tragic inevitability. Parker regards the play's main characters "as symbols of tragic humanity, falling under the weight of unbearable responsibilities, confused by the conflict of passion and reason, blinded by pride, ambition or a self-righteous over-confidence, all erring in the darkness that is human life" ("Henry VIII" 351). Setting the conduct of Enrique and Volseo in the context of seventeenth-century ideas on statecraft allows us to see their errors as constituting an ill-advised but avoidable course of political action. Bacigalupo remarks that "in effect, the role that Fortune has played upon events could have been avoided had Henry not lost sight of the fundamental principles of his office, and had both he and Wolsey not put their faith in their immediate interests or in omens" (214).

Issues of character and political conduct are prominent in the first act of *La cisma de Inglaterra*. As Alexander Parker has observed, the final scene of this act is a "symmetrical counterpart" of the initial one ("Henry VIII" 343), and the two scenes in conjunction define Enrique and Volseo as political figures and introduce the motives that will shape their actions during the play. In spite of certain moral and psychological differences, Enrique and his favorite share a credence in fate and augury that has an adverse affect on their capacity to respond to events with the constancy appropriate to Christian governance.

The king opens the play through a brief exchange with the figure of Ana Bolena, who has appeared to him in a dream as he sits asleep at his writing-table. He tries to command her image to stay in his presence, but it leaves him with the enigmatic words, "yo tengo de borrar cuanto tú escribes" (I am to erase all that you write) (6). Enrique awakens, Volseo enters, and the two discuss the significance of the dream. In his long account of his experience, the king describes what he was doing when he fell asleep:

> ahora que Marte duerme
> sobre las armas sangrientas,
> velo yo sobre los libros,
> escribiendo en la defensa
> de los siete sacramentos
> aquéste con que hoy intenta
> mi deseo confundir
> los errores y las sectas
> que Lutero ha derramado.
>   (77–85)

(now that Mars is sleeping on his bloody weapons, I keep vigil in my library, writing this book in defense of the seven sacraments,

---

La cisma de Inglaterra is one of several plays in which Calderón considers the question of *valimiento* and its consequences. Fox discusses the exemplarity of Alfonso VII and his two favorites in *Saber del mal y del bien* (1628) (*Kings* 25–36); De Armas suggests that Circe in *El mayor encanto, amor* (1635) may be a figure for Olivares, and offers a parallel analysis of Medea's role in *Los tres mayores prodigios* (1636) (*Return* 139–46, 151–59). The general prominence of the relationship between king and favorite in the subgenre of plays on *valimiento* is noted in MacCurdy (77).

with which I hope to confound this day the errors and sects that Luther has brought forth.)

Here Enrique portrays himself as engaged on a project that defines him as a learned and devout monarch. In a period of peace he has set aside the arms that represent the king's traditional role as protector of the nation so that he may exercise his command of letters. In this task he acts as a constant defender of the Catholic faith, and his use of the present tense here reaffirms his commitment by suggesting that he will return to writing the treatise that he has before him. The confutation of Luther is an ongoing project that continues to hold the king's attention. As king and believer, he wishes to refute the "errors" of those who would deny or belittle the power of the Church and its instruments of grace.

As the king's narrative proceeds, however, it begins to show him in a less flattering light. In recalling the female figure who approached him in the dream, Enrique reveals qualities that seem inappropriate in a Christian monarch:

> Aquí el alma
> dentro de mí mismo tiembla,
> barba y cabello se eriza,
> toda la sangre se hiela,
> late el corazón, la voz
> falta, enmudece la lengua.
> (105–10)

(Here my soul trembles within me, my beard and hair stand on end, all my blood turns to ice, my heart pounds, my voice falters, my tongue goes mute.)

This passage describes the effects of sudden and extreme passion. Moved simultaneously by desire and by fear—he insists that his vision is at once a "prodigy" and a "horror" (93–94)—the king has given himself over to the impulses of the moment. And he cannot recall what he has seen without experiencing those emotions once again; here he uses the present tense not to speak of a continuing project, but to describe emotions that return to him with renewed vigor as he remembers the figure in his dream. In the moment of his dream vision, and in his recollection of that moment, he reveals a susceptibility to passion that shapes his conduct despite his faith and resolution. The extremity of his experience causes him to relive his passions and to seek reassurance from his favorite.

Enrique's fears are for both the past and the future. As he recalls the terror of his vision, he is convinced that he has witnessed an omen, and he is determined to interpret what he has seen and to act upon its meaning. As Susan Fischer has noted, the dream sequence now becomes an "inner text," and the king "a reader or a spectator whose task it is to interpret the text being played out before him" (116). The dream indeed anticipates the play's action, both in its solar imagery of light and shadow (Fischer 117–19) and in its augury of the tragic passion that will reverse the king's faith and bring religious division to his realm (Bacigalupo 214). Yet Enrique's attempt to determine its significance is dubious, and begins in a curiously tentative way:

> Si fuera lícito dar
> al sueño interpretación,
> vieras que estas cartas son
> lo que acabo de soñar.
> (141–44)

(If it were permissible to give an interpretation of my dream, you would see that these letters represent what I have just dreamt.)

Enrique has reason to doubt the legitimacy of interpreting the dream, given what he makes of it. Volseo has brought two letters—one from the pope, the other from Luther—and the king proposes that these letters correspond to an image at the dream's end, in which he erased with his left hand what he wrote with his right. The polarity of right and left suggests the opposition between the true doctrine of the pope's letter and the heresy of Luther's. The king intends to exploit this symbolism to reaffirm his allegiance to Rome, placing Luther's letter at his feet and the pope's above his head. Yet he reverses the letters inadvertently, and takes this action for another ill omen. At his favorite's prompting he then contrives a second interpretation, in which he stands as a "pillar" of the faith, with the "foundation stone" of the pope at his feet and the "burden" of Luther's heresy on his shoulders (189–200). The king finds this new correspondence sufficient to calm his fears, and he brings the long process of interpreting the dream to an end.

If examined in detail, this process tells us more about the interpreter than about the object that he intends to interpret. Its inner logic reveals a propensity to force the hand of providence. Enrique proceeds here on two assumptions: that his dream is an omen of future events, and that he can take immediate action to determine and forestall the menace that it holds for him. The second of these assumptions is particularly ill-advised in the world of Calderón's *comedias*. Like Basilio in *La vida es sueño*, Enrique believes that his learning will allow him to understand and counteract auguries of the future, and so to intervene in the providential order of things. And Enrique's intervention is even more precipitate than Basilio's. He is so eager to determine the dream's meaning that he ignores significant parts of its content—he takes no account, for example, of the words that the female figure addressed to him—and he is quick to find correspondences between what he has dreamed and the immediate objects that surround him when he awakens, and to change those correspondences as events evolve.[13] In attempting to understand and defy augury, Enrique displays an imprudent haste that is consistent with his inclination to passion and equally dangerous for his rule.

During most of this scene Volseo seems to distinguish himself from his credulous master. All of his counsel turns against the idea that the dream is prophetic, dismissing what the king has seen as "illusion" (13) and mere "chimeras" (131). Yet when Volseo finds himself alone on stage, he delivers a soliloquy that shows him to rival Enrique in his obsession with fate and augury. He celebrates his accomplishments in rising from humble circumstances to the high estate of a court favorite who trades in the power of kings, and he invokes the forces of political calculation to complete the design that is to place him on the papal throne: "dame la mano, ambición; / lisonja dame la mano" (give me your hand, ambition; flattery, give me your hand) (219–20). His stance throughout is that of a "complete Machiavellian," determined to dominate fortune and to ascend by exercising power and *virtú* to its utmost height (Bacigalupo 215). And in his attempt to command fate Volseo pays heed to augury. He has entered the king's service on the advice of an astrologer, and he continues to fear the same astrologer's prediction that a woman will destroy him. Although he is far more reserved and calculating than the king,

13. Parker has argued that Enrique's procedures for understanding the dream reveal his susceptibility to intellectual error. Each of his interpretations is valid in itself, but the two in conjunction contradict one another and lead to confusion ("Henry VIII" 59).

Volseo is attentive to omens and acts upon what he has learned from them.

Elizabeth Teresa Howe has argued that the characters of Calderón's *comedias* attribute the course of events to fate or fortune, rather than to divine providence, when they live in societies that have inverted the Christian order of values by placing the temporal over the spiritual (108). Through their shared belief in fate and augury, Enrique and Volseo are likely to apply such an inverse system of values to their government, and to forsake the principles of public conduct to pursue immediate personal ends. The final scene of act 1 shows us the king and his favorite at court, acting in their official roles under conditions that reveal what their liabilities have meant for public life.

The scene portrays a formal occasion. Ana Bolena, having entered the royal court as a member of the queen's household, is presented to Enrique for the first time. Ana speaks to the king in the conventional language of courtly compliment; his response, expressed in a long aside addressed in part to Volseo, disrupts the tone of ceremony and decorum:

> ¿Otra vez, alma, os turbáis?
> Ojos, ¿otra vez miráis
> sombras en el aire vano?
> ¿Otra vez, prodigio humano,
> rendido a tu vista estoy?
> Esta es la misma que hoy
> alma de mi sueño ha sido.
> Pues ahora no estoy dormido;
> despierto estoy, vivo estoy.
>   (850–58)

(Once again, soul, are you alarmed? Eyes, do you gaze once again at shadows in the empty air? Once again, human prodigy, am I overcome at your sight? This is the same woman who today was the animating spirit of my dream. Yet now I am not asleep; I am awake, I am alive.)

Enrique sees the unnamed vision of his dream in an external form; from his perspective Ana is now a "human prodigy." His experience of reliving what he has dreamed, and the language that he uses to describe that experience, parallel Segismundo's second liberation from the tower in the last act of *La vida es sueño*. Like Segismundo, Enrique reiterates the phrase "otra vez" as he interrogates himself, considering the possibility that he may be witnessing once again the mere "shadows" of a dream. Yet where the threat of repetition forces Segismundo to conceive of the providential order that stands above earthy appearances, Enrique remains bound by the emotions of the moment, and openly reveals his agitation to Ana: "entre piedad y rigor / me enamoras y me espantas" (between mercy and cruelty, you incite my love and my fear) (865–66). The king's confession exposes a weakness that can only feed Ana's ambitions, and Volseo, ever sensitive to the nuances of power and control, intervenes with the single word that he allows himself during this scene: "Disimula" [Dissimulate] (869). Volseo's command—in itself a precise and calculated gesture of control—heightens the sense of contrast between the irresolute king and his Machiavellian favorite.

Volseo also stands apart from the other members of the court, who respond in diverse ways to the king's confusion and candor. Ana has already voiced resentment at the prospect of humbling herself before the throne (836–38), and despite Enrique's flattery she again vents her bitterness in a pair of asides (846, 890). The princess María resorts to indirection to express her anxiety over the king's words: "Envidiosa / de sus brazos estuviera, / si en la Majestad cupiera / envidia" (I would be envious of her arms, if envy could be reconciled with majesty) (893–96), and the queen immediately adds her own carefully veiled doubts about his constancy: "Y en mis desvelos / pienso que tuviera celos, / si amor hasta aquí supiera" (and in my cares I believe that I would be jealous, if I had known love before) (896–98). These characters all dissimulate to varying degrees: Volseo in dissembling through silence the extent of his influence over the king, Ana in hiding her resentment and ambition, the princess and the queen in masking their emotions behind the language of contrafactual conditions. But these instances of dissimulation differ one from another; Volseo's self-serving pretense cannot fairly be equated with the queen's discreet attempt to make Enrique mindful of what he should render to his family and his crown. Scrutiny of the characters' motives, in this scene and at other decisive moments in the play, suggests that two kinds of concealment are at issue. The first serves to advance the private interests and ambitions of individuals at the court, the second, to minimize the king's weaknesses in order to safeguard royal dignity and the public good. The play's tragic ethos is intimately bound to these two tactics of political concealment. As its action progresses, the first displaces the second with a finality that brings dishonor to king and court and religious division to the realm.

On the question of concealment in statecraft Calderón displays an extensive acquaintance with seventeenth-century political theory. His contemporaries frame their views on this issue in relation to Machiavelli's assertion that the prince must be free to deceive others and to break his word for the sake of political convenience (Fernández-Santamaría 86). Two terms dominate the dispute over this aspect of reason of state: *simulación* and *disimulación* (Fernández-Santamaría 90). These terms shift in their exact meanings with the course of political thought, but they always indicate a general intent to isolate a form of concealment that can be distinguished from sheer deceit and so put at the disposal of the Christian prince. The presence or absence of an intention to deceive weighs heavily on this point; the prince cannot lie outright, but he can withhold information and pursue his affairs in secret without accounting himself responsible for any false inferences that others may draw from his conduct. Pedro de Rivadeneira (1595) advocates such discretion and defends it as a legitimate procedure for shielding public affairs from private interests:

> esto no es mentir, sino hacer las cosas con prudencia para bien de la república. Y como dice el doctor Navarro, hay dos artes de simular y disimular: la una, de los que sin causa ni provecho mienten y fingen que hay lo que no hay, ó que no hay lo que hay; la otra, de los que sin mal engaño y sin mentira dan á entender una cosa por otra con prudencia, cuando lo pide la necesidad ó utilidad. (525b)

> (this is not lying, but rather proceeding with prudence for the good of the commonwealth. And as Doctor Navarro says, there are two kinds of simulation and dissimulation: the first is practiced by those who, without cause or benefit, lie and pretend that there is what is not, or that there is not what is; the second, by those who, without wrongful deception and without lying, prudently imply one thing instead of another, when necessity or utility demands it.)

The emphasis here on Christian prudence is typical of realist political thought, as is the attempt to describe two distinct kinds of statecraft. The evil ruler acts gratuitously in deceiving others through lies and needless inventions; the good prince restricts himself to implying one thing when another is intended and resorts to this device only when he cannot secure the public good by other means. The difficulty of this approach to statecraft is that the prince may overstep the boundary that separates one method from the other, as Rivadeneira acknowledges when he warns against the danger of falling into Machiavellian habits:

> en cualquiera simulacion ó disimulacion que el príncipe cristiano usáre, esté siempre (como dijimos) muy en los estribos y sobre sí, para no dejarse llevar de la dotrina pestífera de Maquiavelo, y quebrantar la ley de Dios y su religion. (525b)

> (in whatever simulation or dissimulation the Christian prince may resort to, he should be [as we have said] in close control and on his guard, so that he will not be led astray by the pestiferous doctrine of Machiavelli, and break the law of God and His religion.)

The limits of proper statecraft, and the best procedure for observing those limits, are clear from this statement. No degree of necessity or utility should persuade the prince to proceed against the claims of religion or of the eternal law that ultimately sanctions secular authority, and the traditional princely virtues of temperance and self-control will enable him to conceal essential affairs of state without trespassing on these forbidden areas. Later thinkers, while sharing the conviction that no concealment is permissible in matters of religion, faith, charity, or justice (Fernández-Santamaría 91), attempt to refine the vocabulary that distinguishes between legitimate and illegitimate conduct. Rivadeneira allows that the prince may resort to both *simulación* and *disimulación*; those who follow him separate the Machiavellian deceit of the former from the prudent secrecy of the latter. In his *Verdadera razón de Estado* (1616) Fernando Alvia de Castro defines *simulación* as "to feign that which is not as if it were" and *disimulación* as "to hide that which is as if it were not"; offering the customary warning about the sanctity of "religion and virtue," he commends *disimulación* as a fair and well-advised political practice: "just as *simulación* is . . . impious and dangerous, *disimulación*, when used properly, is just, prudent, and necessary" (quoted in Fernández-Santamaría 105–6). Juan Pablo Mártir Rizo, in the

Norte de príncipes (1626), states his argument in similar terms. *Simulación* "is to say or promise one thing while intending to do something else"; *disimulación* "consists in not acknowledging what one knows or suspects" and supplies a technique essential to prudence in politics (quoted in Fernández-Santamaría 110).

This vocabulary supplies the terms to articulate a consistent account of political conduct among the major characters of *La cisma de Inglaterra*. At the end of the first act Volseo and Ana indulge in *simulación*, in that they feign a deceitful pose of loyalty and humility to conceal their self-serving ambitions. In contrast, the princess and the queen resort to *disimulación*; they cautiously veil their misgivings about Enrique's emotional condition without feigning false virtues or insincere sentiments. And the course that Volseo recommends to the king is, at least in the first instance, one of legitimate *disimulación*. To urge that the king, in the presence of others, should maintain an impassive demeanor and mask his true emotions is to follow a tenet widely endorsed by the theorists of Christian prudence.[14] As the action proceeds, however, Enrique falls into collusion with Volseo's Machiavellian designs and relies increasingly on *simulación* to pursue dubious personal and political ends. Illegitimate tactics begin to dominate the play's statecraft and to exclude the possibility of prudent *disimulación*. This process is best measured with respect to the king's appearances before the nobility in the final scenes of the second and third acts. Studied in sequence, these two public scenes mark the divisive and irrevocable progress of *simulación* in the politics of the kingdom.

In the second act Volseo contrives an *engaño* (trick or deception) (1385, 1608) to depose the queen and set Ana Bolena in her position. Enrique's unbridled desires simplify this task; having secured Ana's confidence, the favorite has only to supply his master with some practical means for dissolving the royal marriage. To this end he urges the king to summon Parliament and to argue before it that he has found his marriage illegitimate by divine and natural law and so considers himself obliged in conscience to repudiate the bond. As Francisco Ruiz Ramón has noted, when Enrique speaks before Parliament at the end of the act he draws on his gifts as an actor to present the role and the arguments that his favorite

---

14. Saavedra Fajardo, one of the more prominent Spanish theorists of Christian reason of state, insists on the king's prerogative to conceal his emotions: "en los particulares es doblez disimular sus pasiones; en los príncipes razón de estado" (for private individuals to dissimulate their passions is duplicity; for princes, it is reason of state) (1:133).

has set out for him (94). At the climax of his address the king resorts to
the rhetoric of probity and self-sacrifice:

> Esto es ser César cristiano,
> pues a una mujer que adoro
> más que a mí, pues a una santa
> de mis Estados depongo.
> ¡Sabe el Cielo si sintiera
> apartarme de mí propio
> tanto! Pero donde es ley
> es obedecer forzoso.
>
> (1861–68)

(To act in this way is to be a Christian Caesar, since I am banishing
a woman whom I love more than myself—a saint—from my
lands. Heaven knows how profoundly it affects me to set aside part
of myself! But where the law applies it is necessary to obey.)

As Alexander Parker has stated, Enrique claims here to be "sacrificing
his personal happiness to the rule of moral law" ("Henry VIII" 344). This
strategy lays claim on two grounds to the image of the Christian Caesar,
with its overtones of heroic virtue and exemplary restraint: the king
portrays himself as overcoming his love for the queen, and as abjuring
that love out of respect for legal principles. Evidence from other passages
undoes both these claims. The king has revealed to Volseo the intensity
of his passion for Ana, and he is repudiating his wife so that he will be free
to satisfy his illicit desires. He is also aware, as he admits in an earlier
soliloquy (1723–71), that neither natural nor written law offers any
objection to his marriage. Instead of concealing and controlling his
passions, Enrique indulges in *simulación* by misrepresenting the claims
of the law and by feigning virtues that he does not possess.

Susan Fischer has observed that the feigning of convenient sentiments
and convictions is a practice endemic to the play's major characters. She
remarks of the exchanges among Enrique, Volseo, and Ana that "all three
individuals delude themselves into believing that, by adopting a series of
false poses, they will succeed in manipulating others to do as they wish"
(116). This delusion has an adverse effect on the integrity of public life.
As Bacigalupo has argued, by dissembling beyond accepted limits these
three characters "constantly and unwittingly isolate themselves from the

source of legitimate political authority, namely, divine and natural law"
and so induce a condition of disorder in which "the state becomes
tyrannical and finds itself isolated from the Christian community" (216).
Enrique's address before Parliament illustrates his estrangement from
the law; the consequences of that estrangement emerge at the end of the
play, when he summons the nobility to swear obedience to the princess
María. The king has now repented of his illicit love for Ana Bolena, and he
elevates the princess to honor the memory of the queen whom he has
abandoned (1803–7). María initially proves equal to her mother's virtuous example. When the nobles attempt to impose conditions that will
preserve the religious innovations of Enrique's regime, she rejects the
oath and reads her father the fundamental lesson of anti-Machiavellian
thought: "no quiera / que, por razones de Estado, / la ley de Dios se
pervierta" (do not ask that God's law be perverted for reasons of State)
(2923–25). María's reasoning is forceful, and enjoys the unqualified
sanction of Catholic political theory. The king, however, believes that
such an uncompromising ethical stance is no longer tenable, and urges
the princess to conceal her objections: "Callad y disimulad" (Be silent and
dissimulate) (2976). In the play's closing moments María voices her
assent to the oath, excluding in an aside the conditions that she cannot
accept (2983).

When Enrique orders his daughter to dissimulate, the affairs of
England have completed the first circuit of a downward spiral into
disorder and heresy. The king repeats the command that he first heard
from his favorite, but he is repeating it with an ominous difference. The
gesture that Volseo urged upon his master may be construed as prudent
disimulación. The tactic that Enrique imposes on his daughter is an illicit
deception; to profane the oath that guarantees the bond of loyalty
between monarch and subject is to pass from discretion to dishonesty,
from *disimulación* to *simulación*. And the irony here is that María's
attempt to qualify her oath through hidden exclusions will place beyond
her grasp the very end that those exclusions are meant to advance:
England's return to political and confessional unity. As Bacigalupo has
observed, the princess "dissembles in matters pertaining to religion" and
so "divorces herself from the ostensible aim of the ceremony that is being
performed, namely the restoration of a just and legitimate order" (224,
225). Her choice attests to the general decline in the affairs of her
kingdom; under Enrique and Volseo political deceit has so thoroughly
displaced prudent secrecy that María must yield to the force of immedi-

ate convenience. The politics of concealment has reached its inescapable end in self-delusion and social division.

In *La cisma de Inglaterra*, as in *La vida es sueño*, sacrificing the law to interests of state reduces public life to a destructive cycle of calculation and deception. In the history of the English schism Calderón finds support for his skepticism concerning the claims of realist political theory. The degeneration of *disimulación* into *simulación* attests to the instability of the distinction between the two practices and to the fragility of the attempt to find a place for the procedures of secular statecraft within a Christian political order. And the costs of political error are high. The spiral of deception induces division in the realm and draws king and favorite into the vortex of misfortune; at the play's end Enrique has destroyed his reputation as a Christian monarch and the fallen Volseo has abandoned the court to seek a traitor's death in suicide. It is indicative of the distemper that has seized the English monarchy that no character in the play experiences a process of conversion that leads to an apprehension of the force of providence. Yet the absence of a character who parallels Segismundo does not mean that the traditional virtues are left with no voice. The play offers us a positive alternative to Enrique and Volseo in Catherine of Aragon, daughter of Ferdinand the Catholic and queen at England's Tudor court. Calderón's Catalina holds fast to the virtues of constancy and fortitude; she responds to the endemic deception of the court by asserting her steadfast Catholic faith and by reminding others of their obligations to religion and the law.[15] When Enrique yields to his passions the queen resorts to prudent dissimulation, but she openly refuses to accept his willful misrepresentation of divine and natural law, in an address that underscores the contrast between the king's histrionic, duplicitous character and her own "authenticity" and "moral purity" (Ruiz Ramón 95). So forceful are Catalina's virtues that

15. Critical opinion concerning the queen's conduct is both revealing and divided. Alexander Parker has argued that Catalina, in confronting Volseo with his vanity and bad faith, displays a lack of "political prudence" and "charity" that contributes to her personal downfall and to the tragedy of the realm ("Henry VIII" 345–46). Ruiz Ramón, however, finds in the queen a "moral beauty" that allows her to penetrate the deceptive figures around her and to answer Volseo with an exemplary purity and dignity (76–77). I would argue that her proceedings in the play are consistent with Ruiz Ramón's view of her moral excellence. Bacigalupo gives the most cogent analysis of her address to Enrique in the final scene of act 2. He notes that even as Catalina respects and obeys the king's will, she acts upon "her right and duty to impart prudent advice to the king," warning him "to avoid tyranny by following God's laws" (223).

they define the reputation she enjoys among other characters. When
Tomás Boleno introduces his daughter to the court, he urges that she
temper her passions according to the queen's example:

> puesto que cuerda eres,
> sabe vencerte; y pues hoy
> te ponen un transparente
> cristal en la Reina santa,
> mírate en él; que bien puedes
> componer tus pensamientos.
> (746–51)

(since you are prudent, learn to control yourself; and, since the
saintly Queen is set today before you as a flawless mirror, behold
yourself in it; for well may you regulate your thoughts.)

Under the conditions of the play's performance at court, Catalina's moral
authority would have projected itself well beyond the stage. In her ethical
constancy the queen holds up a mirror not only to the members of her
household, but also to the king and the nobility of Hapsburg Spain.
Boleno's instructions as he sets the queen's image before his daughter—
"de sus virtudes aprende" (learn from her virtues) (752)—could apply
with equal force to an aristocratic audience accustomed to a didactic view
of its own past. In the course of the drama Catalina upholds the virtues
that Volseo abuses and distorts, and so joins her father Ferdinand the
Catholic in the pantheon of exemplary Spanish monarchs.

To recognize the opposition between Catalina and Volseo as a relationship of example and counterexample is not to argue, however, that
Calderón offers an explicit or univocal critique of Olivares' influence at
the Hapsburg court. The play was composed during a period of definite
promise for reform and renewal in the Spanish monarchy, when Olivares
could justly be portrayed, in his own writings and in works designed to
promote his reputation, as the antithesis of a false favorite like Calderón's
Volseo.[16] And the positive ideology that the play implies, with its empha-

---

16. Elliott remarks on the "regime of almost spartan austerity" that Olivares adopted
after assuming his high office, and on his "supreme self-control"—a virtue impressed upon
contemporaries by his response to the death of his daughter in 1626 (*Richelieu and Olivares*
19, 16). Stradling comments on his successes, during the years immediately preceding the
first recorded performance of *La cisma de Inglaterra*, in the larger sphere of politics and
international affairs (65).

sis on the favorite's subordinate position and on the exemplary value of
the king's illustrious ancestors, corresponds closely to Olivares's own
conception of the roles appropriate to the king and his chief minister. Yet
Calderón's respect for Olivares' high ideals and initial success does not
render less cogent his treatment of the general dangers of *valimiento*. In
examining the risks that encircle and tempt the favorite, *La cisma de
Inglaterra* anticipates Saavedra Fajardo's trenchant remarks on the office:

> el mayor peligro del valimiento consiste en las trazas que aplica la
> ambición para conservalle, sucediendo a los favorecidos de prínci-
> pes lo que a los muy solícitos de su salud, que, pensando man-
> tenella con variedad de medicinas, la gastan, y abrevian la vida; y,
> como ningún remedio es mejor que la abstinencia y buen gobi-
> erno, dejando obrar a la naturaleza, así en los achaques del
> valimiento el más sano consejo es no curallos, sino servir al
> príncipe con buena y recta intención, libre de intereses y pasiones,
> dejando que obre el mérito y la verdad, más segura y más durable
> que el artificio. (2:262)

> (the greatest danger of *valimiento* consists of the expedients that
> ambition applies to maintain it, since those favored by princes
> experience what happens to those who are overly solicitous of
> their health, who, intending to conserve health with a variety of
> medicines, consume it and shorten their lives; and, just as no
> remedy is better than abstinence and good management, letting
> nature proceed as it will, so in the infirmities of *valimiento* the
> soundest advice is not to treat them, but to serve the prince with
> a good and honest purpose, free of interests and passions, letting
> merit and truth proceed, since these are more secure and lasting
> than artifice.)

Calderón's engagement with contemporary thought concerning the favorite's office and conduct leads to his affinity with Saavedra Fajardo.
Practicing the expedients that ambition supplies to sustain personal
power, applying ill-advised and precipitate remedies to the afflictions of
office, trusting in the devices of statecraft rather than in enduring merit
and truth—these are the faults that Olivares's critics discovered during
the final years of his *valimiento*, and those that Calderón attributes to
Volseo's regime in Tudor England. Through his characteristic strategies

of irony and counterexample, Calderón foresees the most serious failings of *valimiento* even as he endorses Olivares's own view of the virtues appropriate to king and favorite alike.

In *La cisma de Inglaterra* a regime controlled by an impetuous king and a self-serving favorite induces a cycle of negative repetition of the kind that Calderón associates with secular reason of state. Enrique and Volseo stand out as counterexamples whose personal weaknesses and Machiavellian stratagems are to be avoided, and the Neostoic virtues vested in the queen offer the only ethical alternative to the politics of dissimulation. The play's ambivalent stance concerning the rule of Olivares undoubtedly reflects the uneasiness concerning the favorite's prominence that persisted in Spain despite the promise of the early years of Philip IV's reign. In a similar vein, the positive allegory of *valimiento* in *El maestrazgo del Toisón* is clearly related to the structure of the Hapsburg administration in the 1650s and to the conduct of Luis de Haro as the Crown's chief minister. Commentary on the evolution of *valimiento* in the middle decades of the seventeenth century will illuminate the contrasting treatments of the character and office of the favorite in the two plays.

Relations between the favorite and the councils played a central part in this evolution. The regime of Olivares subjected these relations to recurrent stresses and strains, as the favorite pursued his course for remedying the nation's ills, even at the cost of circumventing the mechanisms of government and frustrating the powers of the councils. Under his authority the *valimiento* was "anti-institutional and arbitrary in temper and appointments policy" (Thompson 228), a stance that Olivares himself justified by appealing to the urgent character of the times. Convinced of the necessity for "a revolution imposed from above," Olivares seized on every expedient to advance new measures of governance and taxation and "to inhibit the institutions which safeguarded privilege, legislation and due process" (Stradling 131). Conciliar resistance to these pressures, and to the person who exerted them, must be counted among the factors that moved Philip IV to dismiss his first favorite and so implement new administrative procedures in the 1640s. As Thompson has noted, under Olivares's successors the burden of influence shifted to the councils and traditional rights again commanded respect: "The fall of Olivares, in turn, rehabilitated the *colegial*-dominated conciliar system and represented the triumph of the resistance of customary and legal forms to arbitrary government. Castile, then, also had its Fronde Parlementaire, and after 1643 Castile was run not by the *validos*, epigoni and, after Haro, short-lived, but by the councils and the bureaucracy, and most of all by the Council of Castile" (232).

In opposition to the consensus of opinion among earlier historians, R. A. Stradling has stressed the king's direct involvement in reshaping his government. In the aftermath of Olivares's autocratic regime, Philip IV exercised active direction in his administration, rehabilitating the conciliar system and restoring consultation and debate among the councils (246). During the years of his mature reign effective power lay in the hands of the councillors, rather than in those of a favorite prepared to grant the highest priority to the Crown's interests. These developments had a marked effect on the internal exchange of authority. By the mid-1650s the administration had secured a functional "balance of faction" which ensured that "constant 'opposition' was established as an integral feature of both government and court" (246, 247). Under such conditions Luis de Haro never became *valido* in the sense of the term's application to Lerma and Olivares (266). As the most prominent minister, Haro "achieved the status of *primus inter pares* in Philip's government" (261), but he enjoyed neither the personal influence nor the political dominance of his predecessors. Haro's modest conduct as favorite reflected an institutional shift in the nature of his office.

In *El maestrazgo del Toisón* Calderón responds to the evolution of the Hapsburg administration in the years of Haro's *valimiento*. The allegory of this *auto* defines the proper place of the favorite and presents the Spanish state as structured in accordance with a providential design and so exemplary of Christian politics. As a type of John the Baptist, the favorite subordinates himself to the king's authority; as an institution modeled on the order of Christ's apostles, the conciliar system replicates a sacred pattern and applies it to the practice of government. Through this figural scheme Calderón assimilates the conduct of king, favorite, and councillors in the 1650s to the positive forms of historical repetition that he associates with true reason of state.

In a technique characteristic of his late *autos*—the portrayal of various personages and events as interrelated postfigurations of a single scriptural pattern—Calderón allegorizes the ordering of the Hapsburg state in relation to the founding of the Order of the Golden Fleece by Philip the Good of Burgundy in 1430. The parallels drawn between this order and the Hapsburg state are complex and demand detailed explication, but it is important here to note the association between such late medieval chivalric orders and the ideological ends of the kings and princes who were attempting to restructure European society along the lines of centralized authority. The Golden Fleece can be classified with a number of "secular orders of chivalry," founded by great princes and distinguished from the earlier crusading orders by their aims and conditions of membership and by their submission to secular (rather than ecclesiastical) authority (Keen 179–80). The more prominent among them show an unmistakable dedication to the purposes of "politics, propaganda and diplomacy"; their statutes and ceremonies give "visible and evocative expression to the concepts of loyalty and of alliance, which were key concepts in the late medieval vocabulary of politics and statecraft" (Keen 184–85). Yet for all their commitment to secular ends, these orders also confirm the vitality of Christian ideals and values within the chivalric tradition. A striking aspect of their history is the conjunction of chivalry, religion, and interests of state. Often associated with specific court occasions or political programs, these new orders reinforced allegiance to the princes whose insignia they bore, while honoring various patron saints and promoting Christian heroism and devotion among their members.

The Order of the Golden Fleece, perhaps the most illustrious and influential of the secular orders, exemplifies the principal features of such an institution. Philip the Good established this order on the occasion of his marriage to Isabel of Portugal, and his personal emblem formed part of its insignia: a golden lamb suspended from the duke's flint-and-steel. The order was dedicated to the Virgin and to Saint Andrew, and the early account of its origins in Jean Le Fèvre's chronicle ascribes to it the objectives of sustaining Christian faith, honoring the knights of the past, and promoting chivalry in the present.[17] The political needs of Valois Burgundy also shaped the order's purposes. As Maurice Keen has shown, its ethos helped to foster a sense of allegiance among the local elites of provinces united by marriages and diplomatic means but possessed of "no unitary tradition of obedience and loyalty to a common sovereign" (184). The combination of religious devotion and secular idealism that characterizes the late medieval orders is evident in this varied program.

The religious and political associations of the order persisted when its grand mastership passed into the control of the Hapsburgs with the

---

17. Le Fèvre's description of the religious and chivalric ideals that Philip the Good assigned to the Order of the Golden Fleece at its founding is cited in Domínguez (87).

marriage of Maximilian I to Mary of Burgundy in 1477, and in time they began to serve the imperial aspirations of the dynasty. Frances Yates has written that Charles V's "intensive cult" of the Golden Fleece "tended to restore something of their international character to the Orders of Chivalry and to place Charles himself in an international setting as the Knight-Emperor of Christendom, pledged to maintain the Christianized imperial virtues and to spread them throughout the world" (22). And the continuing importance of the order within the iconography of imperial kingship is apparent from the presence of its insignia in a long sequence of Spanish royal portraits, beginning with three canvasses in which Titian portrays Charles V in the three guises of the ideal ruler—a Renaissance courtier in Bologna, a Christian warrior at Mühlberg, and a grave emperor at Augsburg—and extending through Juan Pantoja's late portrait of Philip II to Velázquez's famous painting of Philip IV in brown and silver. In *El maestrazgo del Toisón* Calderón turns the Golden Fleece to his own allegorical purposes, but his work stands in a series of artistic representations that attest to the prestige of the order in Europe and to its usefulness as a political instrument.

A brief summary of this *auto* will underline its principal techniques and patterns of meaning. In the opening moments the figure of Malice appears, summons his confederate Flattery, and explains that he is fearful of a coming leader or "Duke," who has been announced to the world as a "lamb" destined to remove its "sins." Arguing that such a powerful leader must possess a palace and a court, Malice proposes to Flattery that together they join his retinue, with the intention of scrutinizing and frustrating his designs. After approaching John the Baptist, who attempts to forbid Flattery from serving the Duke, Malice successfully insinuates himself into the corps of councillors. The Duke welcomes his followers and proceeds with his plans for marriage, dispatching Saint Peter to transport his Bride from Lebanon and John the Baptist to invite Synagogue as an honored guest. Swayed by an appeal from Flattery on behalf of her people, Synagogue opposes the announced match, first by releasing storms against the Bride's ship and then, on her safe arrival, by declaring war against the Duke, who responds by inaugurating an order in the Bride's honor, beneath the emblem of the Golden Fleece. After the Duke has set out the heraldry of the order, appointed his followers to its various offices, and asked them to share its first ceremonial meal, Malice flees with one of the insignia and sells it to Synagogue for thirty pieces of silver. Synagogue tests the metal of the insignia with a series of "touchstones"—a cord, a whip, a crown of thorns, a cross with nails, a lance—and discovers it to be an alloy of the human and the divine. As she completes her testing, the earth trembles in what she takes to be a sign of her victory. But in the closing scene the Duke returns in triumph over death, in the company of his faithful councillors, to fulfill his promise to the Bride and to exalt his new order through a series of Eucharistic discoveries.

Certain prominent aspects of the text are evident from this summary. The elements of Calderón's technique for allegorizing the Golden Fleece in relation to the Passion are clear, as is the central role of Malice and Flattery in provoking and sustaining the main action. The conventions of religious drama account in part for the prominence of these two characters. To dramatize the devil by personifying one or more of his attributes is a standard technique in the *autos* written before Calderón (Fothergill-Payne 118), and the pairing of two such figures, or of the devil and one of his principal attributes, is common in both the traditional and the Calderonian *auto* (Fothergill-Payne 126–27; A. Parker, "Devil" 9–10). In *El maestrazgo del Toisón* the contrast between Malice, as the blocking character who takes on the role of Judas, and the rest of the Duke's retinue is central to the development of the text; it is also characteristic of ethicist political theory, with its tendency to set the declining ways of the present against the perfect Christian institutions of the scriptural past. In a typical lament on the failings of contemporary monarchy, the *Política de Dios* explicitly contrasts the position of Christ and his apostles to that of the king and his ministers: "si el Hijo de Dios se recata de sus doze Apostoles, porque entre ellos ay vn Iudas, ¿que han de hazer los Principes seruidos de malos ministros? que entre doze Iudas quiera Dios, que apenas tengan vn Apostol" (if the Son of God is wary of his twelve Apostles, because there is one Judas among them, what are the Princes to do, who are served by evil ministers? for, God willing, they can scarcely find one Apostle among twelve Judases) (100). And if Quevedo can describe the modern state as an inversion of a sanctioned apostolic model, Calderón presents a chivalric order patterned on the life of Christ and his followers as an example of true statecraft, designed to illustrate principles of selection and governance in the conciliar system.

As in *La segunda esposa y triunfar muriendo*, the allegory of this *auto* centers on the figural correspondence of Christ and the King. Malice's opening exposition sets out the terms and assumptions of the allegory. As he informs Flattery of his fears concerning future events, Malice passes

from various intimations of the Incarnation and the Virgin Birth to
another "mystery" that at first he is unable to name:

> vamos
> a otro que no menos turba
> mis atenciones, porque
> consta de mis conjeturas
> aun más que de sus palabras,
> eslabonándose unas
> de otras al mirar las sombras,
> los lejos y las figuras
> de que está llena la Sacra
> página de la Escritura.
>
> (895a)

(let us proceed to another that preoccupies me no less, since it
consists of my conjectures even more than of his words, as some
conjectures link themselves to others, when I contemplate the
shadows, semblances, and figures of which the sacred page of
Scripture is full.)

These lines are of notable thematic and technical interest. In the traditional language of Christian allegory, Malice speaks of the "shadows,"
"semblances," and "figures" that fill the "sacred page" of Scripture, and
attributes his greatest fears to the "conjectures" that he has drawn from
them.[18] The technique in play here has been described as a kind of
psychomachia, which allows the spectators "to follow each step in the
train of thought as it emerges from the mind of a character on the stage
actually conceiving the action before their eyes" (A. Parker, *Allegorical
Drama* 83). As Malice reviews his conjectures about what the Bible may
prefigure for the future, he pursues the strategy of "following the events

18. The word *lejos*, translated here according to its figurative sense as "semblances" or
"appearances," also has an important technical meaning. As Kurtz has noted, *lejos* and *visos*
are terms that Calderón borrows from the language of perspective in visual art; the former
are "the background distances of a painting," the latter, "highlights used to emphasize
background objects" (53). Calderón resorts to these terms frequently in the *autos*, both to
describe his own allegories and to refer to scriptural figures of the Eucharist. Kurtz
comments with care and detail on the significance of this language, arguing that such
"shared perspectival metaphors" suggest an "analogical link" between Calderón's allegorical drama and the sacrament that it celebrates (56–57).

in human history, piecing them together, endeavouring to ascertain what each one is leading to and to what plan providence is fitting it," in an attempt to turn history to the devil's advantage (*Allegorical Drama* 91). His thoughts, as he outlines them here, are the basis of all that follows, and the structure of the *auto* rests largely on his ability to construct from the signs of biblical history a figural allegory.

In the next stage of this process Malice reviews the scriptural figures that have prompted his anxious speculations. The figures that he selects, all from the Old Testament, focus uniformly on the image of the lamb.[19] Moving in sequence through the Bible, he mentions Abel's sacrifice (Genesis 4:4), the paschal lamb of the Exodus and the ceremony instituted in its memory (Exodus 12:1–28), and the lamb portrayed by the prophet Isaiah as both triumphant and meek (Isaiah 16:1, 53:7); he then returns to the Book of Judges, to describe the most explicit and significant of his chosen figures:

> no menor me le da
> que me le esmalte la lluvia
> del rocío de una aurora,
> cuando Gedeón enjuta
> halle la Tierra y a él no,
> en cuyo viso se ocultan
> (bien si la Piel se humedece
> o bien si la Piel se enjuga)
> *Sacramento* que me asombra
> y *Encarnación* que me asusta.
>   (895b)

(it makes me no less fearful that a dawn's shower of dew embellishes the lambskin when Gideon finds the earth dry and it not, in which appearance are hidden [whether the skin turns damp, or whether it stays dry] a *Sacrament* that astonishes me and an *Incarnation* that alarms me.)

19. The early literature of the Order of the Golden Fleece offers precedent for this survey of ovine symbolism. In his chapter on Burgundian revisions and transformations of the Argonautica material, Domínguez discusses Guillaume Fillastre's *Toisón d'or*, a book that proposes to elucidate the symbolic meanings of "the six historical *toisons*, those of Jason, Jacob, Gideon, Mesa of Moab, Job, and David" (105).

In one of the fundamental gestures of figural interpretation, Malice reveals the single end to which all the figures of the Old Testament point and tend. Following an established allegorical reading, he presents Gideon's fleece (Judges 6:36–40) as a sign of the "Incarnation" and, ultimately, of the essential "Sacrament" to be instituted by Christ. The biblical fleece, whose alternations in relation to the earth surrounding it assure Gideon of God's will and favor, offers a sign of the divine sanction bestowed upon Israel and anticipates the elements of the Eucharist; because of this exact sacramental character it provides a fitting culmination to Malice's sequence of ovine images.

As he continues his address, Malice explains why these particular figures concern him so intensely. Noting that he has heard a young leader proclaimed in the desert as "the Lamb of God" (John 1:29), he argues that the unexpected appearance of this "Nazarene" must enclose a great and terrifying "mystery":

> pues al llamarle Cordero
> me oprime, pasma y angustia
> tanto, que al ver que en un Hombre
> temidas sombras concurran,
> al trueno de aquella voz
> el relámpago deslumbra
> mi vista, de suerte que
> ando tropezando a oscuras.
>
> (895b–96a)

(for, on calling him a Lamb, he so oppresses, astounds, and worries me that, when I see the dreaded shadows converge on one Man, at the thunder of that voice the lightning overpowers my sight, so that I wander about in darkness.)

That the numerous figures involving the lamb have centered themselves on a single man is the fundamental motive of Malice's anxiety, and he conveys his confusion through conventional images of light and darkness, portraying himself as blinded by the "lightning" of spiritual awareness that accompanies the "thunder" of the Baptist's voice. Absorbed within the types or "shadows" of the Old Testament, Malice cannot fully foresee the redemptory events that they foreshadow. Like Synagogue, who refuses the Baptist's invitation because she prefers her "shadows" to his truth (904a), he is destined to remain "in darkness," without the benefit of Christ's light.

Malice presents his figural scheme as an attempt to overcome the failings of his "knowledge" through purposeful "ingenuity." He proposes to Flattery that, since his unaided "understanding" cannot penetrate God's designs, they resort to the "subtlety" of an allegory:

> Esta es (pues de Alegoría
> el Sagrado Texto usa
> tantas veces), que nosotros
> usemos, Lisonja, de una.
> (896a)

(That is [since the Sacred Text makes use so many times of allegory] that we, Flattery, make use of one.)

Here the interrelations of history and allegory are clearly indicated. By imitating the methods of Scripture, Malice hopes to construct an allegory that will reveal the providential order of human history and so anticipate the mysterious events that have prompted his fears. He plans to deploy allegory as a method for relating occurrences in history to one another and for projecting the pattern of events to come. And the historical character of Malice's argument continues to assert itself as he sets out the suppositions from which his allegory will depart. He proposes that the forthcoming redeemer is a "noble hero" and "duke" who stands as the leader of his people, that he comes from "Alta Alemania," that he has inherited "absolute majesty" from his father, and that he will be known as Philip, son of Margaret, and surnamed "de Austria." Taken together, these statements have the curious effect of anticipating and compressing the imperial histories of Burgundy and Spain. The ruler whom they describe combines characteristics of Philip the Good, duke of Burgundy and son of Margaret of Bavaria and John the Fearless, with those of Philip IV, who inherited, as the son of Philip III and Margaret of Styria, the imperial majesty vested in the House of Austria. In Calderón's thought the conventional figural associations of monarchy make this conflation possible. Since the true Christian king is himself a type of Christ, Malice can perceive two Christian princes in their figural relationships both to one another and to the central pattern of Christ's existence. This idea is consistent with the historical attitude implicit in figural allegory, and it is crucial to the remainder of the *auto*, in which Malice and Flattery scrutinize the actions of the Duke of Austria—a single character who simultaneously represents Philip the Good, Philip IV, and Christ—in the hope of unlocking the "mystery" attendant upon his name and nature:

> notaremos de más cerca
> sus acciones de que induzcas
> qué misterio es el que inspire,
> qué secreto es el que influya
> en este *Phelippe* nuevo,
> de *Austria* la sacra figura
> que de Cordero le da
> nombre en esa voz que apura
> con sus ecos mis sentidos.
> (896b)

(we will observe his actions at closer range so that you may infer what is the mystery that inspires, what is the secret that informs, this new *Philip*, the sacred figure of *Austria*, to whom the name of Lamb is given in that voice which troubles my sense with its echoes.)

When Malice and Flattery bring their self-serving designs to the Duke's court, they begin to encounter his true apostles, whose conduct exemplifies the virtues of faithful royal service. The conflict between these two sets of servants, and between the principles of good and evil that they represent, provides the main thread of the *auto* and bears directly on the structure and purposes of the Order of the Golden Fleece.

The initial encounter of Malice and Flattery with John the Baptist points to their opposing roles in the central drama, and to the place within that drama of conventional poetic themes and forms. The Baptist himself initiates their dialogue, when he enters with a song inviting others to join his lord's retinue:

> Vengan, vengan a mi voz
> cuantos noble dueño buscan,
> que yo salgo a recibir
> gente en la milicia suya
> a esta tan hermosa orilla,

que están sus arenas rubias,
compitiendo con las salvas
cuando las flores madrugan.

(897a)

(Come, come to my voice, all who seek a noble lord, since I set forth to receive followers into his militia, on this most beautiful bank, for its sands are golden, competing with the salvos when the flowers open at first light.)

Calderón turns here to the *glosa* that he assigns to Man and Sombra in the *auto* version of *La vida es sueño*. As the Baptist summons new followers to his "beautiful bank" whose "golden sands" and early "flowers" rival the bright "salvos" of dawn, he echoes the words of the *glosa* and evokes the green world of Renaissance pastoral. His invitation has a clear doctrinal point to establish—that his master's fold is open to all who wish to serve him—but its most immediate effect is to set out the elements of a conventional pastoral scene.

When they greet one another in song, Flattery and the Baptist preserve the formal structure of the *glosa* and continue to evoke and engage the traditions of pastoral. In the mannered language of seventeenth-century bucolic verse, Flattery hails the Baptist as a "siren" of the adjacent waters, and protests that the birds above, as they "form feathered Aprils" in the air, are unequal to his "rivalry." In response the Baptist addresses Flattery as a "mountain-woman" whose superhuman beauty is welcomed "as the dawn" by the flowers and birds who "paint" the earth and the air. Through its close parallels of theme and of sound (*sirena: serrana*) and its play on the motif of competition or rivalry, this exchange constructs a finely cast artifice that holds the natural, human, and divine in a careful balance.

In the next stanza, also sung, Flattery sustains the tensions and balances of the preceding lines, while attempting to resolve them on the central image of the Baptist:

Hermoso gallardo joven,
la perfección solo es tuya,
pues las flores que te miran
y las aves que te escuchan
por Dios te aclaman, y cuando

su escrúpulo las acusa,
en viendo tus bellos ojos,
quedan vanos de su culpa.

(897b)

(Beautiful graceful youth, perfection is yours alone, since the
flowers that gaze upon you and the birds that listen to you acclaim
you as God, and, when they feel any scruple for adoring you, one
sight of your lovely eyes excuses them of any blame.)

This elaborate compliment is entirely consistent with the conventions of
what has already been said. After praising the wonders of the surrounding nature and hearing her own beauty exalted as "belying" any signs of
humanity, Flattery is entitled to perceive the Baptist as a pastoral deity
whose "perfection" has inspired the ordered display of flowers and birds
around him. In presenting him in this light, as the absolute center of the
scene, Flattery simply extends the rhetoric of their exchange to its logical
endpoint, yet the Baptist is quick to reject any such image of himself.
Changing from song to speech, he abruptly silences her pleasing voice:

¿A mí por Dios? Calla, calla;
tu voz se suspende muda,
que es sacrílega Lisonja
a que mi humildad repugna.
Un Príncipe Soberano
al Mundo mi voz anuncia,
de cuyo coturno aún no
merezco las ataduras
tocar. ¿Cómo será Dios
quien se aniquila y se anula
aun no digno de sus plantas?

(897b)

(Do you take me for God? Be quiet, be quiet; may your voice be
held in silence, for that is sacrilegious flattery which my humility
finds hateful. My voice announces a Sovereign Prince to the
World, the latchet of whose shoe I do not deserve even to touch.
How can one be God who practices abnegation and humility, and
is unworthy even to touch his feet?)

This passsage has a strong corrective intent, in that it reprimands Flattery for attributing divinity to John the Baptist and so exposes the falsity of her assumptions about the conventions inherent in his discourse. Flattery's remarks are appropriate to the green world of shepherds and shepherdesses; the Baptist's rebuke reveals that his interests and concerns lie solely with the one true Shepherd, before whom no lesser gods should be placed. Here, as in the scene involving the same *glosa* in *La vida es sueño*, Calderón conspicuously dramatizes his willingness to accept ۱astoral only in its most Christian form. In interpretive terms, Flattery's main error is her failure to understand the mode of the Baptist's greeting as pastoral *a lo divino*.

Such errors of comprehension and response point, moreover, to the fundamental moral futility of her position. Her attempt to conceal the reprehensible motives of her desire to serve has not persuaded the Baptist, who recognizes her words as "sacrilegious flattery" which he must counter by asserting his own humility in the face of his master's authority. In the context of the *auto*'s concern with political questions, the Baptist's statement resonates with implications for the conduct of royal servants, with a forcefulness that recalls the moral burden of contemporary arguments about the fit order of the state. The *Política de Dios* consistently praises John the Baptist for subordinating his own interests and reputation to the larger purposes of Christ's mission, and proposes this selfless relationship as a perfect pattern of faithful service. In his commentary on the Baptist's encounter with the priest and Levites who would mistake him for Christ (John 1:19–34), Quevedo urges his immediate and exemplary deferral to his Lord upon all who serve wise and powerful masters: "Esto hazen los priuados reconocidos y cuerdos, yd al Rey y enseñarsele: Veisle alli, yo no soy nada, el dà los cargos, solo el es Señor de todo" (This is what grateful and prudent favorites do: go to the King and show him to others; There you see him, I am nothing, he confers all offices, he alone is Lord of all things) (104). And the treatise later returns to the same scriptural authority, to provide a second and more detailed gloss that bears directly on the text of Calderón's *auto*:

> Iuan primero Privado escogido, quando vè vacilar en el reconocimiento del Señor verdadero, de su Rey Eterno, del Rey Dios y Hombre, en estas palabras dize todo lo que se ha de dezir, y todo lo que no se ha de hazer: *No soy digno de desatar la correa de su zapato.* Pues S.P. si Iuan Privado no es digno de desatar la correa

del zapato de su Rey, ¿que serà del criado, que intentare atar con la del suyo a su Rey? ¿Que cosa es atar el criado al Señor? Esso no se ha de presumir de toda la perdicion del seso ambicioso de los hombres: Es menester para tan sacrilega ossadia todo la desverguença del infierno. (251)

(John, the first chosen Favorite, when he sees others hesitate in recognizing the true Lord, his Eternal King, the King both God and Man, in these words says all that must be said, and all that must not be done: *I am not worthy to unloose the latchet of his shoe.* Very well, Holy Father, if John the Favorite is not worthy to unloose the latchet of his King's shoe, what will become of the servant, who attempts to bind his King with his own latchet? What does it mean for the servant to bind his Lord? This cannot be presumed to stem from all the perdition of the ambitious human mind: such sacrilegious daring demands all the shamelessness of hell.)

Quevedo's reading of John 1:27, a verse paraphrased in Calderón's text, presents John the Baptist as the type of the perfect favorite. For Quevedo, the Baptist's refusal to touch the "latchet" of Christ's shoe exemplifies the humility of true service and contrasts sharply with the presumption of any royal servant who wishes to "bind" his master's authority to his own will. The Baptist's line is read here as a rebuke to all who would interfere with the king's sovereignty, either by "binding" his powers or by "releasing" the essential bonds of his office:

Pues si no es licito desatar la correa del zapato, ¿como serà licito desatar al Rey de su alma? ¿Al Rey de sus Reynos? ¿Al Rey de su oficio? ¿Al Rey de la Religion? ¿Al Rey de Dios? Esto el que lo haze, el que desata al Rey destas cosas, no es ministro, no es Privado, no es vassallo, no es hombre: lo que es, digalo por el Bautista el Evangelista San Iuan. (251)

(For if it is not lawful to unloose the latchet of his shoe, how can it be lawful to release the King from his soul? The King from his Realms? The King from his office? The King from Religion? The King from God? He who does this, who releases the King from these things, is neither minister, nor favorite, nor vassal, nor man:

let St. John the Evangelist say what he is on the behalf of the Baptist.)

Indeed, John's first epistle supplies further support for Quevedo's assertion that only hell itself can account for the "sacrilegious daring" of the untrue servant. The passage alluded to here (1 John 4:3) associates the faithless prophet with the most radical sources of evil. In his gloss Quevedo collates the statements of the Evangelist and the Baptist:

> El vn Iuan lo dize, que el que desata a Cristo es espiritu de Antecristo: y el otro Iuan, que vino antes de Cristo, y fue embiado del, quando dize estas palabras, no solo confiessa que no ha de desatar a Cristo, sino que no merece desatar la correa de su zapato. Y el vno que lo haze, fue el Privado: y el otro el querido. Y el que no los imitare, si desata a su Rey, ¿que serà? Ya lo ha dicho S. Iuan. Y si le atare (lo que no se puede creer) serà Iudas. (251)

> (One John says, that he who releases Christ is the spirit of the Antichrist: the other John, who came before Christ, and was sent by him, when he says these words, not only confesses that he must not release Christ, but that he does not deserve to unloose the latchet of his shoe. And the first who acted in this way, was Christ's Favorite, and the other was beloved of Him. And he who does not imitate them, if he releases his King, what will he be? Saint John has already said this. And if he binds him [which cannot be believed] he will be Judas.)

In naming the Antichrist and Judas as the two archetypes of the corrupt servant, Quevedo reminds us again of the moral framework that informs Calderón's *auto*. In his attempt to "bind" the Duke's mysteries to his own fears and desires, Malice acts out the political aspect of his role as Judas, and allows John the Baptist to display the opposing virtues of the true favorite. This idea is entirely consistent with the allegorical scheme that Calderón has proposed; just as the Duke himself is closely associated with both Christ and the king, so Malice's actions have spiritual and political meanings of equal and simultaneous validity. Each stage in the development of the *auto* points in some degree to these two levels of meaning. When, for example, the Duke knowingly accepts Malice into his service so that he may eventually receive the "recompense" appropriate to his demonic impulses (899b), he is both demonstrating the infinitude of divine love and offering, in terms articulated by Quevedo's gloss on John 6:70–71, a lesson to those earthly monarchs who refuse to recognize the evil qualities of their chosen ministers:

> Grande enseñança para los Reyes de la tierra, a quien persuaden que reparen en la eleccion que hizieron del ministro, que se hizo ruin, y traidor, para no castigarle, para no darle a conocer, diziendo, que es el diablo. (181)

> (This is a great lesson for earthly Kings, who are persuaded that they need only take heed of the choice they have made of a minister who has become base, and a traitor, in order that he not be punished, in order that he not be made known by saying that he is the devil.)

In a similar way, the blocking gestures of Malice, Flattery, and Synagogue, and the responses that they prompt in the Duke and his retinue, all address vital issues of kingship and the order of the state.

Of the measures undertaken to counter the *auto*'s forces of evil, the most prominent is the founding of a new order of chivalry, and the significance of this event depends on its place within the main figural allegory. In its structure and purposes, this order is Calderón's major vehicle for aligning the contemporary state with the true apostolic pattern. Its heraldry and offices, as they are set out by the Duke, correspond in general terms to those of the historical order of the Golden Fleece; they also suggest close parallels between the hierarchy of the early Church and the structure of the Hapsburg state.

When he founds the order to aid him in achieving his final triumph of the spirit, the Duke speaks of defending his marriage against those who wish to deny its validity or to dishonor his Bride, and he selects his symbolic arms on this basis. Because Synagogue, the character most strenuously opposed to the match, has taken offense at hearing the Duke called *agnus dei*, he decides to place his new order beneath "the Insignia of the Lamb." Having chosen this emblem, however, he is at pains to dismiss its more questionable associations:

> no porque diga la fama
> en ningún tiempo (al mirar)

que *Toisón de Oro* se llama)
que es por el Vellón de Oro,
que tanto Jassón ensalza,
sino el Cándido Vellón,
que vio Gedeón al alba
cuajar el blanco rocío:
que habiendo de dedicarla
a mi Esposa, y siendo ella
(como es) Gracia de las Gracias,
a ella compete el blasón
del blanco vellón sin manchas.
(906b–7a)

(Not so that at any time fame will say [on seeing that it is called the *Golden Fleece*] that it is named for the Fleece of Gold so exalted by Jason, but for the Snow-white Fleece that Gideon saw collecting the white dew at dawn: for, since I must dedicate it to my Bride, and since she is Grace of the Graces, the device of the white fleece without stain falls to her.)

The immediate classical resonances of the fleece are here set aside in favor of a more acceptable scriptural authority. The particular precedent chosen is a conventional one—Huizinga tells us that Jean Germain, an early Burgundian chancellor of the Golden Fleece, first employed and diffused the term *Gedeonis signa* in relation to the order—but it is nonetheless uniquely appropriate to its context within the *auto*.[20] Gideon's fleece has already appeared at the beginning of the work, among the various lambs and fleeces from the Old Testament that Malice presents as figures of the Eucharist. The Duke's words of dedication continue to stress the sacramental aspect of Gideon's "snow-white lambskin," through a series of ecclesiastical and Marian reminiscences. The Duke's true Bride, herself associated with the Church, merits the honor of a fleece whose purity mirrors the immaculacy of the Virgin. Marked by words and images of nature and by the corrective spirit characteristic of Calderón's *autos*, this passage uses the language of Christian pastoral to

20. The association of the Order of the Golden Fleece with the scriptural figure of Gideon (as opposed to Jason and the pagan fleece of Colchis) is discussed by Huizinga (87–88), Keen (192, 195), and Domínguez (87–91).

extricate the Golden Fleece from the dubious sphere of pagan heroism and presumption.

Christian values and images continue to assert their presence as the Duke outlines the details of the order's heraldry:

> su insignia (pues es mi Amor
> quien constituir la manda)
> será de fuego: y así,
> de pedernales la banda
> (de que penderá el cordero)
> se ha de labrar, engastada
> de eslabones de oro, que
> estén exhalando llamas,
> con una letra que diga:
> *Herido luce*; a que añada
> otra en respuesta, diciendo
> (pues para ti se Consagra):
> Tú sola y no otra; con que
> del Collar, medida y tasa
> siempre será una, advirtiendo
> que en mi Amor no habrá mundanza.
>
> (907a)

(its insignia [since it is my Love which orders that it be established] will be of fire: and thus, the chain [from which the lamb will hang] must be made of flints, mounted with links of gold emitting flames, with a motto that says: *It sparks when struck*; and let another motto be added in response, saying [since it is consecrated to you]: You alone and no other; such that the measure and value of the Collar will always be one, giving notice that there will be no change in my Love.)

This account of the insignia assigned to the Order of the Golden Fleece sets the personal emblems and mottos of Philip the Good within the traditions of Christian iconography. His flint-and-steel suggests the "fire" of divine love, as displayed in such examples as the flames of Pentecost (Acts 2:1); his verbal device "Autre n'aurai Dame," paraphrased here in Spanish, is presented as a statement of Christ's commitment and devotion to the one true Church. This element of love is essential to the meaning

of the order; the founding of the Fleece, like the Pentecost, is a moment
of consecration and renewal that prepares the apostles for the work of
their master. Taken together, the various aspects of the order's insignia—
its materials, its design, its "measure" and "value"—all point to the power
and constancy of the love that will inspire its members.

The order also resembles the Church in that it attempts to embody this
love in outward regulations and structures, and the Duke now discusses
the forms of authority best suited to his purposes. After explaining some
principles of maintenance and recruitment, he describes his preferred
structure of command:

> Cinco oficios principales
> ha de tener en su Casa
> el *Maestre del Toisón*:
> asesor para sus causas,
> gran canciller, secretario,
> tesorero y rey de armas.
> (907b)

(The *Master of the Fleece* must have five principal offices in his
House: an assessor for his causes, a great chancellor, a secretary,
a treasurer, and a king of arms.)

He then turns to his followers and distributes these offices among them,
on the basis of functional analogies between the tasks undertaken by the
various apostles and the duties necessary for maintaining a chivalric
order. Saint Andrew is to act as assessor, pronouncing upon the justice of
the order's causes; John the Baptist, who "imprints the seal" of Christ's
redemptory "character," as chancellor; Saint John, who will record the
testimony of his faith in the Book of Revelation, as secretary; Saint James,
whom the armies of imperial Spain will invoke in battle, as king of arms;
and Saint Peter, to whom Christ will grant the "golden key" of his
kingdom, as treasurer. To the five original positions the Duke finally adds
a sixth, that of chronicler, which he assigns to Saint Matthew. These key
offices, all well suited to the attributes of the saints who hold them,
comprise the structure that will fulfill the order's imperial destiny.

This scene casts the religious claims of chivalry in exact typological
terms. That the apostles can execute the offices specified here points to
the figural significance inherent within the order. As he attempts to

impart a sense of mission and form to his order, the Duke defines its duties so that they correspond precisely to those of the first saints. Acting in his role as founder of the Golden Fleece, he re-creates the structures devised by Christ for the early Church. Patterned repetition of this kind is characteristic of Calderón's figural view of history, and here, as elsewhere in the *auto*, the implications of the allegory extend beyond chivalry itself. The prominence of the chivalric orders in Spain's official life, and the parallels between the attributes of the Duke and of Philip IV, suggest that the apostolic analogy applies not only to the Order of the Golden Fleece but also, in another temporal frame, to the structure of the Spanish state. This idea reflects the prevalent values of Catholic political theory, as well as the specific conditions under which the *autos* were performed. Quevedo argues that the proper order of the state is embodied in Christ's example: "Diga a vozes la vida de Christo, que cosa ha de encargar vn Rey a su criado, y que han de ser los criados de los Reyes" (Let the life of Christ say in full voice, what a King should entrust to his servant, and what the servants of Kings should be) (104). And Calderón's audience at the Alcázar consisted in part of chancellors, secretaries, and treasurers who could find their own functions mirrored here in the apostles and the officers of the Golden Fleece, while his larger public included citizens who might presumably benefit from seeing the officials of their society cast in such exalted roles. At a single stroke, Calderón has portrayed Christ assigning duties to his apostles, Philip the Good founding the Order of the Golden Fleece, and Philip IV ordering the affairs of Spain.

The closing moments of the *auto*, with the death of the Duke and his final victory over Synagogue, reinforce the patterns that link the Order of the Golden Fleece to the Passion on the one hand and to the Spanish monarchy on the other. Synagogue's testing of the order's insignia is a striking dramatization of the Crucifixion that turns traditional techniques to unexpected figural ends. Her "touchstones" are conventional objects in Spanish religious drama, often used to suggest or represent Christ's sufferings and sacrifice, as in Gómez Manrique's *Representación del nacimiento de Nuestro Señor* of the late fifteenth century, in which the Christian martyrs offer the instruments of the Passion as gifts to the infant Jesus.[21] Calderón, however, uses the objects for the unusual

21. Foulché-Delbosc prints the text of Manrique's *Representación* in the second volume of his *Cancionero castellano del siglo XV* (53–56).

purpose of establishing that the emblematic lamb of the Golden Fleece is an exact figure of the *Agnus Dei*, in which Christ's dual nature is perfectly represented. And Malice's part in stealing the fleece and selling it to Synagogue is consistent with his place in the drama of the Passion, as he himself suggests in his last words:

> y así, el dinero arrojado
> a los umbrales del templo,
> moriré a mis proprias manos,
> desesperado, advirtiendo,
> mortales, que lo que no
> pudiera hacer por sí mesmo
> el demonio, pudo hacer,
> tomando por instrumento
> a la malicia de un hombre.
>
> (911b)

(and so, having thrown the money at the threshold of the temple, I will die in desperation by my own hands, giving warning, mortals, that what the devil could not achieve on his own, he was able to achieve by taking the malice of a man as his instrument.)

Malice now recognizes that he has taken the part of a particular man who serves as the "instrument" of the devil's designs. His confession confirms him in the role of Judas, while echoing Quevedo's assertion that demonic impulses invariably lie behind the actions of the false favorite. And his death (Matthew 27:3–5), like that of Volseo in *La cisma de Inglaterra*, illustrates the fate that awaits the unfaithful; in suicide he receives the "reward" that the Duke has promised him. In setting the offices granted to the apostles against the price of Malice's betrayal, Calderón, like Quevedo, points to the contrast between the exaltation of those who serve their master in good faith and the infamy visited upon the evil servant:

> Dos criados tuvo Cristo: vno, que fue Iuan, se disminuyò, para que creciesse el Rey: y este fue hombre embiado de Dios, y entre los nacidos ninguno mayor que èl. ¡Gran cosa! Nadie mayor que el disminuido. Otro quiso crecer èl, y que no creciesse el Señor: y este fue Iudas, hijo de perdicion, y que le valiera mas no aver

nacido. De aquel primero pocos imitadores se leen, y se ven: De
este su fin, sus cordeles, su horca, su bolsa, su venta, su beso se
precia de gran sequito, y de larga imitacion: y toda su vida
presume de señas de muchos, y de original de muchas copias por
lo propio justiciadas. (249)

(Christ had two servants: one, who was John, made himself lesser,
so that the King would be greater: and he was a man sent by God,
and among mortals none was greater than he. A wondrous matter!
None was greater than the lesser. Another wanted to be greater
himself, and that the Lord should not be so: and this one was
Judas, son of perdition, who would better have remained unborn.
Of the former few imitators are read about, and seen: of the latter
his end, his cords, his gallows, his purse, his sale, his kiss, all can
boast of a great retinue, and of enduring imitation: and his life as
a whole displays a pattern for many other men, and is the original
of many who copied and were put to death on their own account.)

This passage once again draws the political aspect of Calderón's allegory
to our attention, by reasserting the implications of the fundamental
opposition of John the Baptist and Judas. Throughout the *auto* the Baptist
has acted as the Duke's true minister, humbling himself to the work of his
master; here Malice, having shown his colors as a "son of perdition,"
realizes the futility of his mission and the curse of his birth. His example
bears on the politics of Calderón's Spain in two ways. In the first instance,
his death stands as a warning to any who might be tempted to join
the "great retinue" of his imitators. More significant, the *auto* as a whole
shows that Philip the Good (and, by extension, Philip IV) has followed the
prudence of Christ Himself in excluding such ruinous councillors from
his presence. According to the terms that the text offers us the Spanish
state, like the Order of the Golden Fleece, has drawn its structure from a
divine pattern that preserves and guarantees its sovereignty and its
imperial destiny.

   This last issue, that is, the privileged place of the Golden Fleece among
the emblems of Spain's Christian empire, is the theme upon which the
auto closes. When the Duke returns to his faithful Bride, drawing the
knights of the order in his triumphant train, Synagogue protests that her
powers, as embodied in a "lion of Judah" that stands crowned on her cart,

will ensure that his victory is of brief moment. The Duke replies that her claim to this emblem is no longer valid:

> No es tuya desde este tiempo,
> que pasando a ser blasón
> del auto que hoy represento
> pasará a ser León de España,
> en mi lugar, sucediendo
> *El Maestrazgo del Toisón,*
> la fe, religión y celo
> de sus católicos reyes,
> archiduque de Austria.
>
> (913a)

(From now on it is no longer yours, since by becoming the device of the *auto* that I present today, it will become the Lion of Spain, when my place, in *The Mastership of the Fleece* and as archduke of Austria, passes to the Catholic kings in their faith, religion, and zeal.)

The succession of the Duke's order will transfer the emblem of the lion from Judah to Spain. As the mastership of the Golden Fleece passes from Maximilian I, archduke of Austria, to the "Catholic kings" of the peninsula, the order will add the imperial lion to its heraldic arms. When Synagogue questions the "contradiction" of juxtaposing lion and lamb, the Duke asserts that these creatures represent two aspects of the one true God. The crowned lion then opens to reveal a lamb, which opens in turn to disclose, in sequence, the bread and wine of the Eucharist and a child bearing the bonds of the Passion. This set of discoveries confirms Calderón's typological view of history by two related means. It traces a retrograde temporal series that leads from the lion of Spain and the lamb of the Golden Fleece to the Eucharist and the Crucifixion, and it reveals Christ as the ultimate source and referent of the various figures and figural patterns presented in the course of the *auto*. As the discoveries progress from lion to child, they illustrate the allegorical patterning that has allowed Calderón to dramatize the events and structures of European history in their common relationships to the central fact of the Incarnation.

The allegory of *El maestrazgo del Toisón* attributes a special status to the government of Philip IV. By describing the personages and institutions of that government in figural terms, it aligns the Hapsburg state with the unfolding of providence in human history. Read in its immediate context, however, Calderón's allegory offers something more complex and pressing than a dramatic compliment to the king. Like the *Política de Dios* it insists that the Christian monarch must rule according to the pattern of Christ's own governance, and the burden of this argument is that the king will lose his authority if he departs from the highest standards of fortitude and justice. In addition, this *auto* was presented to king and country at a time of balance and due process in the central administration, following the changes in the conciliar system and in the powers of the favorite that the Crown had introduced in the years after the fall of Olivares. In response to these reforms Calderón praises king and favorite for honoring the law and for respecting the institutions traditionally empowered to guarantee the rule of law in its territories. If *La cisma de Inglaterra* attests to the anxieties concerning the favorite that persisted during the early years of Philip IV's reign, *El maestrazgo del Toisón* reflects the new order of the *valimiento* and the councils in the 1650s. Through its allegory of the state, this *auto* reiterates the fundamental lesson of Calderón's political theater: that fidelity to the law will accommodate the king's proceedings to the positive patterns of providence and so ensure the conservation of his realm.

4

**ALLEGORY AND
AFFAIRS OF STATE**

El nuevo palacio del Retiro
and *El lirio y la azucena*

Calderón's political theater presents a critical view of seventeenth-century statecraft and projects a Christian vision of universal history. The *comedias* and *autos* concerned with kingship and the state turn on central issues in contemporary political thought. Many of the questions that commanded the attention of Spanish theorists—the role of the prince as Stoic exemplar and Christian sovereign; the problem of defining a Christian reason of state; the position of the favorite and the royal councillors; the uses of dissimulation in affairs of state—have a place in Calderón's understanding of politics. And a providential view of history, centered on the Incarnation and dedicated to tracing the unfolding of God's plan for Creation, informs his work. It is Calderón's position that the king can best secure the destiny of his realm by attending to the eternal order and by governing in accordance with the laws that allow men and women to participate in the ways of providence. The approach to these issues varies from one text to another. *La vida es sueño*, as both *comedia* and *auto*, addresses the necessity of accommodation to the hierarchy of laws; *A Dios por razón de Estado* and *La cisma de Inglaterra* explore the ways of humanity and of providence at specific moments in biblical and modern history. And *El maestrazgo del Toisón*, through its allegory of the Order of the Golden Fleece, traces a providential pattern in the ordering of the Spanish state. In applying Christian typology to the progress of official life in Spain, Calderón extends his theory of history to contemporary affairs. He follows this method consistently in the various *autos* that he wrote to commemorate state occasions. In the cases where we can document the events that Calderón has chosen to celebrate, these *autos* allow us to study the application of his historical perspective, and of his views on kingship, to specific individuals, actions, and institutions. *La segunda esposa*, with its allegory of matrimony and revival, marks Calderón's response to the second marriage of Philip IV. In this chapter I shall discuss two further *autos*—*El nuevo palacio del Retiro* (1634) and *El lirio y la azucena* (1660)—that represent his treatment of important state occasions at two distinct moments in his career.[1] Analysis of these two plays will again emphasize Calderón's careful attention to the changing political conditions of the Hapsburg regime; it will also illustrate his increasing command of the techniques and conventions of political drama.

In the *autos* that he composed for the Corpus festival of 1634, Calderón turned to biblical history and to contemporary events at court. *La cena del rey Baltasar* draws its argument from the book of Daniel; *El nuevo palacio del Retiro* commemorates the festivities held in December 1633 to mark the opening of the buildings and gardens that had been added under Olivares's direction to the Royal Apartment of San Jerónimo in Madrid. First planned as the latest in a series of such additions, the new

---

1. In selecting these *autos* I have followed Kurtz's definition of the "circumstantial or topical *autos*" as "those in which the dramatist allegorizes events and personages of secular, usually contemporaneous, history in order to analogize Christian *Heilsgeschichte*" (131n). *Autos* that conform to this definition appear at intervals throughout Calderón's career; Valbuena Prat provides a partial listing under the classification "autos de circunstancias" (34a–b). As Kurtz has noted, the circumstantial and the historical *autos* are not easily distinguished, since Calderón frequently uses historical persons and events as a mirror for the Spanish monarchy in the present; see, for example, Kurtz's discussion of the *loa* to *El Santo Rey Don Fernando, Primera Parte* (150–52).

structures proved sufficiently impressive (at least from the Crown's perspective) to justify renaming the Royal Apartment the Palace of the Buen Retiro.[2] Events designed to inaugurate the new palace extended over several days. On December 1 Olivares received the king and queen at the palace; the official festivities followed on December 5 and 6 as king and court gathered to admire the skills of bullfighting, to enjoy the pleasures of the table and the stage, and to participate in a number of martial games on horseback presented in the courtyard of the palace. In his account of the occasion the annalist León Pinelo dwells on the details of these games; he identifies the various aristocratic participants, and he describes the king and Olivares competing side by side at the head of the royal quadrille in a *juego de cañas* and the king himself taking a prize in a game of running at the ring.[3] Calderón's *auto* follows the general outline of these events. Man (Olivares) welcomes the King (Philip IV) and the Queen (Isabel of Bourbon) to the new palace; the King holds a royal audience, shares with Man both his livery and his place of honor in the procession of knights, and takes part in the contest of the ring. In this argument Calderón has carefully preserved the significant features of the inauguration of the Retiro, an occasion of obvious prominence in the official calendars of court and city alike.

Calderón was by no means alone in commemorating this occasion, and

2. The Royal Apartment of San Jerónimo was constructed in 1561–63 at the command of Philip II, for the purposes of religious retreat in the Easter season and for the observance of state occasions. It was twice expanded and renamed in the 1630s, in the service of Olivares's program to restore and glorify the Spanish monarchy. The first significant additions were made in 1632–33, when Olivares ordered the name changed to the Royal House of the Buen Retiro; the far more ambitious building program of May–December 1633 led to the final and definitive change in its name, announced by royal proclamation on 1 December 1633. Brown and Elliott comment on the significance of this change: "in the minds of the king and the minister, it must have seemed that the new court had become an imposing edifice in its own right and, thanks to the surrounding rooms, could even be used like a palace for indoor activities" (71). The successive additions to the apartment are discussed by Brown and Elliott (55–74).

3. In his headnote to this *auto* Valbuena Prat reprints the appropriate sections from León Pinelo's description of the inaugural festivities (131a–b). For the details of the occasion, see also the concise account in Brown and Elliott (68). The *juego de cañas* is an equestrian exercise of Moorish origin, popular as a festive entertainment among the nobles of early modern Spain. The participating riders carried shields marked with heraldic devices and mottoes; they divided themselves into a number of quadrilles (usually eight) and executed a series of ritualized skirmishes, casting lengths of cane in an imitation of armed combat. The *Diccionario de Autoridades* supplies a detailed account of the ceremony and order of the exercise, under the term *cañas* (2:128a–b).

works by other authors indicate the tactics that could be used to praise
the monarchy's achievements in the Retiro and to elide its potential
misjudgments and failings.[4] In his "Versos a la primera fiesta del palacio
nuevo" Lope de Vega presents the image of the sun rising on the wonders
of the palace and its gardens, and offers an idealized account of the
martial games. As in many panegyrics of the palace, the king and his
favorite hold the poet's attention. Lope's verses applaud Olivares's heroic
appearance at the king's side:

> Iba a su lado el conde,
> que méritos y amor igualan tanto,
> porque llegar adonde
> a la misma fortuna causa espanto
> es virtud, es valor: que no hay estrella
> de más felicidad que merecella

(At his side rode the count, rendered his equal through excellence
and love, since it requires virtue and courage to ascend to the
point where fortune itself stands astonished: for there is no
happier star than merit)

and they describe the martial skills and regal authority that Philip
displayed in the ritual combat of the ring:

> Alentado, valiente,
> atento a su rëal naturaleza,
> bizarro, indeficiente,
> igualó su poder con su destreza:
> que cuando la virtud máxima crece,
> de toda envidia y deslealtad carece.
>   (2:373, 377)

(Proud, valiant, mindful of his regal nature, gallant, faultless, he
showed strength and skill in equal measure: for at its apex virtue
is beyond all envy and disloyalty.)

---

4. Brown and Elliott survey the panegyrics of the Retiro and its patrons that appeared in
the 1630s, including *El nuevo palacio del Retiro* and Lope's commemorative verses (229–
31); they also quote at length from Olivares's own defense of the palace (233–34).

The prominence that Lope accords to the court favorite is consistent with the demands of the occasion. Olivares had presided over the additions to the Royal Apartment in order to create a space that would lend itself to spectacle and pageantry on a grand scale, and he promoted the inevitable association between the new palace and his own ambitious program for reforming the Spanish monarchy. Lope resorts to the terms of Olivares's Neostoic ideology when he chooses to assert that the favorite has astonished fortune through his bravery and virtue and to commend the king's public triumph over envy and disloyalty. Yet such admiration for the palace and the program that it embodied was far from universal. For all the official praise that the Retiro attracted, other voices did not hesitate to question or belittle what the favorite had achieved. An iron aviary that had been constructed as an earlier addition had saddled Olivares's architectural project with the dismissive title of the *Gallinero* (Chicken Coop), and the name stuck to the new palace despite all efforts to improve and ennoble its image. The general resentment of Olivares made the palace unpopular—the British envoy Arthur Hopton remarked of the citizens of Madrid that "they suffer worse because it is attributed to a fancy of the Conde's, whose judgment they approve not in this as in many things" (quoted in Brown and Elliott 68)—and specific objections centered on the questionable course of building a pleasure-palace at a time of fiscal constraint at home and military challenges abroad.[5] From the perspective of the regime's critics, the Retiro was a house of seductive or superfluous delights that Olivares had constructed at public expense to divert the king from his duties in maintaining and defending the realm. Serious panegyrists had to confront the difficulties of reasserting that the palace had been designed for higher purposes and of showing that the pleasures of the senses—often associated with princely negligence or with the rebellious energies of popular carnival—could be reconciled with those purposes.

Calderón meets the challenges of his material by establishing a figural allegory that applies to the Retiro and to the king and court who have gathered within its precinct. In the first instance this allegory centers on the relationship of king and favorite; Man has constructed the Retiro as an "immortal temple" of the law of grace, in order to honor his King and Creator and the Queen. The text as a whole, however, is relentless in

---

5. For the articulation and the motives of the widespread hostility to the construction of the Retiro, see Brown and Elliott 228–29.

assigning figural significance to each aspect of the inaugural festivities and to each of the aristocratic participants. As in other *autos* that commemorate state and historical occasions, the techniques of moral allegory outline and complement a central figural pattern.

Moral allegory, however, has a second important function in this work. Through one of the distinctive techniques of the mode, Calderón presents the five human senses as personified abstractions who offer their services to the King, both in supplying pleasures for the palace and in executing his will during the royal audience. This treatment of the senses appeals to the Neostoic values of service and self-sacrifice that Olivares himself endorsed, but it tends to stand apart from the central allegory. Although the ideal of service converges with the figural pattern in the course of the *auto*—particularly in the description of the Retiro's gardens and in the allegory of the martial games—the Neostoic image of the heroic favorite is not easily reconciled with the portrayal of the King as a type of Christ. The focus on the favorite and his chosen ideology is appropriate to the *auto*'s occasion, but it leads to tensions in the structure and development of its allegory.

This outline points to three aspects of *El nuevo palacio del Retiro* central to its significance: the allegory that presents the palace and the monarchy in figural terms, the role of the favorite in the king's service, and the contribution of the senses to the immediate pleasures and spiritual purposes of the occasion. Each of these has a prominent place in the unfolding of the *auto*, and during the conclusion they are drawn together in an elaborate dramatization of the martial games. My analysis will address each aspect in turn, and then consider the articulation and interplay of all three in the *auto*'s closing scenes.

The figural allegory begins as a mystery or enigma encoded in the edifice and gardens of the Retiro. In the opening scene Judaism approaches the palace and expresses wonder at findings its splendors in the barren land where his synagogue once stood. His insistent questioning summons Man, and the two characters address one another in two set speeches that review the order of providential history and define the place of the Retiro within that order. Judaism's account extends from the Creation through the Exodus to the death of Christ. As in *A Dios por razón de Estado*, Judaism does not recognize the significance of the Crucifixion and insists on his own privileged role in the historical record of the Old Testament. He presents the transition from natural law to written law as the pivotal event in human history, and he dwells on the numerous signs of divine favor that have marked the chronicles of his people. In his response Man completes the history that Judaism has begun. Man explains that the law of grace has now transcended the written law of Moses, and that Judaism cannot comprehend the design of the Retiro because he has tried to repudiate the new law it enshrines.

To expound the Retiro's significance Man draws on the multiple techniques of etymology, heraldry, and typology. He offers a series of glosses on the names of the King and the Queen (139a). In its Greek roots "Philip" signifies "tamer of beasts," a phrase appropriate to the domestication of nature in the gardens and aviaries of the palace. More important, in its Spanish form this name signals the faith (Felipe > Fe) that is the object of the King's devotion. And the Queen is identified with that faith, both through her name and through the heraldic devices that she is entitled to display. Deriving Isabel from Elizabeth, Man argues that her name signifies the new covenant or "oath of God" that has been offered to humanity in the Church, and to reinforce this association he asserts that the three lilies of the Queen's arms represent the theological virtues. Taken in conjunction, these etymologies and exegeses confirm Calderón's typical allegory for royal marriage, in which the bond between the faithful king and his chosen queen represents the marriage of Christ and the Church. As he concludes his remarks on the patrons for whom he has built the Retiro, Man makes this dual significance explicit: "que son Cristo y la Iglesia, / y son la Reina y el Rey" (since they are Christ and the Church, and they are the Queen and the King) (139b).

The allegory elaborated in Man's address, however, does not end with this typology. The Church has a twofold presence here, in that Man finds it figured forth in the Queen and in the Retiro itself. A second set of correspondences establishes this second typology for the Church. The Retiro represents the "triumphant Jerusalem" of John's Apocalypse (139a), and its gardens enclose the variety of Creation and recall the selection of animals for the biblical ark that bore man and the creatures above the Flood. Indeed, the parallel between the Retiro and Noah's ark is the most carefully developed typology in the *auto*'s exposition:

> y así, en aqueste edificio,
> de que fue figura aquél,
> se mira el estanque grande
> diversas fuentes correr,
> se ve el cuarto de las fieras,

y el de las aves también,
porque aquí tiene su estancia
la fiera, el ave y el pez;
ya que la fábrica altiva
toca con el capitel
al cielo, porque triunfante
hoy, y militante estén
dadas la manos.

(139b–40a)

(and so in this structure, of which that ark was a figure, the great
pool runs with several fountains, and the dwelling of the beasts is
present, as is that of the birds, because beast, bird, and fish all find
their abodes here; since this proud edifice touches the sky with its
capital, so that the triumphant Jerusalem and the militant may
today join hands.)

Here Man confirms the spiritual significance of the Retiro by defining its
exact place within a temporal sequence of figures for the Church. In its
artificial watercourses, and its collections of beasts and birds, the palace
reproduces and preserves the order of Creation. This function marks its
position in providential history. The palace fulfills the figure of Noah's
ark, and its "proud edifice" is in turn a figure for the triumphant Church
of the Apocalypse. Its design looks back to Noah's ark and to the
Creation, and forward to the vessel that will safeguard the faithful at the
end of time. The splendors of palace and garden do not exist merely to
serve the king's pleasure; they indicate the prominence of the Retiro in
the divine order of things. The new palace is neither the "unexampled
marvel" that Judaism first takes it to be (137a), nor the *Gallinero* that
contemporary critics held up to public mockery.

The figural view of history also informs the *auto*'s allegorization of the
favorite. The text tells us that Man's role as divine favorite has changed
over time, with the progression from one dispensation of the law to
another, and that history offers many examples of government by king
and favorite. Calderón sets out this context in order to assign a unique
place to the King's regime. All prior instances of *valimiento* are related to
Man's role in the King's service as the gardens and temples of the Old
Testament are to the Retiro, that is, in a pattern of figure and fulfillment.

In a series of passages Calderón presents the substance and the consequences of this argument.

Judaism makes the first reference to the favorite in the opening section of his expository address. His account of Creation reviews God's acts in dividing the world and assigning its parts to the various creatures, ending with the placement of Man in Eden:

> Al hombre, que su valido
> y que su privado es,
> hizo alcaide desde entonces
> de este divino vergel;
> del bien y del mal llegó
> en poco tiempo a saber;
> pero ¿cuál privado, cuál
> no supo del mal y el bien?
>
> (138a)

(From that time on He made man, His minister and favorite, the governor of this divine garden; man soon came to know of good and evil, but who among favorites has not learned of evil and good?)

Judaism locates the institution of *valimiento* within the order of Creation. Man exists to assist God as the first favorite. Under natural law he performed this service by presiding over the "divine garden," a site that in its ordered selection of created things figures forth both Noah's ark and the Retiro. Yet from Judaism's perspective this office was bound to defeat its holder. In the course of his duties every favorite must come to know good and evil, and for humanity the cost of such knowledge has been the loss of paradise. The assignment of Eden to human governance has created the office of the favorite, but it has also revealed the dangers that make the favorite's tenure fragile and uncertain.

Like many of the blocking characters in Calderón's *autos*, Judaism reasons on the basis of his own interests and assumptions. In this case he misrepresents the nature of *valimiento* because he will not admit that the law of grace, introduced through the King's regime, has brought to an end the cycle of changes from one law to another that began with Adam's infidelity to natural law alone. Man himself refers to the constancy of the new law to explain his position in the King's service. When Taste reminds

him that other favorites have declined with the alterations of time and the
law, Man replies that the Retiro stands for a more enduring rule:

> que ha de vivir eterna
> esta fábrica, que hoy sube
> al sol, porque aunque a la vista
> de otras privanzas se funde,
> no la amenaza el peligro,
> porque esta es en quien se cumplen
> misterios que en otra fueron
> solo rasgos y vislumbres.
>
> (143b)

(for this edifice which rises today to the sun will live eternally,
since, although it may seem to be founded like the regimes of
other favorites, no peril threatens it, because in this edifice mysteries are fulfilled which in any other were only sketches and
semblances.)

Here Man extends the argument about the Retiro's position in history to
describe the institution that binds him to the King. The "edifice" of the
palace will stand "eternally" because in it the "mysteries" of the new law
have found fulfillment. And the institutions associated with the Retiro
share in its stability. Until this moment the favorite's role has been subject
to the imperfections of the earlier kinds of law; with the sublimation of
natural and written law, *valimiento* has assumed its final and lasting form.
The Retiro represents a new dispensation, one that has freed the King's
regime from the dangers of time and change.

In ascribing permanence to the *valimiento* of Man and the King, this
auto pays an elaborate compliment to Olivares. It also echoes the
ideology that Olivares invoked to justify his position in the Hapsburg
regime. The ideal of the Stoic favorite, present by implication in *La cisma
de Inglaterra*, is here made explicit. Man's dedication to the King and the
law exemplifies the spirit of service and self-sacrifice that characterizes
true *valimiento*. And the *auto*'s treatment of the senses follows from its
commitment to this ideal. Man himself stresses the role of the senses
when he summons them to aid him in the royal audience:

> atentos, pues, y rendidos
> me asistid todos, que es ley

que el Hombre sirva a su Rey
con todos cinco sentidos.
                                    (143a)

(attentive, then, and humble, all lend me your service, since it is
decreed that Man should serve his King with all five senses.)

Man's appeal implies a hierarchy of service sanctioned by divine law. The
five exterior senses are subordinate to Man's will, and Man is obliged in
turn to direct his senses in accordance with the interests of the King. This
imperative invites us to consider how the senses may best serve these
interests, and the text explores the uses of the senses and of sensual
pleasure in the affairs of court and king. The initial disposition of the
court characters helps to determine the true role of the senses. At the
end of the *auto*'s exposition Man announces the entrance of the Queen
and the King, who arrive in a triumphal procession accompanied by the
theological virtues and the human senses. As members of the royal
retinue the virtues and the senses will act together in the King's service.
And the *auto* suggests that the senses can contribute their part in two
ways: either by cooperating among themselves to offer the King pleasure
or aid, or by competing with one another to attract the favor of the virtues.
The complementary processes of cooperation and competition should be
examined with care, since both are central to the direction and legitima-
tion of the senses.

The Retiro itself illustrates the benefits of cooperation among the
senses. After the Queen has entered she commends Man before the King
for his labors in constructing the palace and its gardens. Her praises
dwell on what the senses have offered toward the completion of this task:

Bien los Sentidos, que han sido
sus deudos, y sus criados,
logren todos sus cuidados,
pues todos han prevenido
sus riquezas: el Oído,
músicas a tus enojos;
ricos hermosos despojos,
en blandos lechos, el Tacto;
frutas, el Gusto; el Olfato,
rosas; matices, los Ojos.
                                    (141b)

(How well the Senses, who have been his kin and his servants,
have achieved all his ends, since all have provided their riches:
Hearing, music to ease your troubles; Touch, the welcome spoils
of rest in soft beds; Taste, fruits; Smell, roses; Sight, colors.)

This description combines the ethos of service with the conventions of
pastoral literature. As Man's "servants" the senses have together made
provision for the King's repose and recreation. Each of the five has
enriched the Retiro by supplying the objects that will ensure his delight,
and these objects are pleasing in themselves and harmonious one with
another. Through their offerings the senses have transformed the palace
into a garden paradise, a pastoral site that enshrines the symmetry and
order of the divinely created world of nature.[6] Yet here, as in many of his
autos, Calderón evokes the models of classical pastoral with a corrective
intent. For all its sensual delights, the Retiro is no pagan garden of ease.
The palace that stands before the King has been ordered for his pleasure,
but the Queen is quick to remind him of its larger spiritual significance:

> y así, pues el Hombre fue
> alcaide de aquel primero
> jardín, más feliz espero
> que hoy el cargo se le dé
> deste más feliz, porque
> si allí padeció privanza,
> en su privanza hoy alcanza
> el Hombre tanto favor,
> que ya sin aquel temor
> ha de gozar tu privanza.
>
> (141b)

(and so, as Man was governor of that first garden, more propi-
tiously I hope that he will be given charge of this happier garden,

---

6. Alban K. Forcione has studied the classical antecedents of the garden paradise and its
various appearances in the works of Cervantes (212–45). The gardens of the Retiro, as
Calderón renders them here, correspond to the Valley of the Cypresses in the *Galatea*,
which Forcione characterizes as "Cervantes' most concentrated expression of the harmony
between the creator, nature, and man" (222). In this connection it is significant that nature
is described in the *Galatea* as the "mayordomo de Dios" (God's steward) (221).

since if there he suffered as favorite, Man will attain today such
favor in his office that, free of his old fear, he will enjoy your trust.)

The Queen elaborates on the idea that Adam was God's favorite in Eden.
In presiding over the Retiro, Man has reenacted and perfected Adam's
role as the first favorite. Man as Adam fell from Eden because he yielded
to the temptations of its garden; as favorite to the King he will flourish
in the new palace because he has ordered the senses and subordinated
them to his master's service. The sensual pleasures of the Retiro will
offer rest and entertainment, but not temptation. The care of this "happier
garden" is the highest achievement of Man in his office as favorite, and
the continuance of that care is the most secure expression of the King's
favor. In his ordering of the Retiro, Man has overcome the failings that
beset him as Adam.

If the senses can cooperate to extend their pleasures to the King, they
can also aid him in attending to the business of the state. They offer
service of this kind during the royal audience. As Man reads the
memoranda in which the petitioners have stated their written requests—
Apostasy for freedom of conscience, Gentility for conquest, the Occident
for Baptism, Africa for Christian ports in her lands, and Judaism for
permission to trade within the kingdom—the senses respond to each
petition according to the King's commands (145b–46b). The cooperation
and obedience of the senses is not, however, the sole point at issue. The
senses respect and enact the King's will, but the will in turn must bend to
the influence of the Church and its virtues. In each case the senses' initial
response is one of refusal; only the intervention of the Queen and the
virtues persuades the King to respond with due care and attention to the
petitions. The conduct of this audience clearly reflects bureaucratic
practices at court, as well as contemporary thought concerning the
powers and responsibilities of the monarch. Man performs the favorite's
task of presenting written memoranda to his master, and the Queen
asserts that the King will exercise his authority with a "providence" that
follows the higher order of the eternal law (145b). The progress of the
audience as a whole suggests that this law demands the subordination of
the senses and the will to the theological virtues.

In its treatment of cooperation, the allegory of the senses in this *auto*
confirms the Stoic lesson of such *comedias* as *El príncipe constante* and *El
mayor encanto, amor*: that the king and his servants must control the
senses and subordinate their energies to the legitimate interests of the

realm. In the case of competition, doctrinal questions become more prominent. In the course of the text the senses compete for superiority on two occasions, and in both cases Faith acts as the arbiter of their contest and judges in favor of Hearing. This pattern follows in part from the conventions of Spanish sacramental drama. Louise Fothergill-Payne has shown that the motif of competition among the senses is a topos in the tradition of the *autos* written before Calderón, as is the preference of Faith for Hearing (161, 162–66). Through these topoi Calderón elaborates the figural allegory that establishes the correspondence of the King and Christ. Their contest leads in the last analysis to an apprehension of the *auto*'s central mysteries.

The first competition occurs after the triumphal entrance and the initial speeches of the King and the Queen. When the monarchs and the favorite leave the stage, the senses find themselves in the company of the virtues, and the former begin to compete for the attention and approval of Faith. Sight, Touch, Smell, and Taste present themselves in turn, each making a persuasive case for superiority and each meeting with Faith's refusal (142a–b). Hearing is the last to speak, and he alone is doubtful of his precedence in relation to the others:

> ve la Vista sin dudar
> lo que ve, huele el Olfato
> lo que huele, toca el Tacto
> lo que toca y gusta el Gusto
> lo que gusta, siendo justo
> el objeto con el trato;
> pero lo que oye el Oído
> solo es un eco veloz
> que nace de ajena voz
> sin objeto conocido.
>
> (142b)

(Sight apprehends what she sees without doubt, as does Smell what he smells, Touch what he touches, Taste what he tastes, since in each case the object corresponds to its perception; but what Hearing hears is only a fleeting echo, born of another's voice and with no known object.)

In emphasizing the relationship between each sense and its object, this passage parallels Scholastic thought on the functioning of the senses.

Aquinas maintains that sense-perception depends on the "immutation" of the organs of sensation by an object or "exterior cause." He distinguishes between "spiritual immutation," in which a form is passed from the object to the appropriate organ "according to a spiritual mode of being," and "natural immutation," in which the form is passed through a change in the physical state of the object or the organ (*Basic Writings* 1:739). Spiritual immutation occurs in all of the senses, but some senses depend on natural immutation as well. Sight functions by spiritual immutation alone; hearing and smell by natural immutation of the object; touch and taste by natural immutation of the organs of sensation. These distinctions imply a hierarchy among the senses, one that places hearing and smell in a middle register between the spiritual sense of sight and the material senses of touch and taste. In Aquinas's words "the sight, which is without natural immutation either in its organ or in its object, is the most perfect, and the most universal of all the senses" (1:739). Calderón of course departs from the Scholastic hierarchy in granting Hearing superiority among the senses. Indeed, Faith favors Hearing precisely because of his inexact stance in relation to the objects of sensation. As Hearing himself explains, his incertitude inspires a salutary "mistrust" of the potentially deceptive appearances of the phenomenal world:

> luego estoy bien corrido,
> pues no tienen mis errores,
> como la Vista, colores;
> como el Tacto, variedades;
> como el Gusto, suavidades,
> ni como el Olfato, olores.
> (142b)

(so I am truly humbled, since my errors do not possess the colors of Sight, the variations of Touch, the delicacies of Taste, or the fragrances of Smell.)

That sense-perceptions are hazardous and conducive to error is a stock theme of the Spanish baroque. Here Calderón articulates this theme in relation to a specific topos of the Christian tradition. The affinity of Faith and Hearing is present in various sources, including Aquinas's own liturgical compositions and a long series of scriptural passages.[7] The books of wisdom and of prophecy in the Bible repeatedly describe hearing as the medium through which men will know wisdom and the message of salvation. The Psalmist commands, "Give ear, all inhabitants of the world," for "my mouth shall speak wisdom; the meditation of my heart shall be understanding" (Ps. 49:1–3); the sage in the book of Proverbs instructs his pupil to "Incline your ear, and hear the words of the wise" (Prov. 22:17); in the letter to the Church of Ephesus, the angel of Revelation asserts "He who has an ear, let him hear what the Spirit says to the churches" (Rev. 2:7). The capacity of hearing to receive the lessons of salvation and of providential history is particularly clear in Isaiah's exhortation to Israel:

> Incline your ear, and come to me;
> hear, that your soul may live;
> and I will make you an everlasting covenant,
> my steadfast, sure love for David.
>
> (Isa. 55:3)

In Christian thought hearing's association with evangelism reveals its affinity for the mysteries offered to humanity in the Eucharist. Fothergill-Payne has noted the presence of this affinity in the traditional *auto sacramental* (163). In *El nuevo palacio del Retiro* Calderón presents the final martial games as a complex allegory of the Eucharist and its mysteries. After the King has made himself incarnate by uniting with his favorite at the head of the royal quadrille, he raises the circular form of the Host as the target for the contest of the ring. This sequence recapitulates the progression from Christ's first act of Incarnation to the regular repetition of that act in the rite of the Mass. The martial games thus end in the discovery of the sacrament that celebrates the pivotal event of Christian history. And to each of the characters present at the games—the King and his favorite, the aristocracy, the virtues and the senses—Calderón assigns a role that confirms the centrality of that sacrament in the functions of the Retiro and the ordering of the Hapsburg state.

---

7. In her commentary on faith and hearing Fothergill-Payne cites the relevant lines from Aquinas' *Adoro Te*: "Visus, tactus, gustus, in te fallitur, / sed auditu solo tuto creditur" (Sight, touch, taste are in your case deceptive, but through hearing alone comes sure belief) (163).

During the martial games, as in the opening exposition, Calderón puts Judaism's isolation and ignorance to dramatic use. At the end of the royal audience Judaism is the only petitioner who meets with an unqualified refusal; the King dismisses his request to trade within the realm and banishes him from the court.[8] Judaism harbors both resentment and curiosity toward the King's proceedings, but since he cannot enter the palace he must observe the games from a distance and rely on the spoken commentary of others if he is to grasp their significance. Faith agrees to supply the gloss that Judaism requires, and together they assume a prominent role as projecting characters who describe and explain the course of the final scenes. Although the *auto* resorts to stylized representation to dramatize certain central events—most notably the King's appearance at Man's side and the contest to capture the ring—we can comprehend the games in their entirety only through the description and commentary that Faith and Judaism offer to us. This device allows Calderón to delineate the allegory of the martial games by playing one perspective against another, as he contrasts Judaism's questioning with the secure knowledge of Faith.

At the beginning of the games the projecting characters turn their attention to the prominent members of the aristocracy, who form the primary audience for the occasion and parade together in the quadrilles of the *juego de cañas*. Such treatment of the audience is typical of literature produced for court festivities. Lope's panegyric of the new palace describes the noble statesmen and diplomats seated in their ranks above the games:

> Sus lugares tenían
> consejos, reino, nuncio, embajadores;
> la esfera componían
> graves ministros, nobles senadores:
> que son las armas y las santas leyes
> potencia de las almas de los reyes.
>
> (2:373)

---

8. Brown and Elliott refer to the exclusion of Judaism as "a pointed reference to the attempts of Jews and crypto-Jews to settle and trade in the king's dominions" (230). They also discuss the role of Portuguese bankers (often suspected of *converso* status) in the financial affairs of Philip IV's government (100).

(The Councils, Crown, Nuncio, and ambassadors all had their places; grave ministers and noble spectators made up the outer ranks: for arms and holy laws are the power of kings' souls.)

To describe the offices of the aristocracy Lope resorts to the metaphor of the state of an organism. The king is the soul that gives life to the monarchy, and it is incumbent upon the councillors and ministers of the realm to wield the arms and laws through which that soul exercises its power. Calderón intensifies the emphasis on divine law implicit in Lope. According to Faith's commentary on the scene, the aristocracy has promoted Spain's role as the vessel of the new law, both by modeling its institutions on those of the early Church and by offering new correspondences between the personages of sacred history and the councillors in whom the state has vested its authority. Two kinds of analogies support these notions. As in *El maestrazgo del Toisón*, Calderón consecrates the Spanish state by finding functional analogies between the responsibilities of the standing councils and the tasks of Christ's apostles. As Faith reviews the councillors present for the games (148a–b), she associates each of them with an apostle whose duties, as recorded in Scripture or in the apocryphal tradition, parallel those of a conciliar office. Faith begins with the heads of the prominent councils—Saint Paul, the "supreme" apostle, presides over the Council of State; Saint Matthew, who conveyed the word of the Church to Ethiopia, governs the Council of the Indies— and proceeds through Saint Peter (the Military Orders), Saint James (War), Saint Andrew (the Inquisition), Saint Philip (Finance), and Saint John (the Chamber of Castile). A further set of onomastic analogies confirms the aristocracy's position within the succession of figures in providential history. When Faith describes the entry of the equestrians for the *juego de cañas*, she associates the influential noblemen at the head of each quadrille with historical personages from the order of priests and prophets. Calderón returns here to the techniques of etymology. The Count of Niebla is identified with Dionysius the Areopagite, who came to know the divine cause through the "cloud" (*niebla*) of unknowing, and the Count of Peñaranda with Moses, who recognized the "rock" (*peña*) that was "to be ploughed" (*aranda*) to release water for Israel during the Exodus (149a). The names and offices of the aristocracy, as Faith elucidates them here, complement the *auto*'s central allegory. Just as the Retiro is a figure of the Church, so the noblemen assembled in its courtyard stand in a figural relationship to the patriarchs and apostles.

Faith's commentary on the aristocracy illustrates the general truth that she enunciates to Judaism at the beginning of this scene: "has de hallar en el cristiano imperio, / hoy en todo alegórico misterio" (today you will find allegorical mystery in every part of the Christian empire) (146b).

The "mystery" that inspires the order and the mission of the "Christian empire" asserts its presence most forcefully at the end of the martial games. When Faith announces the game of running at the ring, she sets out the correspondences that will define the sacramental significance of this contest:

> Y así, en místico sentido,
> y alegórico concepto,
> siendo las lanzas las voces,
> y la sortija un pequeño
> círculo breve, en que está
> cifrado el mayor secreto,
> correrán hoy en las tablas,
> que son las gradas del Templo.
> (149a–b)

(And so, in a mystical sense and through an allegorical conceit, in which lances are voices and the ring is a small compact circle which encodes the greatest mystery, they will run today in the theater formed by the steps of the Temple.)

Faith describes an ingenious metaphor or "conceit," in which the *auto*'s personified characters will take the "steps" of the palace as a "theater" for martial exercise, while they direct their "voices" as "lances" toward the "circle" that stands before them as the "ring" or target of their competition. And like the *auto* as a whole this conceit turns the devices of moral allegory to explicitly Christian purposes. Its technique is that of a psychomachia, a battle among abstract forces over matters concerning the fate of the human soul; its meaning lies in the "mystical sense" that can be discerned beneath its surface. Through visual and conceptual means the contest focuses our attention on the sacred form of the Host, in which the radical "secret" or mystery of the Church is "encoded," and the task of apprehending that secret is the true challenge that confronts the *auto*'s characters when they undertake to seize the ring.

This challenge induces a range of significant responses. Its most immediate effect is to drive Judaism into confusion and silence. When the Host appears before him, Judaism addresses it directly in a series of anguished questions, attempting to identify it as a sacred object from the history of Israel (149b–50a). In this response he reveals the failing that consistently besets the Judaic characters of Calderón's *autos*: the denial of Christian fulfillment, expressed as a preference for the incomplete figures of the Old Testament. Here Judaism confesses before the Host his incapacity to receive the words of Faith—"yo no te alcanzo ni tu enigma sé / porque a la Fe he escuchado sin la Fe" (I can neither grasp you nor know your enigma, because I have listened to Faith without Faith) (150a)—and abandons speech for the rest of the *auto*. And as Judaism contemplates the "enigma" of the Host, the five senses enter into the contest to possess it. For this device, the second instance in the *auto* of competition among the senses, the Christian tradition supplies both general and specific precedents. Faith herself refers to Saint Paul's exhortation in 1 Corinthians 9:24 that the faithful must act as athletes in a race for the "prize" of salvation (149a), and the spoken *loa* to Lope's *Las bodas entre el alma y el amor divino* describes the senses as five "cross-bowmen" who aim and release their bolts unsuccessfully at the Host, since Faith alone is capable of seizing its mystery.[9] In his *auto* Calderón carefully adapts the device of the contest to mirror the circumstances of the games at the Retiro. The King acts as "defender" of the ring, while the senses appear as five "challengers" who compete to capture it (150a). When the contest begins the King enters the Host through transubstantiation, in an action that has both topical and theological significance. The King's capture of the Host's substance corresponds to Philip IV's triumph at the inaugural games; this seizure also forces the senses to pursue the consecrated Host by identifying its transformed substance despite its unchanged species or accidents. The contest here follows the course of the earlier competition before Faith. A misplaced reliance on appearances causes four of the senses to fail, and Hearing succeeds because he attends to the King's words rather than to the evidence of immediate perceptions:

9. Fothergill-Payne discusses the motif of rivalry among the senses in the traditional *auto sacramental* and the dramatization of that motif through the metaphor of athletic competition, with appropriate citation from Lope's *loa* (161–62).

debajo de aqueste velo
—que son especies de pan—,
está consagrado el Cuerpo
de Dios, y que por la Fe
de esta manera lo entiendo,
que yo no he menester más
de oírlo para creerlo.

(151a)

(beneath this veil of the species of bread the Body of God is consecrated, and I understand this to be so through Faith, since I need only hear to believe.)

In contrast to the pattern of Lope's *loa*, Calderón grants victory to Hearing, in order to reaffirm the connection between the human ear and the divine word. Whereas Judaism has listened without credence to Faith's praise of the Host, Hearing has penetrated the "veil" of appearances and captured the Host through his steadfast allegiance to Faith.

After this victory the other senses, acting at Man's command, acknowledge Hearing's precedence. Through this gesture they set themselves in a hierarchy that subordinates the lesser senses to Hearing and Hearing to Faith. The affirmation of appropriate relationships among the *auto*'s personified characters is an important result of the martial games. Man and the King unite in the mystery of the Incarnation; the aristocracy assembles to order and consecrate the state; the senses compete for the last time and yield to Faith's authority. And the King's final task is to enact and explain the sacrament that informs each of these interrelated hierarchies. In the *auto*'s closing moments the stage machinery elevates the King so that he may appear within the circle of the Host and address the court from that good eminence:

en ese breve RETIRO
del Pan constante me quedo
para siempre, en Cuerpo y Alma,
de la forma que en el Cielo
estoy, ocupando iguales
dos lugares en un tiempo.

(151b)

(in that brief RETIREMENT of the Bread I remain ever constant in
Body and Soul, in the form that I hold in Heaven, occupying two
coequal places at one time.)

Here the text assigns the highest spiritual meaning to the name of the
Retiro. The Host is a site of sanctified "retirement," to which the King
resorts in body and soul alike. In this process he does not divide or
diminish himself, since the mystery of transubstantiation allows him to
enter the Host without abandoning his seigniory in heaven. And the
Eucharist is important for the progression of divine laws, since the King,
by offering himself to the faithful in this sacrament, will honor the new
covenant of grace:

> porque así la Ley de Gracia
> me tenga siempre en el NUEVO
> PALACIO del Buen Retiro,
> que es la fábrica del Templo
> que del Testamento Antiguo,
> que fue aquel campo desierto,
> en NUEVO PALACIO pase
> a ser Nuevo Testamento.
>   (151b)

(so may the Law of Grace keep me always in the NEW PALACE of
Good Retirement, which is the fabric of the Temple, and may the
barren field of the Old Testament be transformed into the NEW
PALACE of a New Testament.)

Calderón elaborates his interpretation of the Retiro's name to confirm its
figural significance. According to the pattern of figure and fulfillment that
governs the relationship of the two testaments of Judeo-Christian scripture, the "temple" and "wasteland" of Judaism have been transformed
into the "new palace" where the king now makes his retreat. The favorite,
the aristocracy, and the senses have all contributed to the palace, and
during the martial games they have assumed their proper places within
the sacramental order that it enshrines. And the final discovery of the
Host confirms the unique status of the Retiro. While other princely
dwellings may tempt their patrons to withdraw from the duties of office,
the "new palace" is the site of a "good retirement" in service to the law of

grace. As the King presents himself to the faithful in the Host, he offers the most eloquent defense of the Retiro's dedication to spiritual purposes.

From the perspective of its critics the Retiro was a symbol of Olivares's ascendancy in the royal court, and of the afflictions that his regime promised to visit upon the realm. Absorbed in the delights and novelties of his pleasure-palace, Philip IV would give little thought to resisting the devices through which his favorite threatened to undermine the fiscal well-being of the Crown's subjects at home and the spartan virtues and Christian probity that had sustained its reputation abroad. To put the matter in the terms of Calderón's political thought, the opponents of Olivares attributed the construction of the Retiro to Machiavellian stratagems that in due course would diminish the king's authority and reduce public life to a cycle of political intrigues and domestic disturbances.

In *El nuevo palacio del Retiro* Calderón counters this position by locating the inauguration of the palace within the beneficial cycles of providential history. And the text employs a broad range of techniques and arguments to sustain this argument. Parallels drawn to the Old Testament associate the Retiro with Eden and with Noah's ark and the favorite with Adam; interpretations based on etymology and heraldry identify the King and Queen with Christ and the Church; functional analogies link the prominent royal councillors to the apostles and the Spanish state to the early Church; the conventions of Christian pastoral and the terms of Scholastic psychology assign the senses their proper role in the ordering of the Retiro and the final discovery of the Eucharist.

The comprehensive character of this text is significant for our understanding of its place in the evolution of the *autos* that Calderón wrote on the basis of state occasions. As one of the first *autos* of this kind, *El nuevo palacio del Retiro* explores the various strategies that can be used to allegorize contemporary events, but it does not articulate the kinds of allegory and their respective techniques in an entirely consistent way.[10] Unlike *El maestrazgo del Toisón* it does not elaborate at length the figural

---

10. The difficulties of developing a consistent allegory on the basis of an argument drawn from contemporary events account in large measure for the critical hostility to the topical *autos* of Calderón and the other major dramatists of the Golden Age. Although Kurtz is generally sympathetic to the genre, her discussion of *El nuevo palacio del Retiro* reflects the general suspicion concerning the "aesthetic or theological value" of plays so closely associated with important persons and events at court (131–32). I would argue that this *auto* is of greater interest, on literary and historical grounds, than Kurtz allows; it is nonetheless not so accomplished as Calderón's later works in the same genre.

parallels between the state and the early Church, and it resorts to a separate correspondence to describe the role of the favorite. Its Neostoic lesson in the appropriate use of the senses is not fully integrated into the larger figural patterns that inform and sustain its central allegory. These tensions can be attributed in part to the relative novelty for Calderón of the occasional *auto* and in part to the difficulties of an event so closely associated with the rule of Olivares. The general suspicion of the favorite and his office made the task of writing in his praise unusually challenging. In contrast, Calderón's later occasional *autos* respond to different political circumstances and display a mature technical expertise. Written after the fall of Olivares and the subsequent changes in the conciliar system and the institution of *valimiento*, these works employ a more selective range of allegorical strategies, and each one presents a consistent internal development.[11] The late reign of Philip IV offers Calderón a series of occasions for sophisticated *autos* devoted to the ideals of Christian statecraft.

The selectivity of the later *autos* is apparent in *El lirio y la azucena* or *La paz universal*. Here Calderón dramatizes the negotiations and ceremonies through which Spain and France concluded the Treaty of the Pyrenees during the winter and spring of 1659–60.[12] In its allegory this *auto* is attentive to the personages and events of its historical occasion. Luis de Haro and Cardinal Mazarin—the court favorites who sued for peace on behalf of the two monarchs—appear as the Secular Arm and the Ecclesiastical Arm, and the course of the *auto*, like that of the diplomatic proceedings, ends in a dynastic marriage that secures the concord of the two realms. In its emphasis on the role of the favorite, and on the spiritual significance of the royal marriage-bond, *El lirio y la azucena* parallels *El nuevo palacio del Retiro*, but it is more consistent in developing and articulating its political themes. Luis de Haro is presented as a type of the perfect favorite in the mold of John the Baptist, and the diplomacy that he

11. Kurtz has noted a similar course of development in the *autos* that present Calderón's allegories of classical mythology. Comparing the two versions of *Psiquis y Cupido* (1640?, 1665) she emphasizes the heightened abstraction and complexity of the later work, in which the classical material is reworked as "a symbolic logic of Christian theology, founded on the analogy of soul, sacred history, cosmos, and godhead" (96).

12. The negotiations for peace between France and Spain, and the dynastic marriage designed to seal that peace, were significant events in the life of the Hapsburg court. For details of the diplomatic betrothal of María Teresa to Louis XIV in June 1660, and of the impressive ceremonial prepared for the occasion by Diego Velázquez, see Elliott, "Twilight" 1.

practises with Mazarin as exemplary of true reason of state. These strategies are consonant with the *auto*'s central argument, which proposes that demonic opposition has disrupted the natural harmony between the Christian kingdoms of France and Spain, and that the marriage of Louis XIV to the princess María Teresa is an expression of Christian love that will restore the two nations to their due state of concord. And the high promise of this bond offers proof of probity for the statecraft of the two favorites; in seeking to reconcile their kingdoms through marriage, they have promoted God's plan for the universal peace of Christendom. In *El lirio y la azucena*, as in *A Dios por razón de Estado*, Calderón shows that true reason of state cannot be severed from the designs of providence.

I begin my discussion of this *auto* with a brief summary of its content. In the opening scene Discord appears and summons her companion War, to whom she presents, through her demonic arts, two visions of events that have inspired her with fear. The first vision portrays the miracle of the dove that descended bearing oil for the baptism of Clovis, the first of the Frankish kings; the second dramatizes a legend concerning the piety shown by Rudolph I, the founder of the Hapsburg dynasty, in escorting a priest to an isolated hermitage during a violent storm.[13] In each vision a messenger gives the appropriate monarch a flower as the emblem of his domain—the iris of France and the lily of Navarre—and promises that in due time these two flowers will be intertwined in a single symbolic garland. This promise of union has prompted Discord's fears. As she explains in a long expository address, Discord associates herself with the written law (or Synagogue) and Clovis and Rudolph with, respectively, natural law and grace. She thus perceives herself as brack-

13. Soons discusses the persistence of these pious legends in histories of the two dynasties (185–86). The legend of Rudolph's piety, with its promise for the imperial future of his dynasty, also figures in works of political theory, as in Botero's *Della ragion di stato*. In his chapter on religion (II.15) Botero supports his argument for the religious basis of all power and sovereignty by citing the example of the Hapsburgs, who have gained an empire through Rudolph's pious deed. He then relates the legend that Rudolph dismounted in the storm to offer himself as escort to the priest and the Host, and concludes that God has created the Hapsburg empire as a sacred trust for Rudolph and his descendants: "Cosa mirabile! fra poco tempo Rodolfo di conte divenne imperatore, i suoi successori arciduchi d'Austria, principi de' Paesi Bassi, regi de Spagna, colla monarchia del mondo nuovo, signori d'infiniti stati e di paesi immensi" (A wondrous affair! in a short time Rudolph rose from the rank of count to that of emperor, and his successors became archdukes of Austria, princes of the Low Countries, kings of Spain, with the empire of the new World, lords of infinite states and of immense lands) (87). This legend, and the political lesson that Botero draws from it, are repeated in Rivadeneira's *Tratado del príncipe cristiano* (480b).

eted between the kingdoms of the iris and the lily, and believes that their union will enslave her. In answer to her fears, she proposes to War that together they attempt to foresee the future peace between the two realms, so that they may take action to forestall it.

The rest of the *auto* depends on this initial exposition. Following Discord's anticipatory scheme, Rudolph and Clovis now emerge as Philip IV and Louis XIV, and proceed to arrive at a reconciliation despite the obstacles erected by the two blocking characters. In a series of movements suggestive of diplomatic overtures, the characters of Peace and Ease cross from one kingdom to the other, in the hope that one of the Christian kings will offer them refuge. Rejected by both sides, they find themselves isolated in the middle of the staging area, where they are able to generate a spontaneous and "popular" call for concord. The kings then dispatch their two chief ministers to a central Temple of Peace, which seems to arise from the waters of a river. Here a peace is concluded, the terms of the treaty are announced, and the King of Natural Law is joined with his beloved María in marriage. As they celebrate their union, the temple opens to reveal a globe emblematic of the universal Christian empire that will now envelop the world.

This outline indicates some of the parallels between *El lirio y la azucena* and Calderón's other late *autos*. Like *El maestrazgo del Toisón*, this work personifies two attributes of the devil and uses these characters to project and describe the unfolding of providence in human history. Because providence works against the devil's designs, the demonic characters attempt to alter the course of history for their own benefit. To present the prophetic visions that Discord offers to War, and to dramatize the unrelenting opposition of both characters to the destiny of Christendom, Calderón makes full use of the elaborate stage resources available for the Corpus plays of the later seventeenth century. In the coherence of its central conflict, and the complexity of its staging, this *auto* claims our attention as an outstanding work of drama. Unlike *El nuevo palacio del Retiro*, which unfolds on stage in a series of set speeches and tableaux, *El lirio y la azucena* uses the resources of dialogue, song, and spectacle to advance a compelling dramatic argument.

As in *El maestrazgo del Toisón* the demonic characters also set out the main figural scheme, through their efforts to foresee and prevent unfavorable events in the future. To establish their role in projecting the action of the *auto*, they begin by defining the relationship between history and Christian allegory. In a key passage from her initial exposition, Discord explains to War that the paired visions of Clovis and Rudolph must be interpreted as anticipatory of the concord between the two dynasties:

> intento
> que pasando a Alegoría
> hoy la Historia, imaginemos
> que en felice sucesión
> nos representen los mesmos
> que hemos visto, los que quieran
> en los siglos venideros,
> unir *Azucena* y *lirio*,
> porque una vez previniendo
> por dónde nos viene el daño,
> acudamos al remedio.
>
> (921a)

(I intend that today, by turning history into allegory, we imagine that those whom we have seen—whose descendants may wish in the coming centuries to unite the *Lily* and the *Iris*—present themselves to us in a happy succession, so that having once foreseen where the harm comes from, we may attend to the remedy.)

These lines may appear to announce a shift from historical fact to poetic fiction, but on closer scrutiny Calderón's terms here prove to be figural and exact. Discord is proposing that her visions anticipate the future union of France and Spain, just as certain events in the Old Testament prefigure others in the New. Using the imagination (the faculty of mind that forms, reproduces, and arranges images)[14] Discord and War may "image forth" the lines of kings proceeding from Clovis and Rudolph, and so perceive how they are to converge. While the word *sucesión* refers primarily to a dynastic line, in this context it also suggests a continuous

14. In this definition of the imagination I follow Alexander Parker, who describes the function that the Scholastic tradition assigns to this faculty in the processes of perception and cognition: "the perception of an object through the senses is effected by the formation of a pictorial reproduction or image of it. This is the work of the imagination which, by forming such images (or 'phantasms'), enables us to retain the knowledge of things, to know them when they are no longer present to the senses, and to reproduce and associate them" (*Allegorical Drama* 74).

series of allegorical figures. Since each successive monarch is, in figural terms, a type of Christ, a dynastic progression may be seen as a sequence of such types, extending from the past to the present and into the future. Allegorical techniques will thus enable the demonic characters to envision Louis XIV and Philip IV—the kings who are to reconcile France and Spain—as future "portraits" of Clovis and Rudolph (921a). In accordance with the figural mode, the allegory announced here begins and ends in history.

The central scheme of this *auto*, then, proposes that Discord and War, looking forward in time, can construct from the visions of Clovis and Rudolph—referred to explicitly as "una y otra historia" (one history and another) (919b)—an "allegory" of the peace to be concluded between France and Spain. Its main conflict arises in turn from the attempts of these blocking characters to prevent such a union. In dramatizing this opposition Calderón pursues his engagement with contemporary political theory, particularly as it addresses the issues of the favorite and of reason of state. In the course of the *auto* each of these phenomena is presented in a demonic version, and is then corrected in order that the final reconciliation may be achieved.

The *auto*'s key political terms first appear in Discord's expository address. To define her place in Synagogue's regime, and to describe the tactics that she intends to deploy against the two Christian kingdoms, Discord resorts to the vocabulary of seventeenth-century statecraft. Her discourse takes this lexical turn when she recounts the events that have led to her intimate association with Synagogue:

> La Sinagoga, que entonces
> dominatriz de su pueblo
> en él reinaba, me dio
> tanto lugar en su pecho,
> que no mentiré aunque diga
> que pudo mi valimiento
> asentar para adelante
> el ser un solo supuesto
> ella y yo, pues transformada
> yo en ella y ella en mí a un tiempo,
> vivió un cuerpo con dos almas
> y animó un alma en dos cuerpos.
> (920b)

(Synagogue, who then reigned as empress over her people, granted me such favor that I will not lie even in asserting that my *valimiento* established thenceforth that she and I assumed one form, since, she being transformed into me and I into her at the same time, one body lived with two souls and one soul gave life to two bodies.)

The powers of which Discord presumes to boast expose her influence as *valimiento* of the most dangerous kind. Instead of maintaining her integrity as sovereign of the Written Law, Synagogue has granted such favor to Discord that the two have become as one, bound together in body and soul. This process has had grave consequences for the politics of her realm. "Transformed" in this way, Synagogue can no longer exercise power as the unique and supreme governor of the kingdom, nor can she ensure that her regime's proceedings will not violate the form of divine law that she recognizes. Like such false favorites as Alvaro de Luna and Cardinal Wolsey, Discord has failed to respect the sanctity of royal authority, and her encroachments have diminished the realm through the division of sovereignty and the invention of illegitimate political stratagems.

Discord reveals the first principles of her statecraft when she reviews the achievements and aims of her *valimiento*. She claims that through her position she has incited Synagogue's people against Christ and the new law of Christian grace, and she proposes that her powers can now avert the diplomatic union of the dynasties descended from Clovis and Rudolph. Although she concedes that the shared piety of these founders holds the promise of a profound spiritual affinity between their kingdoms, Discord insists on her capacity to sunder one from the other by political means:

> ¿cómo yo impedirles puedo
> la amistad de dos hermanos?
> Mas responderé a eso,
> que aunque no se opongan nunca
> en Fe, Religión ni celo,
> la razón de Estado puede
> Guerra introducir entre ellos:
> y la mayor, sin que toque
> en la Ley ni el parentesco,
> es la de la antipatía.
>
> (921a)

(How can I impede the friendship of two brothers? But I will reply, that although they may never oppose one another in Faith, Religion, or zeal, reason of State can introduce War between them: and the greatest pretext of state, without resorting to Law or kinship, is that of antipathy.)

This argument is Machiavellian in its terms and assumptions. It proposes that politics and religion can exist as separate orders, and that political manipulation can undermine the fundamental concord of Christendom. Despite the ordained amity of Clovis and Rudolph, Discord believes that "antipathy" in the distinct sphere of politics will divide their dynasties and draw them into armed conflict. From the central misconception that Machiavelli's critics attributed to his political thought—the denial of the supremacy of providence in human affairs—Discord had derived an unquestioning trust in reason of state.

Discord proceeds on the assumption that reason of state is a purely secular device that she can exploit to further the aims of her *valimiento*. She does not believe that statecraft can promote the designs of providence in the affairs of nations, nor does she concede that an ethos of service and self-sacrifice can inform the favorite's relationship to the monarch. In their selfless pursuit of universal peace, the Arms Secular and Ecclesiastical offer a positive alternative to this demonic conception of politics. Through their exemplary conduct and their skillful diplomacy, the two Christian favorites reconcile their kingdoms and expose the errors of Discord's political thinking.

To exalt the role of the true favorite Calderón appeals to a factor that the court favorites of early modern Europe frequently mentioned in their own defense: hard work.[15] When the two favorites reject the initial overtures for peace between their nations, Ease describes himself regretfully as "quien siente en extremo / saber cuán poco conocen / al Ocio los valimientos" (one who feels great regret at knowing how unfamiliar *valimientos* are with Ease) (924a), and when the negotiations at last begin Ease abandons the Temple of Peace, "que Ocio no ha de haber, / donde hay validos" (since there can be no Ease where there are favorites)

15. In *Richelieu and Olivares*, Elliott remarks that "by identifying themselves so closely with the service of the crown, as wise and disinterested ministers uniquely equipped with the necessary qualities of industry and prudence, the Cardinal and the Count-Duke hoped to exorcise the image of the favourite" (57).

(934b). While these brief references apply generally to both of the Christian favorites, the scenes that present *valimiento* in the most favorable light center on the Secular Arm. As in *El nuevo palacio del Retiro*, Calderón uses his figural allegory to define the place of the current favorite in the Spanish administration.

In one of the text's first gestures of peace, the Secular Arm approaches Discord on behalf of the King of Grace and offers her the sacrament of Baptism. The exchange that follows reflects on the favorite's identity and function:

> Disc. ¿Tú eres aquel, si traduzco
>   en *luo Luis* latino verbo,
>   que significa lavar,
>   al gramático concepto,
>   el que Luis o lavas?
> Segl.   Sí,
>   pues por agua imprimo el sello,
>   carácter de nuevo mundo,
>   como chanciller supremo
>   de las Indias de su Ophir.
>   (922b)

(Discord. Are you the one who, if I translate the Latin verb that means "to wash" as *luo Luis*, signifies grammatically he who *Luis* or washes? Secular arm. Yes, for with water I imprint the seal, that mark of the new world, as the supreme chancellor of the Indies of his Ophir.)

Following an etymological program that is present throughout this *auto*, Calderón translates the name *Luis* as "el que Luis o lavas," and so connects Luis de Haro with John the Baptist. The image of the Baptist as Christ's "chancellor," and the analogy between his duties and those of the favorite, are both familiar from *El maestrazgo del Toisón*. And the allegory here is appropriate to Haro's prudence and discretion in several ways. From the typology of *El nuevo palacio del Retiro* the unfortunate implication might be drawn that the favorite (Man) holds authority only as the personal creation of the monarch (God). The association of Haro and John the Baptist avoids this possibility, and points more precisely to the ministerial character of the favorite's role. This association also accords well with the official titles that Haro had begun to use sparingly at the time of the *auto*'s composition. As *Canciller Mayor y Registrador de las Indias*—a title first bestowed upon Olivares in 1623—the favorite may be depicted as "imprinting the seal" that grants admission to the "new world" of the redeemed. Finally, the allusion to 3 Kings 9:26–28 (1 Kings 9:26–28 in the RSV) underscores the allegorical scheme of the *auto* as a whole. The biblical passage describes the building and despatch of Solomon's navy, and ends with a count of the wealth that it has brought him: "And they went to Ophir, and brought from there gold, to the amount of four hundred and twenty talents; and they brought it to King Solomon." In its riches the scriptural land of Ophir prefigures the Indies of which Luis de Haro is chancellor, and Solomon, associated in late sixteenth-century Spain with Philip II, is a type both of Christ and of the Spanish king.[16]

In fulfilling their duties to the realm, the Christian monarch and his true favorite have placed themselves within the order of providential history. Discord errs above all in believing that she can pursue her interests in defiance of that order and of the divine law that sustains it. This error is particularly apparent in the political program that she has contrived to divide the two Christian kingdoms. Calderón presents Discord's reason of state as flawed in its internal logic and as contrary to the force of external historical events. The inner contradictions of her program, and its collapse in the face of the divine plan for peace and concord, are elaborated in the rest of the *auto*.

Discord's misjudgment begins in her conception of the natural antipathy between the dynasties of Clovis and Rudolph. In explaining to War the basis of her political strategy, Discord appeals to the theory of the four elements. She associates France with the cock, who displays the qualities of fire, and Spain with the lion, a beast who presides as monarch over the earth. Her intention is to convince War that the opposition in nature of the elements of fire and earth will predispose the two nations to international rivalry, and that the demonic characters can foment this conflict and exploit it for their own purposes. In the innate "character" of the two kingdoms, Discord claims to have found sufficient "reason" to proceed with her statecraft (921b).

16. For the association of Philip II and Solomon, see the closing tercet of Góngora's "Sacros, altos, dorados capiteles" (1589?), written in praise of the Escorial: "Perdone el tiempo, lisonjee la Parca / la beldad desta Octava Maravilla, / los años deste Salomón Segundo" (Let time pardon and Fate favor the beauty of this Eighth Wonder, the years of this Second Solomon) (*Sonetos completos* 58).

The idea that gives Discord her point of departure—the existence of a natural antipathy between France and Spain—is a seventeenth-century commonplace. In part 1 of Gracián's *Criticón* (1651), when Critilo lists for Andrenio the contraries of which the universe is composed, he includes this example of opposition among nations:

> En la edad, se oponen los viejos a los moços; en la complexión, los flemáticos a los coléricos; en el estado, los ricos a los pobres; en la región, los españoles a los franceses; y assí, en todas las demás calidades, los unos son contra los otros. (quoted in Greer, "General Introduction" 146)

> (Among ages, the old are opposed to the young; among temperaments, the phlegmatic to the choleric; among estates, the rich to the poor; among regions, the Spanish to the French; and so, in all other qualities, some are against others.)

This statement, however, does not offer an unqualified endorsement of Discord's reasoning. Critilo understands that a larger symmetry encompasses the particular opposition of the two kingdoms, and such an insistence on the universal order of things renders suspect the proposition that Franco-Spanish hostility can be taken in isolation and exploited for immediate political gain. In addition, the affinities that Discord herself has drawn between the elements and the character of nations suggest that France and Spain enjoy the potential for both conflict and concord. According to the traditional cosmology that Calderón invokes in the *auto* of *La vida es sueño*, fire and earth are adjacent elements in the tetrad that maintains the equilibrium of natural forces or qualities in Creation. Although earth is cold and will repel the heat of fire, the two elements possess in their dryness a common quality that exerts a countervailing force of attraction between them. The balance of forces in earth and fire, and in the nations that possess the qualities of these elements, exposes the self-destructive aspect of demonic statecraft. Through the logic that she has used to posit a natural antipathy between the Christian kingdoms, Discord has revealed unwittingly the bond of sympathy that will secure their diplomatic concord.

Discord misconstrues the disposition of the elements because she has refused to recognize the order of providence in Creation. This denial also prevents her from understanding the providential succession of the laws that God has given to humanity. As Calderón shows in the final discoveries of *A Dios por razón de Estado*, the three kinds of law are concordant one with another. In the unfolding of human history each kind of law sublimates but does not negate the one that has preceded it. In her belief that she can aggravate a radical opposition between the Kingdoms of Natural Law and Grace, Discord again betrays her ignorance of the divine order. Like the other demonic blocking characters in Calderón's *autos*, she contemplates without full comprehension the signs and mysteries that announce the course of providential history and attempts to forestall adverse events through fruitless remedies. As she confronts the numerous signs of future concord between the Christian kingdoms, Discord acknowledges the precarious character of her statecraft:

> Temo
> que haya significación
> adelante en todo esto;
> pero la necesidad
> no elige el mejor consejo,
> sino el más pronto.
>   (923b)

> (I fear that all this anticipates the future, but necessity does not
> choose the best counsel, but the most expedient.)

In this statement Discord reveals herself as a true Machiavellian and exposes once again the liabilities inherent in the doctrine of bad reason of state. Even in the face of mounting evidence against her cause, she refuses to take "better counsel" for reasons of political "necessity."

The two Christian favorites counter Discord's stratagems by pursuing the concord that has been ordained for their kingdoms. In the proceedings that lead to this end the Spanish princess has a pivotal role. In a carefully ordered sequence of scenes Calderón portrays María Teresa as a figure of the Church. Following the typology conventionally applied to royal weddings, this allegory relates the reconciliation through marriage of the two nations to Christ's union with the Church, and presents Franco-Spanish diplomacy as Christian statecraft devoted to fulfilling God's will in the affairs of nations. Instead of denying the order of providence, this true reason of state promotes the divine design for humanity.

Peace and Ease play a central part in the program that relates María Teresa to the Church. In their flight from Discord and her demonic forces, the two pacific characters first seek refuge with the King of Grace. As they approach his residence, they describe it as a "good refuge" (*Buen-Retiro*) and as a "pattern" of the "strange and beautiful city" of John's Apocalypse (924b–25a). This exchange draws on the typology from *El nuevo palacio del Retiro* that portrays the pleasure-palace as a "shadow" and "figure" of the New Jerusalem (140b–41a). Peace now reiterates this allegory, adding that the "royal architecture" of the palace recalls the beauty of the Bride to whom John compares his heavenly city (925a). Justice, the porter who hails the visitors in a long responsorial passage reminiscent of the liturgy, then names the princess who lives in the palace:

> ¿Quién, sin que tema desgracia.
> llama con tanta osadía
> a este cuarto de María,
> Hija del Rey de la Gracia?
> (925b)

(Who, without fearing disgrace, hails with such daring this apartment of María, the Daughter of the King of Grace?)

This greeting completes a figural pattern. The palace, itself a "figure" of the "singular Bride," contains the "apartment of María," the "Daughter of the King of Grace" whose marriage will ensure the concord of her father's realm with the Kingdom of Natural Law. Through its bridal imagery, and its parallels with liturgical language, this scene introduces María Teresa and associates her with the Church in its guise as the Bride of Christ.

A subsequent scene reinforces this figural correspondence through another allusion to the diplomatic proceedings. When Peace and Ease make their overtures to the King of Natural Law, they find him in a garden of fleurs-de-lis, gazing attentively at a portrait of a young woman whose likeness alone has enamored him. Explaining that the picture has come into his hands by chance, he laments that its subject is unknown to him; Peace then reveals that the woman portrayed is the princess María. This stage business probably dramatizes an incident from the recent negotiations. During a series of secret conferences with Luis de Haro in

1656, the diplomat Lionne, a delegate of Mazarin, caught sight of a medal bearing an image of the princess and remarked, "If your king would give to my master for his wife the original of the portrait . . . peace might soon be made" (quoted in Trevor Davies 69). Calderón has recast this incident as a direct expression of Louis XIV's love for María Teresa. And he accommodates it to the allegorical scheme of his *auto* by using it to emphasize María's role as a type of the Church. When the King of Natural Law asks if the princess is equal to her likeness, Peace replies that the subject is superior to the portrait:

> PAZ.   Y aún más bella
>   que grosero ese matiz
>   no la pintó tan hermosa
>   como el día que la vi
>   en poder de Salomón.
> CLOD.   ¿Cómo puede ser?
> PAZ.   Así;
>   que pues es de sus cantares,
>   con ellos lo he de decir.
>   (927b–28a)

(PEACE. And even lovelier, for this coarse palette did not paint her with the beauty she possessed on the day I saw her in Solomon's power.
CLOVIS. How can that be?
PEACE. As I will say, and since she is the bride of Solomon's songs, I must use them to speak of her.)

In a long exchange that is once again responsorial in form, Peace and the King now compare the portrait to its original (928a). Taken together, their couplets place phrases from the Song of Songs within a strain of conventional poetic language characteristic of the Petrarchan love lyric. Reminiscent of such Spanish devotional lyrics as sonnet 46 of Lope's *Rimas sacras* (1614), this passage reflects significantly on the entire range of bridal imagery in the *auto*.[17] The King of Natural Law, related here to

17. For the text of Lope's sonnet ("No sabe qué es amor quien no te ama"), which juxtaposes imagery from the mystical, meditative, and Petrarchan strains of Golden Age lyric poetry, see his *Obras escogidas* 2:138.

the perfect type of the Christian king in Solomon, praises his beloved in language traditionally interpreted as representing Christ's union with the Church. And Calderón's presentation of the portrait is emblematic of the sophisticated integration of literary and visual imagery in his late *autos*, in that it gives equal weight to painting and poetry. Considered in isolation, neither portrait nor verse can discover the true nature of the princess; only in conjunction do they reveal the crucial allegory.

The final scenes of the *auto*, which converge on the sacramental moment of the dynastic wedding, recapitulate the correspondences already established and find new figural patterns in the diplomacy of the two favorites. For their conferences Peace orders a temple to arise between the two kingdoms "on the waves of the Bidasoa" (930a). This location corresponds to the Isle of Pheasants on the Franco-Spanish border, where the favorites met to negotiate and the kings to confirm the peace; it also recalls the biblical waters of Jordan (930a) and of tribulation (933a). A set of internal typologies that relate objects in the *auto* to one another and to figures of the Christian sacraments from Old Testament history now comes into play. The floating temple is a figure of Noah's ark and of the monstrance conveyed by the priest in the legend of Rudolph's piety; Peace appears above the proceedings in a rainbow that looks back to the dove of Clovis's baptism and to God's covenant with Noah in Genesis 9:8–17 (Soons 186). To the Temple of Peace, surrounded by figures of divine sacraments and covenants, the two monarchs come to seal their union. The King of Grace arrives with the Bride in "Ezekiel's chariot," while the King of Natural Law approaches in a "mystical ship" (936a). The two vehicles meet in front of the temple, which opens at Fame's bidding to reveal a globe elevated by the two favorites, crowned with a representation of the Host, and encircled by seven ribbons. Fame glosses this final *apariencia* as she explains that the once fragile temple will now withstand the forces of Discord and War:

> Columnas en ella habrá
> que la sabrán defender
> de sus ráfagas, supuesto
> que hoy en su albergue se ve
> aquella pasada sombra
> que de un Sacramento fue
> orbe, y ya de siete, cuya
> propagada redondez

Eclesiástico y Seglar
Brazo sustentan.
(936b–37a)

(It will contain columns to defend it from their blasts, since today
we see lodged within it that shadow which was once the orb of a
Sacrament, and is now that of seven, an orb whose perfected
roundness is now supported by the Ecclesiastical and Secular
Arms.)

In a triumph of Christian diplomacy over false reason of state, the Temple
of Peace stands sustained by the "columns" of a faith now strengthened
by the union of the Kingdoms of Natural Law (France) and of Grace
(Spain). In the same moment the Church, associated throughout the *auto*
with María Teresa, has been united with Christ and glorified in the Host,
which rests securely on the Arms Secular and Ecclesiastical. The appearance here of the Host fulfills the figures of the sacraments displayed and
evoked in the course of the *auto*, and confers a sacramental aura on
the peace of the two kingdoms. And the visual spectacle points to the
universal scale of this achievement; as Alexander Parker has noted, the
"pictorial symbolism" of this *apariencia* shows us "the Church filling
the world with grace through the sacraments she administers" (*Allegorical Drama* 98). The peace celebrated at the *auto*'s conclusion is part of
God's plan for harmony among the nations of Christendom. Presented in
this light, as the fulfillment of a providential design, the Treaty of the
Pyrenees becomes a triumph for the faith that the Spanish Hapsburgs
had long identified with their own imperial regime.

The idea that Spain must be faithful to its place in the order of
providence is common to *El nuevo palacio del Retiro* and *El lirio y la
azucena*. The two *autos* propose that actions taken by the state can fulfill
some part of the design that God has ordained for humanity, and that on
particular occasions the proceedings of the Spanish monarchy have
promoted this end. In each work an extensively elaborated typology
traces a providential pattern in contemporary events, and each typology
consecrates the favorite's role as a servant to the Crown and the state.
Taken together these *autos* illustrate the conjunction of providential
history and Christian statecraft in Calderón's political theater. Yet they
also display significant differences, due in part to the author's increasing
skill in composing *autos* of this kind and in part to the potential of their

distinct historical occasions. *El nuevo palacio del Retiro* deals with politics primarily at the level of symbols and abstractions; it uses a diverse range of allegorical techniques to defend the palace that Olivares had constructed to enshrine his controversial program for restoring Spain's imperial grandeur. Although it has the abstract quality of all allegorical drama, *El lirio y la azucena* dramatizes a specific series of political proceedings that led to a well-received victory for Spain's diplomacy in Europe, and Calderón takes this opportunity to praise Spanish statecraft for honoring the principles of true reason of state.[18] The contrast between the two *autos* points to the strong sense of occasion that informs and shapes them. Considered in the light of contemporary reactions, the Treaty of the Pyrenees is more promising material for festive drama than the inauguration of the Buen Retiro, and Calderón responds to this material by writing an *auto* that is more selective in its techniques, more compelling in its dramatic structure, and more cohesive in its engagement with political theory.

18. Although its terms were not wholly favorable to Spain, the Treaty of the Pyrenees was welcomed in the peninsula as an endpoint after two decades of "total war" in western Europe (Domínguez Ortiz 98). The concord with France was widely celebrated as offering a prospect of the universal peace that Calderón mentions in his subtitle, and on his return to Madrid, Luis de Haro was hailed as the Prince of the Peace (Trevor Davies 70).

✛ ✛ ✛ ✛ ✛ ✛

CONCLUSION

Spanish political thinkers consistently favor the idea that divine providence has taken special care for their nation and its empire. A long tradition of Christian ideology informs this conception of Spain's position in human history. The Carolingian revival of empire appealed to a Christian revision of the theory of imperial *translatio*, and Charlemagne himself "regarded his imperium, not as a *civitas terrena* in opposition to the *civitas Dei*, but as a city representing the earthly portion of the church, the kingdom of eternal peace in this world" (Yates 3). The circumstances that brought Charles V to the head of an empire that embraced two worlds also made him heir to the tradition that united the cities of God and man, and spiritual ideals of unity and concord exerted a persistent influence on the imperial vision of

Hapsburg Spain.[1] Possessed of "a powerful strain of messianic nationalism," Castilians cast themselves as "the chosen people of the Lord" and claimed a privileged place in the "grand design" of Christian conversion and dominion (Elliott, "Self-Perception" 46). Through aligning true statecraft with providence, and tracing figural patterns in the proceedings of the Hapsburg state, Calderón sustains the conceptual framework of Christian empire and applies it to the political conditions of his own time. This continuity with the imperial tradition has prompted Calderón's interpreters to view his political theater as subservient to the dominant ideological ends of the monarchy. In a characteristic statement on this subject, Barbara Kurtz has described the "political typology" of the *autos* on state occasions as "an apologetic defense of the visionary, providentialist goals of imperial policies in contemporary Spain" (152–53).

To regard Calderón as an apologist for the late Hapsburgs is to exclude the possibility that his theater offers genuine criticism or counsel concerning political affairs. Kurtz has remarked that the sacramental allegory of *El nuevo palacio del Retiro* strains the limits of belief and taste, and that "the topical referent of such an allegory served a memorialist—and politically opportunistic—function for a genre that was, throughout Calderón's career, increasingly linked with and dependent upon royal and municipal patronage" (132). Criticism of the *comedias*—particularly of the late plays written for court performance—presents a similar prospect of ideological conformity and aesthetic diminution. Hildner asserts that through "artistic spectacle and verbal artifice" Calderón's theater turns the spectators' attention from the actual conditions of life in society to "ethical hypotheses" that confirm doctrines favorable to the ruling powers of church and state (95–96). Cascardi stresses the "gaudy showmanship" of both *comedias* and *autos*, and contrasts the response to "social and moral obligations" among earlier authors of the *comedia* with Calderón's abandonment of the genre's "critical functions" (120, 162). For Cascardi the king in Lope is subject to "possible failure" and "must be trained in his office," while in Calderón's late plays "the King need not study" since "government is neither taught nor learned" (119). These readings of Calderón follow a general line of historical interpretation that

1. Yates has traced the descent of the ideology of Christian empire from the debate between the papacy and Frederick II of Sicily (1194–1250) through Dante's program for the founding of a world monarchy in the *De Monarchia* to the imperial ambitions of sixteenth-century Spain. Her study emphasizes the diffusion of Dante's ideas in the court of Charles V, principally through the influence of the king's chancellor, Mercurio Gattinara (21–22).

regards all public forms of art and spectacle in early modern Spain as instruments for the guidance and control of a subject populace by the authority of an absolutist state.[2] An approach that assumes an increasing consolidation of power on the part of the Crown and the aristocracy, and grants the arts a central role in that process, will stress the aspects of conformity and praise in Calderón's theater.

Yet Calderón's ideological ends are not limited to the defense of high personages and official proceedings. In her careful analysis of his court drama, Margaret Rich Greer has argued that three features of composition and performance—the "polyphony" of the "dramatic idiom," the "physical space" of staging at court, and the "political context" of contemporary affairs—allow us to comprehend the complex "discourse of power" through which Calderón addresses political issues of current concern even as he elevates the authority of the king and his circle (*Play*, 199–201).[3] And in responding to specific issues and events Calderón appeals to a broad theoretical position that consistently informs his political theater. This position insists on the assimilation of true reason of state to providence, and on the accommodation of the state's institutions and actions to the ordered unfolding of human history. The idea of Christian dominion, as it descends through the influence of ethicist political thinkers, leads Calderón to reassert the moral and legal limits of royal authority. To assess the ideological force of his position, we must consider both his stance concerning the primary audience of political drama and the place of his providential theory of kingship in relation to

2. José Antonio Maravall has proposed and elaborated this argument concerning the instrumental character of the arts in the society of Hapsburg Spain. He presents his views on theater and public spectacle in *Teatro y literatura* and in the final chapter (on the social uses of novelty, invention, and artifice) of *Culture of the Baroque* (225–47). The latter work also sets out his general theory of the Spanish baroque as a culture "directed" from above: "what characterized that seventeenth-century absolutist order was the dissemination of the principle of absolute power throughout the entire social body, integrating all the manifestations of authority, strengthening them, and (by means of such manifestations) being present in many spheres of social life and to a certain extent inspiring them" (71–72).

3. Among current scholars of Golden Age literature Greer is not alone in emphasizing the theater's potential as a medium for offering counsel and critical comment on princely conduct. Dian Fox has studied Calderón's view of the virtues and afflictions of monarchs, with particular attention to his scrutiny of the reputations traditionally accorded to the kings who appear in his history plays (*Kings*). Parallel work with a more general focus can be found in Teresa Soufas's recent article on the carnivalesque role of the *gracioso* and in Robert Lauer's monograph on tyranny and its remedies in drama and political thought. A formative project is also at work in the subgenre of plays on *valimiento*.

other strains of political thought available in late Hapsburg Spain. Calderón addresses king and court with a marked formative intent, and his
case for Christian government must compete with other views that offer
less resistance to the Machiavellian line.

Recent scholarship on the conditions of staging in royal venues has
emphasized the king's privileged place as the dual focus of the dramatic
representation. Exact circumstances vary between genres, but the prominence accorded to the king is a constant factor. In the case of the *autos*,
the royal court enjoyed the honor of receiving the first performance, and
the king viewed the action from a special platform. In the courtyards and
theaters of the palaces in Madrid, the production formed "part of the
court ritual," and the placement of the king favored his perspective on the
stage and focused part of the court's awareness on his person.[4] These
conditions allowed playwrights to presume upon the king's attention and
to assume a hearing for such counsel as they might offer. Calderón
readily accepts the opportunities afforded by political theater; he is fully
engaged in the discourse of the education of princes, and he resorts to
formative methods that make strong claims on the royal conscience,
particularly in the *autos*. Wardropper has noted that Calderón's reference
to "composición de lugares" (composition of places) in the prologue to
the 1677 collection of *autos* asks readers to imagine for themselves the
sound and spectacle of dramatic performance by conducting an interior
meditation according to the principles of the *Spiritual Exercises* of Saint
Ignatius Loyola; Kurtz has explored in detail the hypothesis that the
prologue may extend "a veritable exhortation to true meditative reflection upon the *autos*, to a genuine use of meditative technique in apprehending and interpreting the plays" (168).[5] Kurtz's argument invites us to
consider the potential combination of political counsel and meditative
reception in the *autos* devoted to issues and occasions of state. As both
mirror of princes and spiritual exercise, the sacramental play is a persua-

4. The staging practices that elevated and favored the king are discussed for the *auto* by
Shergold (esp. 452–53) and for the various forms of secular court plays by Varey ("The
Audience and the Play" 401–2). Varey comments that under the conditions of performance
at court "the dramatist writes with an audience of one primarily in mind, just as the courtier
sees the King, not the play, as the thing" (405).

5. Wardropper discusses the Ignatian terminology of the 1677 prologue in "Calderón de
la Barca and Late Seventeenth-Century Theater" (37b). Kurtz's final chapter ("*Auto* as
Spiritual Exercise" 164–204) carefully considers the potential presence of meditative
methods in the composition and reception of Calderón's *autos*.

sive vehicle for directing the king's mind to the force of providence and its laws in the affairs of nations.

In asserting the priority of law and ethics in political matters, and appealing to the king's moral judgment, Calderón endorses the ethicist view that success in statecraft depends on religious probity. John Elliott has argued that "this direct equation between national mortality and national fortune was one that weighed heavily on the rulers of Spain," and that such a "supernatural" account of political events tended to attribute Castile's imperial decline to divine disfavor and to advocate spiritual and ethical renewal ("Self-Perception" 47). God's actions, however, did not exhaust the field of potential explanations for historical change. An alternative account of Spain's condition accepted an "organic conception of the state" and regarded political entities as subject to the "cyclical process" of "growth, maturity and decay" ("Self-Perception" 48). The measures associated with this "naturalistic" approach are frequently at odds with the program of Christian remedies that Calderón's theater attempts to sustain.[6]

The objectives and limitations of naturalistic interpretation are apparent in Gracián's *El político Don Fernando el Católico* (1640) This treatise presents Ferdinand as the highest exemplar of true statecraft, and a consciousness of the temporal contingency of all political arrangements shapes its definition of the qualities appropriate to successful rule and its choice of a model prince. Given the dominant processes of change and decline in the fate of empires, Gracián adopts a realist stance concerning the character and labor of kings, and the central dilemmas of the realist school make themselves felt in his thought.

The opening sections of *El político* describe the vicissitudes that time has brought to the regimes of the past and observe repeatedly that monarchs will flourish only if their gifts correspond to the political circumstances that prevail when they reign. Periods of increase favor a ruler's reputation, and periods of decline and lethargy undermine it (38), although princes of exceptional caliber will respond to the challenge of renewal (40). Different times demand different talents (48), and kings in whom a certain trait of character is dominant tend to coincide during a

---

6. Elliott isolates three strains of explanation for decline in the thought of the Spanish *arbitristas*: supernatural, naturalistic, and scientific. The first two have produced the stronger resonance in works of literature; the third, which defines decline "in terms of mistaken policies which could be changed for better ones" ("Self-Perception" 56), has had less literary influence.

single period, so that the bellicose rulers have their era, as do the pious and the hedonistic (50–51). These axioms suggest that Ferdinand enjoyed a twofold advantage, in that he governed during the initial years of Castile's imperial ascendancy, in an era of monarchs adept at statecraft (38, 51). The full measure of his success, however, followed from his ability to turn this advantage to account through his exemplary political gifts.

For Gracián the essential attribute of all successful rulers is *capacidad*. Intended to encompass a broad range of political skills and virtues, this term refers in the first instance to a mental agility that is conducive to acuity of intellect and maturity in judgment (55). Gracián supplies a supporting catalogue of rulers who have prevailed through *capacidad* or failed for lack of it; Ferdinand's name crowns the list of true monarchs, and the eulogy of his character stresses the comprehensive nature of this attribute and its preeminence in the vocation of politics:

> Este príncipe comprensivo, prudente, sagaz, penetrante, vivo, atento, sensible y, en una palabra, sabio, fue el Católico Fernando, el rey de mayor capacidad que ha habido, calificada con los hechos, ejercitada en tantas ocasiones; fue útil su saber, y aunque le sobró valor, jugó de maña. No fue afortunado Fernando, sino prudente, que la prudencia es madre de la buena dicha. Comúnmente, es feliz, así como la imprudencia es desgraciada: todos los más prudentes príncipes fueron muy afortunados. (58)

> (This prince—understanding, prudent, astute, clear-sighted, alert, attentive, responsive and, in a word, wise—was Ferdinand the Catholic, the king of the greatest *capacidad* that has existed, a *capacidad* proven by his deeds and exercised on many occasions; his knowledge was useful and, although he was possessed of ample valor, he also made use of guile. Ferdinand was not fortunate, but prudent, since prudence is the mother of good luck. In most cases prudence brings happiness, just as imprudence brings misfortune; all the most prudent princes were very fortunate.)

This defense of *capacidad* marks a significant departure from the ethicist position. Gracián reiterates the conventional view that true princes do not depend on fortune, but he has little confidence in the virtues traditionally assigned to kingship. The excellence of *capacidad* arises from the ruler's need to match the means at his disposal to the changing occasions of government. Under the pressure of this contingency Gracián accepts that the true prince must have recourse to measures that no ethicist thinker would allow; "guile" has its political moment, as does "valor." Security of rule lies not in moral constancy, but in intellectual readiness and agility.

The tension between traditional thought and realist innovation can be traced through the text of *El político*. Gracián rehearses the standard arguments concerning the role of providence in the rise and fall of empires (40), the importance of avoiding cunning and deceit (51), and the privileged place of the Hapsburg dynasty in the order of history (81–82). He is nonetheless quick to recognize the challenges that rulers confront and the priority that they should grant to strictly political considerations. The treatise touches on such topics as the difficulties of initiating a new regime (34) and the predilection of the governed for change and variety (35, 75). In accordance with his conception of *capacidad*, Gracián consistently praises the ability to evaluate and respond to shifting circumstances. He remarks of Ferdinand "no hubo hombre que así conociese la ocasión de una empresa, la sazón de un negocio, la oportunidad para todo" (there was no man so aware of the occasion for an undertaking, the time for a transaction, the opportunity for all things) (63). In its intellectual cast, and its insistence on flexibility in the face of time and change, *El político* shows a marked affinity with the Machiavellian politics of calculation.

Gracián's realism represents one extreme in the spectrum of Spanish political thought. At the other end lies an obdurate conservatism of the kind that Quevedo attributes to the court of the grand Turk in *La hora de todos* (1650): "si hemos de permanecer, arrimémonos al aforismo que dice: *Lo que siempre se hizo, siempre se haga*; pues, obedecido, preserva de novedades" (if we are to persist, let us hold fast to the aphorism that says: *May what always was done, always be done*; since if it is observed this aphorism averts innovations) (304).[7] In relation to these contrasting positions Calderón occupies the middle ground. He denies that human foresight and intelligence can empower the prince to meet all contingencies, and advocates instead a moral respect for providence and the hierarchy of laws. His stance is conservative in its fidelity to the tradi-

---

7. Elliott cites this passage from Quevedo, in connection with "the reinforcement of the stockade mentality in Castilian society" through military reversals and the failure of Olivares's ambitious program for reform ("Self-Perception" 61).

tional virtues and limits of kingship, but it is not hostile to all forms of change in government. Calderón follows the shifting relations of the Crown, the councils, and the office of the favorite, and he values the political balance that arose among these institutions during the mature reign of Philip IV. The creation of a theater that sustains the anti-Machiavellian argument for Christian statecraft and limited sovereignty, and adapts that argument to the changing conditions of politics in seventeenth-century Spain, is a striking achievement in his long dramatic career.

Select Bibliography

✢   ✢   ✢   ✢   ✢   ✢

Abbreviations

BAE   Biblioteca de Autores Españoles
B Com   *Bulletin of the Comediantes*
BHS   *Bulletin of Hispanic Studies*
HR   *Hispanic Review*
IEP   Instituto de Estudios Políticos
MLN   *Modern Language Notes*
MLR   *Modern Language Review*
NBAE   Nueva Biblioteca de Autores Españoles
PIMS   Pontifical Institute of Medieval Studies
PMLA   *Publications of the Modern Language Association of America*
RCEH   *Revista Canadiense de Estudios Hispánicos*
RH   *Revue Hispanique*
ZRPh   *Zeitschrift für Romanische Philologie*

Primary Sources

Aquinas, Saint Thomas. *Basic Writings*. Edited by Anton C. Pegis. 2 vols. New York: Random House, 1945.
——. *On Kingship, to the King of Cyprus*. Translated by Gerald B. Phelan. Revised by I. Th. Eschmann. Toronto: PIMS, 1949.
Botero, Giovanni. *Della ragion di stato libri dieci*. Milan: Bettoni, 1830.
Calderón de la Barca, Pedro. *Autos sacramentales*. Vol. 3 of *Obras completas*. Edited by Angel Valbuena Prat. 2d ed. 3 vols. Madrid: Aguilar, 1967.
——. *La cisma de Inglaterra*. Edited by Francisco Ruiz Ramón. Madrid: Castalia, 1981.
——. *El médico de su honra*. Edited by D. W. Cruickshank. Madrid: Castalia, 1981.
——. *La vida es sueño*. Edited by Albert E. Sloman. Manchester: Manchester University Press, 1961.

Cancionero castellano del siglo XV. Edited by R. Foulché-Delbosc. 2 vols. NBAE 19 and 22. Madrid: Bailly-Bailliere, 1912–15.

Cartas de Sor María de Jesús de Agreda y de Felipe IV. Edited by Carlos Seco Serrano. 2 vols. BAE 108–9. Madrid: Atlas, 1958.

Covarrubias, Sebastián de. *Tesoro de la lengua castellana o española.* 1611. Madrid: Turner, 1977.

Diccionario de Autoridades. 1726–39. 6 vols. in 3. Madrid: Gredos, 1964.

La Estrella de Sevilla. Edited by R. Foulché-Delbosc. *RH* 48 (1920): 497–678.

Furió Ceriol, Fadrique. *El concejo y consejeros del príncipe.* BAE 36: 317–37. Madrid: Rivadeneyra, 1855.

Góngora y Argote, Luis de. *Sonetos completos.* Edited by B. Ciplijauskaité. Madrid: Castalia, 1969.

Gracián, Baltasar. *El político.* Edited by E. Correa Calderón. Salamanca: Anaya, 1973.

Machiavelli, Niccolò. *Il principe.* Edited by L. Arthur Burd. Oxford: Clarendon, 1891.

Mártir Rizo, Juan Pablo. *Norte de príncipes* and *Vida de Rómulo.* Edited by J. A. Maravall. Madrid: IEP, 1945.

Mira de Amescua, Antonio. *La segunda de don Aluaro* [*Adversa Fortuna de don Alvaro de Luna*]. Edited by Nellie E. Sánchez-Arce. Mexico: Jus, 1960.

The New Oxford Annotated Bible with the Apocrypha. Edited by Herbert G. May and Bruce G. Metzger. Expanded ed. New York: Oxford University Press, 1977.

Quevedo Villegas, Francisco de. *Cómo ha de ser el privado.* In *Obras completas,* edited by Felicidad Buendía, 2:592–635. Madrid: Aguilar, 1961.

———. *La Hora de Todos y la Fortuna con seso.* Edited by Jean Bourg, Pierre Dupont, and Pierre Geneste. Madrid: Cátedra, 1987.

———. *Política de Dios, Govierno de Christo.* Edited by James O. Crosby. Urbana: University of Illinois Press, 1966.

Rivadeneira, Pedro de. *Tratado de la religión y virtudes que debe tener el príncipe cristiano.* BAE 60: 449–587. Madrid: Rivadeneyra, 1868.

Saavedra Fajardo, Diego de. *Idea de un príncipe político cristiano representada en cien empresas.* Edited by Vicente García de Diego. 4 vols. Madrid: Espasa-Calpe, 1927–30.

Seneca. *On Clemency.* In *The Stoic Philosophy of Seneca,* edited and translated by Moses Hadas, 137–65. New York: Norton, 1958.

Simón Díaz, José, ed. *Relaciones breves de actos públicos celebrados en Madrid de 1541 a 1650.* Madrid: Instituto de Estudios Madrileños, 1982.

Téllez, Gabriel [Tirso de Molina]. *El burlador de Sevilla y convidado de piedra.* Edited by Joaquín Casalduero. Madrid: Cátedra, 1980.

Vega Carpio, Lope Félix de. *El mejor alcalde, el rey.* Edited by José María Díez Borque. Madrid: Istmo, 1974.

———. *Obras escogidas.* Edited by F. Sainz de Robles. 2 vols. Madrid: Aguilar, 1946.

Secondary Sources

Allen, Don Cameron. *Mysteriously Meant: The Rediscovery of Pagan Symbolism and Allegorical Interpretation in the Renaissance.* Baltimore: Johns Hopkins University Press, 1970.

Auerbach, Erich. "Figura." In *Scenes from the Drama of European Literature,* 11–76. New York: Meridian, 1959.

Bacigalupo, Mario Ford. "Calderón's *La cisma de Inglaterra* and Spanish Seventeenth-Century Political Thought." *Symposium* 28 (1974): 212–27.

Barney, Stephen A. *Allegories of History, Allegories of Love.* Hamden, Conn.: Archon, 1979.

Blue, William R. *Comedia: Art and History.* University of Kansas Humanistic Studies 55. New York: Peter Lang, 1989.

Brown, Jonathan, and J. H. Elliott. *A Palace for a King: The Buen Retiro and the Court of Philip IV.* New Haven: Yale University Press, 1980.

Cascardi, Anthony J. *The Limits of Illusion: A Critical Study of Calderón.* Cambridge: Cambridge University Press, 1984.

Chabod, Federico. "Esiste uno Stato del Rinascimento?" In *Scritti sul Rinascimento,* 591–623. Turin: Einaudi, 1967.

Cilveti, Angel L. "Dramatización de la alegoría bíblica en *Primero y Segundo Isaac* de Calderón." In *Critical Perspectives on Calderón de la Barca,* edited by Frederick A. de Armas, David M. Gitlitz, and José A. Madrigal, 39–52. Lincoln, Neb.: Society of Spanish and Spanish-American Studies, 1981.

Cohen, Walter. *Drama of a Nation: Public Theater in Renaissance England and Spain.* Ithaca: Cornell University Press, 1985.

Connolly, Eileen M. "Further Testimony in the Rebel Soldier Case." *B Com* 24 (1972): 11–15.

Copleston, F. C. *Aquinas.* Harmondsworth, Middlesex, Eng.: Penguin, 1955.

De Armas, Frederick A. "'El planeta más impío': Basilio's Role in *La vida es sueño.*" *MLR* 81 (1986): 900–11.

———. *The Return of Astraea: An Astral-Imperial Myth in Calderón.* Lexington: University Press of Kentucky, 1986.

Díez Borque, José María, ed. *Una fiesta sacramental barroca.* Madrid: Taurus, 1983.

Domínguez, Frank A. *The Medieval Argonautica.* Potomac, Md.: José Porrúa Turanzas, 1979.

Domínguez Ortiz, Antonio. *The Golden Age of Spain, 1516–1659.* Translated by James Casey. London: Weidenfeld and Nicolson, 1971.

Donovan, Richard B. *The Liturgical Drama in Medieval Spain.* Toronto: PIMS, 1958.

Elliott, J. H. *Imperial Spain, 1469–1716.* Harmondsworth, Middlesex: Pelican, 1970. (Originally published 1963).

———. "Quevedo and the Count-Duke of Olivares." In *Quevedo in Perspective,* edited by James Iffland, 227–50. Newark, Del.: Juan de la Cuesta, 1982.

———. *Richelieu and Olivares.* Cambridge: Cambridge University Press, 1984.

————. "Self-Perception and Decline in Early Seventeenth-Century Spain." *Past and Present* 74 (1977): 41–61.

————. "The Twilight of Hapsburg Spain." In *Painting in Spain, 1650–1700, from North American Collections*, by Edward J. Sullivan and Nina A. Mallory, 1–5. Princeton: The Art Museum, Princeton University, 1982.

Fernández-Santamaría, J. A. *Reason of State and Statecraft in Spanish Political Thought, 1595–1640*. Lanham, Md.: University Press of America, 1983.

Fiore, Robert L. *Drama and Ethos: Natural-Law Ethics and Spanish Golden Age Theater*. Lexington: University Press of Kentucky, 1975.

Fischer, Susan L. "Reader-Response Criticism and the *Comedia*: Creation of Meaning in Calderón's *La cisma de Ingalaterra.*" *B Com* 31 (1979): 109–25.

Forcione, Alban K. *Cervantes, Aristotle and the "Persiles."* Princeton: Princeton University Press, 1970.

Foster, David. "Calderón's *La torre de Babilonia* and Christian Allegory." *Criticism* 9 (1967): 142–54.

Fothergill-Payne, Louise. *La alegoría en los autos y farsas anteriores a Calderón*. London: Tamesis, 1977.

Fox, Dian. *Kings in Calderón: A Study in Characterization and Political Theory*. London: Tamesis, 1986.

————. *Refiguring the Hero: From Peasant to Noble in Lope de Vega and Calderón*. University Park: Pennsylvania State University Press, 1991.

Frye, Northrop. *Anatomy of Criticism: Four Essays*. Princeton: Princeton University Press, 1957.

Gilbert, Felix. *Machiavelli and Guicciardini: Politics and History in Sixteenth-Century Florence*. Princeton: Princeton University Press, 1965.

Glaser, Edward. "Calderón de la Barca's *Sueños hay que verdad son.*" *ZRPh* 82 (1966): 41–77.

Gordon, D. J. "Poet and Architect: The Intellectual Setting of the Quarrel between Ben Jonson and Inigo Jones." In *The Renaissance Imagination*, edited by Stephen Orgel, 77–101. Berkeley and Los Angeles: University of California Press, 1975.

Greer, Margaret Rich. "General Introduction." *La estatua de Prometeo*, by Pedro Calderón de la Barca, 1–187. Kassel: Reichenberger, 1986.

————. *The Play of Power: Mythological Court Dramas of Calderón de la Barca*. Princeton: Princeton University Press, 1991.

Halkhoree, P. "A Note on the Ending of Calderón's *La vida es sueño.*" *B Com* 24 (1972): 8–11.

Hall, H. B. "Segismundo and the Rebel Soldier." *BHS* 45 (1968): 189–200.

Hall, J. B. "The Problem of Pride and the Interpretation of the Evidence in *La vida es sueño.*" *MLR* 77 (1982): 339–47.

Hamilton, Bernice. *Political Thought in Sixteenth-Century Spain*. Oxford: Clarendon, 1963.

Heiple, Daniel L. "The Tradition behind the Punishment of the Rebel Soldier in *La vida es sueño.*" *BHS* 50 (1973): 1–17.

Heninger, S. K., Jr. *Touches of Sweet Harmony: Pythagorean Cosmology and Renaissance Poetics*. San Marino, Calif.: Huntington Library, 1974.

Hesse, Everett W. "Calderón's Concept of the Perfect Prince in *La vida es sueño*." In *Critical Essays on the Theatre of Calderón*, edited by Bruce W. Wardropper, 114–33. New York: New York University Press, 1965.

Hildner, David Jonathan. *Reason and the Passions in the Comedias of Calderón*. Purdue University Monographs in Romance Languages 11. Amsterdam and Philadelphia: John Benjamins, 1982.

Hillach, Ansgar. "Calderón antimaquiavélico: El auto sacramental *A Dios por razón de Estado*." *Iberoromania*, N.S., 14 (1981): 87–97.

Howe, Elizabeth Teresa. "Fate and Providence in Calderón de la Barca." *B Com* 29 (1977): 103–17.

Huizinga, J. *The Waning of the Middle Ages*. Garden City, N.Y.: Anchor, 1954. (Originally published 1924).

Keen, Maurice. *Chivalry*. New Haven: Yale University Press, 1984.

Kennedy, Ruth Lee. "*La Estrella de Sevilla* as a Mirror of the Courtly Scene—and of its Anonymous Dramatist (Luis Vélez?)." *B Com* 45 (1993): 103–43.

Kurtz, Barbara E. *The Play of Allegory in the Autos Sacramentales of Pedro Calderón de la Barca*. Washington: Catholic University of America Press, 1991.

Lauer, A. Robert. *Tyrannicide and Drama*. Stuttgart: Steiner-Verl. Wiesbaden, 1987.

Lefort, Claude. *Le Travail de l'oeuvre: Machiavel*. Paris: Gallimard, 1972.

Lipmann, Stephen H. "Segismundo's Fear at the End of *La vida es sueño*." *MLN* 97 (1982): 380–90.

Loftis, John. *Renaissance Drama in England and Spain: Topical Allusion and History Plays*. Princeton: Princeton University Press, 1987.

Lubac, Henri de. *Exégèse médiévale: Les quatres Sens de l'Ecriture*. 4 vols. Paris: Aubier, 1959–64.

Lynch, John. *Spain under the Hapsburgs* 2d ed. 2 vols. Oxford: Blackwell, 1981.

MacCurdy, Raymond R. *The Tragic Fall: Don Alvaro de Luna and Other Favorites in Spanish Golden Age Drama*. North Carolina Studies in the Romance Languages and Literatures 197. Chapel Hill: University of North Carolina Press, 1978.

Manent, Pierre. *Naissances de la politique moderne: Machiavel, Hobbes, Rousseau*. Paris: Payot, 1977.

Maravall, José Antonio. *Culture of the Baroque: Analysis of a Historical Structure*. Translated by Terry Cochran. Minneapolis: University of Minnesota Press, 1986.

———. *Teatro y literatura en la sociedad barroca*. Madrid: Seminarios y Ediciones, 1972.

———. *La teoría española del estado en el siglo XVII*. Madrid: IEP, 1944.

May, T. E. "Segismundo y el soldado rebelde." In *Hacia Calderón*, edited by Hans Flasche, 71–75. Coloquio Anglogermano. Exeter, 1969; Berlin: de Gruyter, 1970.

Meinecke, Friedrich. *Machiavellism: The Doctrine of Raison d'Etat and its Place in Modern History*. Translated by Douglas Scott. New Haven: Yale University Press, 1957.

Mesnard, Pierre. *L'Essor de la philosophie politique au XVIᵉ siècle*. Paris: Vrin, 1951.

Montgomery, Robert L., Jr. "Allegory and the Incredible Fable: The Italian View from Dante to Tasso." *PMLA* 81 (1966): 45–55.

Neumeister, Sebastián. "Las bodas de España: Alegoría y política en el auto sacramental." In *Hacia Calderón*, edited by Hans Flasche and Robert D. F. Pring-Mill, 30–41. Quinto Coloquio Anglogermano. Oxford 1978; Stuttgart: Steiner-Verl. Wiesbaden, 1982.

Oestreich, Gerhard. *Neostoicism and the Early Modern State*. Edited by Brigitta Oestreich and H. G. Koenigsberger. Translated by David McLintock. Cambridge: Cambridge University Press, 1982.

Orgel, Stephen. *The Illusion of Power: Political Theater in the English Renaissance*. Berkeley and Los Angeles: University of California Press, 1975.

Parker, Alexander A. *The Allegorical Drama of Calderón: An Introduction to the Autos Sacramentales*. Oxford: Dolphin, 1943.

———. "Calderón's Rebel Soldier and Poetic Justice." *BHS* 46 (1969): 120–27.

———. "The Chronology of Calderón's *Autos Sacramentales* from 1647." *HR* 37 (1969): 164–88.

———. "The Devil in the Drama of Calderón." In *Critical Essays on the Theatre of Calderón*, edited by Bruce W. Wardropper, 3–23. New York: New York University Press, 1965.

———. "Henry VIII in Shakespeare and Calderón: An Appreciation of *La cisma de Ingalaterra*." *MLR* 43 (1948): 327–52.

Parker, Geoffrey. *Europe in Crisis, 1598–1648*. London: Fontana, 1979.

Paterson, Alan K. G. "The Traffic of the Stage in Calderón's *La vida es sueño*." *Renaissance Drama*, N.S., 4 (1971): 155–83.

Pocock, J. G. A. *The Machiavellian Moment: Florentine Political Thought and the Atlantic Republican Tradition*. Princeton: Princeton University Press, 1975.

Pring-Mill, Robert D. F. "La 'victoria del hado' en *La vida es sueño*." In *Hacia Calderón*, edited by Hans Flasche, 53–70. Coloquio Anglogermano. Exeter, 1969; Berlin: de Gruyter, 1970.

Raab, Felix. *The English Face of Machiavelli: A Changing Interpretation, 1500–1700*. London: Routledge and Kegan Paul; Toronto: University of Toronto Press, 1964.

Rivers, Elias L. "The Pastoral Paradox of Natural Art." *MLN* 77 (1962): 130–44.

Ruiz Ramón, Francisco. *Calderón y la tragedia*. Madrid: Alhambra, 1984.

Sasso, Gennaro. *Niccolò Machiavelli: Storia del suo pensiero politico*. Bologna: Mulino, 1980.

Seznec, Jean. *The Survival of the Pagan Gods: The Mythological Tradition and its Place in Renaissance Humanism and Art*. Translated by Barbara F. Sessions. Princeton: Princeton University Press, 1953.

Shergold, N. D. *A History of the Spanish Stage from Medieval Times until the End of the Seventeenth Century.* Oxford: Clarendon, 1967.
———, and J. E. Varey. "Some Early Calderón Dates." *BHS* 38 (1961): 274–86.
Skinner, Quentin. *The Foundations of Modern Political Thought.* 2 vols. Cambridge: Cambridge University Press, 1978.
Soons, Alan. "Dogma and Metaphysical Politics in Calderón's *El lirio y la azucena.*" In *Estudios sobre el Siglo de Oro en homenaje a Raymond R. MacCurdy,* edited by Angel González, Tamara Holzapfel, and Alfred Rodríguez, 181–91. Albuquerque: University of New Mexico Press; Madrid: Cátedra, 1983.
Soufas, C. Christopher, Jr. "Thinking in *La vida es sueño.*" *PMLA* 100 (1985): 287–99.
Soufas, Teresa S. "Carnival, Spectacle and the *gracioso*'s Theatrics of Dissent." *RCEH* 14 (1989–90): 315–30.
Stradling, R. A. *Philip IV and the Government of Spain, 1621–1665.* Cambridge: Cambridge University Press, 1988.
Thompson, I. A. A. "The Rule of Law in Early Modern Castile." *European History Quarterly* 14 (1984): 221–34.
Tomás y Valiente, Francisco. *Los validos en la monarquía española del siglo XVII.* Madrid: IEP, 1963.
Trevor Davies, R. *Spain in Decline, 1621–1700.* London: Macmillan; New York: St. Martin's, 1957.
Varey, J. E. "The Audience and the Play at Court Spectacles: The Role of the King." *BHS* 61 (1984): 399–406.
———. "Calderón's *Auto Sacramental, La vida es sueño,* in performance." *Iberoromania,* N.S., 14 (1981): 75–86.
———. "Social Criticism in *El burlador de Sevilla.*" *Theatre Research International* 2 (1977): 197–221.
Vicens Vives, Jaime. "The Administrative Structure of the State in the Sixteenth and Seventeenth Centuries." In *Government in Reformation Europe, 1520–1560,* edited by Henry J. Cohn, 58–87. London: Macmillan, 1971.
Wardropper, Bruce W. "Calderón de la Barca and Late Seventeenth-Century Theater." *Record of the Art Museum, Princeton University* 41, no. 2 (1982): 35–41.
———. *Introducción al teatro religioso del Siglo de Oro: Evolución del auto sacramental antes de Calderón.* 2d ed. Salamanca: Anaya, 1967.
———. "El tema central de *El burlador de Sevilla.*" *Segismundo* 17–18 (1973): 9–16.
———, ed. *Critical Essays on the Theatre of Calderón.* New York: New York University Press, 1965.
Wilson, Diana de Armas. *Allegories of Love: Cervantes's "Persiles and Sigismunda."* Princeton: Princeton University Press, 1991.
Wilson, E. M. "The Four Elements in the Imagery of Calderón." *MLR* 31 (1936): 34–47.
———, and Jack Sage. *Poesías líricas en las obras dramáticas de Calderón.* London: Tamesis, 1964.
Yates, Frances A. *Astraea: The Imperial Theme in the Sixteenth Century.* London: Routledge and Kegan Paul, 1975.

Index

✛   ✛   ✛   ✛   ✛   ✛